TROUBLED
★ TIMES ★
— IN —
TENNESSEE

TROUBLED ★TIMES★ — IN — TENNESSEE

JAMES B. JONES

AMERICA
THROUGH TIME®
ADDING COLOR TO AMERICAN HISTORY

America Through Time is an imprint of Fonthill Media LLC
www.through-time.com
office@through-time.com

Published by Arcadia Publishing by arrangement with Fonthill Media LLC
For all general information, please contact Arcadia Publishing:
Telephone: 843-853-2070
Fax: 843-853-0044
E-mail: sales@arcadiapublishing.com
For customer service and orders:
Toll-Free 1-888-313-2665

www.arcadiapublishing.com

First published 2021

Copyright © James B. Jones 2021

ISBN 978-1-63499-305-0

Typeset in Sabon 9.5pt on 12pt
Printed and bound in England

Contents

1

Drug Use and Abuse, Tennessee, c. 1830–1920

Tennessee history is abundant with information about the abuse and control of alcohol.[1] Yet there is virtually no coverage of the use or abuse of other narcotics. This is because there was thought to be a dearth of evidence and because the use of narcotics was not at first considered to be under the regulatory power of cities or the state in the late nineteenth and early twentieth centuries. Narcotics, as we are familiar with them today, were medicines and were also used as intoxicants.

The first source of information on narcotics in Tennessee was in *Gunn's Domestic Medicine, or Poor Man's Friend. In the hours of Affliction, Pain and Sickness* (1830). It was a bestseller and, by 1840, reached its nineteenth printing. In Knoxville, John C. Gunn, MD, had determined to bring the practice of medicine to the common men in the Southern and Western frontier states and territories. His book provided descriptive and cautionary advice on opiates leaving twenty-first-century readers with the notion that the use and abuse of drugs were neither ordinary nor extraordinary.[2]

Besides recommending a plethora of homeopathic cures, Gunn included references to opium. The first thing he wrote about it shows how common it was among doctors and the lay public of the 1830s and 1840s. "Without this valuable and essential medicine," he wrote, "it would be next to impossible for a Physician to practice his profession with any ... success: it may not improperly be called ... the soothing angel of moral and physical pain."[3] Opium and laudanum were remedies for a long list of maladies including: fear, diarrhea, grief, ague and fever, bilious fever, nervous fever, colic, rheumatism, flooding, sleeplessness, consumption, diseases of the liver, dysentery, "constant looseness of the bowels," inflammation of the kidneys, bladder inflammations, being "overheated," catarrh, kidney stones, "sore legs," ear-aches, lock jaw, cancer, diseases of pregnancy, a child's fever, and "hooping cough."[4] Gunn illustrated that opium had long been in use in the United States, for example, as the main ingredient of Bateman's Drops and Godfrey's Cordial, "both of which have

... for near a century[,] have opium as their bases or principal parts ... they are ... valuable medicines."[5]

Opium was pervasive in America and the most common ingredient in all medicines aimed at abating pain. The use of opium was "the result ... of a continuous growth ... since colonial days."[6] It was commonly used on southern plantations where opiates eased slaves' aches and pains.[7] It was the nineteenth-century medical profession's prescription of choice. Dr. Gunn then tackled the question about the physiological and recreational differences between wine and whisky on the one hand and opium on the other.

The excitement produced by alcohol "is a flame which soon subsides, and leaves nothing" intoned Gunn, "but ashes of self-reprehension and bitter reflection behind it...." Opium, however, gave a "steady, agreeable, and permanent glow of pleasure, [both] physical and intellectual which lasts from ten to twelve hours." Alcohol, wrote the Tennessee physician, confused the mind, but opium, "if taken in the proper quantities," created "order, harmony and pleasurable serenity, [it] produces a just equipoise between our intellectual strength and sensibilities [and] arouses all our dormant faculties, and disposes them to harmonious and pleasurable activity."[8] Gunn defined what may have been the proper medicinal dosage for opium and laudanum. He also gave directions on how laudanum was made: "... by dissolving an ounce of Opium in a pint of good spirits of any kind—it is generally fit for use in five or six days." Paregoric was similarly made, but with "one drachm of Opium."[9] After this rhapsodic endorsement, Dr. Gunn issued a note of contradictory caution to his readers: oftentimes the pleasurable effects were accompanied by a grave disadvantage, namely addiction. "Opium, if habitually taken, in other words when it is made of as a stimulant or luxury, and not as a medicine, affects the physical system ... the mind becomes weak, irresolute, heavy, dull, and languid" and was followed inevitably by addiction and death.[10] Nevertheless, Gunn approved of opium as a mental and pleasure stimulant "if taken in the proper quantities." That this East Tennessee doctor sanctioned the drug in medical and recreational ways shows how commonly available it was to Tennesseans, and all frontier Americans.

Many believe that addiction to opium did not appear as a social problem until the Civil War. Morphine was common at battlefield hospitals. That the narcotics were common is demonstrated by the fact that the Union Army procured over 9 million opium pills and over 2,840,000 ounces of other opium products, including laudanum, powdered opium, opium with ipecac, and paregoric, while 29,828 ounces of morphine sulfate were issued to the medical corps.[11] The Medical Inspector of the Federal Army reported in 1863 that he had been informed "by Dr. Th. L. Maddin, professor of surgery in the Shelby Medical College, Nashville ... that later in the season, congestive fevers of a highly pernicious type occur in ... [the Tennessee River] valley ... as an internal remedy, he recommends a powder composed as follows: Take quinine, 1 drachm; calomel, ½ scruple; opium 5 grains; cayenne pepper, 12 grains.... The reputation for skill and scientific attainments which Dr. Maddin enjoys ... entitle his opinions to special consideration."[12]

Because of its efficiency as a numbing agent it was freely given to battlefield casualties on both sides.[13] That opium was commonly and widely available, despite the Federal naval blockade, can be demonstrated by an entry in Sergeant John

Coffee Williamson's wartime journal. While serving with General Joseph Wheeler's 5th Tennessee Cavalry, on a raid into middle Tennessee in 1864 Coffee noted on August 29 that after a triumphant dash into Sparta, the cavalry made it to Smithville at nightfall. Williamson's journal notation is indicative of an addict's "habit," and reveals that narcotic use was not unknown: "I have been very sick all day, and at night I was perfectly worn out.... I took a dose of morphine and slept soundly." Nor was opiate use confined to soldiers. Ms. Mary L. Pearre, of Williamson County, tired of the medicines prescribed by her physician noted in her diary on March 27, 1863: "Not another pill will I swallow except opium. I rather like its effect." On June 15, 1863, author Lucy Smith French, in McMinnville, while suffering from writer's block, confided in her journal: "I sat down in the morning to do my writing—about 9 o'clock [I] began to feel sick and at 10 was obliged to undress and go to bed. Took laudanum and brandy—lay in bed all day...."[14]

Physicians in blue and gray prescribed opium for diarrhea and dysentery, arguably the most common diseases in the war. William H. Taylor, a Confederate assistant surgeon, revealed how freely opium was dispensed for intestinal ailments. According to Taylor, while on the march, he carried in one pocket a ball of a laxative called blue mass and in the other a ball of opium. Each morning at sick call, he would first ask each soldier: "How are your bowels? If they were open, I administered a plug of opium, if they were shut I gave a plug of blue mass."[15] Given the ubiquitous presence of malaria, dysentery, and diarrhea (or the "Tennessee Trots") and the almost cavalier issuance of opium, one may begin to understand the ease with which soldiers on both sides of the conflict contracted the "soldier's disease." Yet the Civil War did not cause drug addiction in Tennessee or in the United States, but only quickened its pace. Addicted veterans, for example, may have "spread addiction by recruiting other users."[16] On March 19, 1863, Confederate Army Surgeon-General Samuel Preston Moore issued a circular, which aimed to enlist women in opium production. It was necessary to "induce the ladies throughout the South to interest themselves in the culture of the garden poppy. They may thus render the Confederacy essential service ... furnish the ladies with the seeds of the poppy ... and ... instruct them that the juice exuding from the punctured capsules, when sufficiently hardened, should be ... forwarded to the nearest purveying depot."[17]

Rare surveys by public health officials conducted in Michigan in 1878, Chicago in 1880, and Iowa in 1885, for example, demonstrated that nearly 75 percent of all drug addicts were women who took it to ease neuralgia, painful menstruation, and even morning sickness. There is no basis to precisely determine the number of addicted Civil War veterans, and as one study put it: "Rather than dismissing the war as a 'scapegoat,' we should understand it as one of several causes of opiate addiction in late nineteenth-century America."[18] A rapid rise in opiate consumption began in the early 1870s, while a concurrent rise in morphine use began in the late 1870s. *Per capita*, consumption peaked in 1896. Yet another cause for increased consumption was the ubiquitous use of opiates by medical doctors and the presence of opium in patent medicines. Moreover, some "cures" for the habit contained opiates or cocaine.[19]

It is difficult to determine the number of opiate addicts in nineteenth-century Tennessee. Many addicts concealed their dependence on the drug and so cannot be tallied. How many Tennessee Civil War veterans were addicted? There are no records to begin answering this question, although it has been convincingly stated that opium addiction increased largely as a factor of the therapeutic use of the drug—that is, in the treatment of disease and less due to chronic opium "recreational" intoxication.

In the late nineteenth century, the practice of smoking opium was closely associated with the Chinese. The glut of cheap Chinese labor threatened the American worker. Often opium smoking was thought of as one way in which xenophobic and racist Americans believed the Chinese were plotting to overthrow and destroy American morals.[20]

There is convincing anecdotal evidence providing a rare glimpse into the nontherapeutic use of opiates in the Volunteer State, particularly in Memphis. One newspaper report complained: "At the Chinese opium dens of this city, it is not unusual to see a fast man and lewd woman resting on a dirty couch and smoking together from a dirty pipe, fixed up by a dirtier Chinaman [*sic*]."[21] A widely reported incident in Memphis in late June 1879 spelled out that opium smoking was rampantly on the increase in the city.[22] Reports explained how three prostitutes, escorted by two "sports" were discovered smoking opium in the back room of Henry Ying's laundry on 207 Main Street. One article, entitled "CRACKING A JOINT [*sic*]," told how two Memphis policemen acting upon their suspicions entered the opium den at Ying's establishment after midnight where a "strange sight met their eyes." According to the account:

> Several parties were seated in the room, including several of the demimonde and three sports, who were watching with great interest a bed in the farther end of the apartment. Upon this bed was lying a Chinaman and a white nymph du pave.... The girl held between her lips an uncouth-looking pipe ... upon which was sizzling a gummy substance ... applied from the end of an iron wire, which he heated in a small lamp placed in a waiter on the bed, and then dipped in a small wooden box which contained the substance referred to. From the top of the pipe a thin blue flame ascended, and large puffs of smoke came from the lips of the girl as she lay in the dreamy happiness produced by the drug ... like that of the hashheesh [*sic*] eater of the East.[23]

Upon seeing the police, the startled "sports" broke out, but the three courtesans and Mr. Ying were taken to police headquarters and posted bail. Ying's paraphernalia were confiscated. According to the reporter, whose account seemed to misrepresent his innocence, each application of opium consisted of three drops, which in the opium-smokers vernacular was called a "joint." The process of smoking the opium was called "cracking a joint." Fifty cents bought three joints. Whether or not a joint was the standard non-therapeutic criterion for "cracking a joint" is not known. But it was known that there were several opium dens in the city in 1879, "all situated in Chinese laundries." More revealingly impressive about this nineteenth-century social behavior was the assertion that "the practice of smoking opium is largely on the increase, not only amongst 'the gang' but also among a class of people considered respectable."[24] Consequently, the recreational abuse of opium, in Memphis at least, was not circumscribed to prostitutes, Chinese launderers, and "sports," but apparently cut across class, racial, and gender divisions, and may have included any number of respectable citizens such as clerks, housewives, attorneys, cotton brokers, policemen, engineers, newspaper editors, judges, merchants, writers, bankers, and the idle rich.

The editor of the *Memphis Daily Appeal* was outraged at the number of "Chinese opium dens at present in this city." The principal dens of opium smoking iniquity were located at Ying's laundry, on Main Street, on the corner of the alley between Second and Third Streets, on Monroe Street between Main and Second, on Jefferson Street, and on the corner of the alley between Second and Third Streets. "In fact," claimed the editor, "every Chinese laundreyhouse [sic] is an opium den. Within the past six months opium smoking has increased to a wonderful [sic] extent in this city, especially among women of the town and their male friends."[25]

Of a diametrically opposed view was the worldly editor of the Memphis *Public Ledger*, who wrote that Mr. Ying "during his leisure moments indulges in the pleasurable Chinese custom of whiffing the fumes of opium. He also favors any curious friends with a dose, provided their curiosity leads to his hospitable den."[26] Neither Ying nor the three prostitutes, however, were prosecuted because there was no law against opium smoking. The dismissal of the four prompted the editor of the *Public Ledger* to observe: "Why people haven't a right to smoke opium, eat hashish, or chew hen manure if they desire, is a question in many circles at present. Tobacco chewers, cigar smokers—especially in the street car—and bibulous people have no more right to satisfy their appetites than opium smokers."[27]

It was thus up to the Memphis legislators to enact an ordinance against opium smoking in order to demolish "these nefarious and immoral dens, which have a most baleful effect upon public morals."[28] And they did too, on June 28, when the following amendment was inserted in the public health law:

> Nor shall anyone keep for sale, give away, or have or loan or loan for use, with or without hire or reward, any opium or any deleterious drug, to be smoked, inhaled, or otherwise used, nor any pipe, instrument or receptacle by which such thing may be done; and if such instrument, receptacle or pipe is at any time found by the police, they shall take the same to police headquarters, that the same may be destroyed under orders of the chief of police, nor shall any opium smoking be permitted or done by anyone at his or her business house, place of business, boarding house, dwelling house, or other place.[29]

This was the first attempt at controlling drug abuse and protect public morals through legislation in any city in nineteenth-century Tennessee. While the editor of the *Daily Appeal* was placated, a letter in the *Public Ledger* perhaps written by one "among a class of people considered respectable," represented a more jaded and annoyed constituency, and pointed out a certain hypocritical attitude expressed in this law:

> Is it not strange that they will allow druggists or anyone else that may desire to do so to sell morphine, opium, or any other deadly poison to anyone that may have the money to pay for it? And because the Chinese and perhaps a few others, that may wish to have an easy time for a while by smoking their opium—something that will not kill one in five thousand to its use otherwise—morphine and opium

by the mouth or skin—our city dads kick at it with both feet and say you shall not smoke your opium. We allow you, however, to take it internally or by the skin, and if it kills you, all right, we are not to blame.[30]

The distinction between opium smoking and the consumption of other opiates may have rested on a racial bias, inasmuch as opium dens were closely associated with the Chinese. In any event, the prohibitive ordinance, while it certainly did not prohibit opiate consumption except by smoking, may have been responsible for an improvement of public morals inasmuch as by mid-July the *Daily Appeal* reported: "Nearly every member of the demi-monde has left this city."[31] It is more likely that the more immediate threat of yellow fever prompted their exodus, and not a legislated termination of opium consumption by smoking or any other means in the Bluff City. Certainly the city would be a cleaner, less exotic place in the future.

Yet, this was not the case and the abuse of opium did not cease in Memphis. Such activities were more common than might be imagined. Six years after the "Ying incident," in late August 1885, another Bluff City newspaper reporter was acquainted with an opium den by a reformed addict he met in a saloon. His guide took him down a filthy little side street, and the two stopped at a laundry where, characteristically enough, stood "Chinaman John" ironing a shirt. John nodded to the guide and the two entered and ascended the stairs to the opium den. The reporter related the descriptions of opium pipes. It took years of practice, he learned, to make an opium pill, and their Chinese host and his African-American wife were very skilled at the peculiar art. The reporter watched as "Chinaman John" smoked the opium. Asking him if it were good, John replied: "Oh yes, any kind of sickness no hurtee s'long [sic] you got pipes." Both John and his spouse claimed that they could work for twenty-four hours at a stretch without feeling any fatigue after they had smoked opium. Having seen enough of the opium panorama, the reporter and his guide returned to the saloon and over a schooner of beer, their drug of choice, the reporter learned more about the world of the opium habit and narcotic addicts in Tennessee.

According to the report, the use of morphine and opium were greatly on the increase in the Volunteer State and the nation as a whole. Just as had been reported in 1879, "Votaries are to be found in 'good society' as well as among the 'shady kind.' In opium dens the so-called 'respectable' ladies and actresses of note can be seen mingling with outcasts of their own sex, and with all classes of men in silent fellowship. In business and social life, in body and mind, the opium user grows rapidly weaker and worthless and useless until … the day of agony and death are at hand." In what sounded much like a *Police Gazette* recanting of Dr. Gunn's discourse fifty-five years earlier, the article went on to explain that the drug produced different effects upon different people. It stimulated both physical and mental performance. Some were aroused to carry out great physical work while others were lulled to sleep. Still others were capable of carrying out literary accomplishments with great ease, using their fantasies to soar with their muse.

It was estimated by the ex-addict that there were 1 million narcotic abusers in the United States, most of them were in the South. In Memphis, the population of opium fiends was "upwards of 1,000, mostly white and including four negro women and twelve Chinese men. No negro man uses it.…" The reformed addict claimed to know one man who smoked a pound of opium a day, and another, a "professional type" who hypodermically injected an astonishing 60 grains of morphine a day. Hundreds of ladies used the drug as well because "they suffer some intense pain of some sort, and a physician will prescribe morphine and administer it hypodermically. They find immediate relief and bless the drug. The next time the feel the pain they don't wait for the physician, but take it on their own responsibility, and in this way become confirmed opium fiends." Some smoked gum opium, some drank, inhaled, or injected morphine, while others became addicted to paregoric or laudanum. It affected the whites the worst "as it attacks the brain first." Mongolians and Chinese were next, while African Americans were least affected by the drug, claimed the erstwhile addict. Yet, despite the grip the narcotic had on its abusers there was help in various sanitariums.[32] Consequently the non-medicinal use of opium and its derivatives—either to sustain an addiction or as an intoxicant—constituted an increasing presence in the lives of some Tennesseans, including many classes, races and both genders. It was a genuine social problem with which the public was not yet prepared to cope, and which legislation could not abate. Nor was it limited to Memphis.

Evidence that opium smoking was common in nineteenth-century Tennessee cities indicates that the problem was common in Nashville, Knoxville, and Chattanooga. Additionally, the use of cocaine made its appearance in the 1880s. Smoking opium was a specialized narcotic that was meant only for recreational use, a characteristic that did not diminish its addictive qualities. Morphine and laudanum and a host of patent medicines contained the addictive substance. An alarming headline in the March 30, 1888 Nashville *Daily American* read "THE HASHEESH EATERS." A druggist explained how the opium habit was increasing in the Capitol City. Addicts, especially white middle-class women, veiled their habits by seeking out opium and morphine from drugstores in the suburbs.[33] The Nashville centenarian Miss Jane Thomas related in her book of nineteenth-century reminiscences that at about the time "they had just begun inhaling morphine here," she was invited to a fashionable party. One of the guests complained of a headache. She was advised to take morphine, which caused her to swoon. She feared she would die, but ice water and rest on a couch evidently saved her.[34] In the Capitol City in the early spring of 1895, a young woman, Juliet Bridges of New Middleton, Smith County, died as a result of an overdose of morphine. Ms. Bridges, a graduate of a noted female college in Nashville, was the victim of a runaway accident "which left her in pain so intense that only morphine could ease her pains." She became a slave to the drug and the habit finally grew to have so powerful an effect on her that she was sent to the Tyson Sanitarium" in January 1894. Apparently cured, she was sent home in September 1894. She soon returned to Nashville, to the Douglas Sanitarium, for another attempt at a remedy. In March, she escaped from the sanitarium because Dr. Douglas "wouldn't let her have enough morphine...." She quickly marched to Nashville and bought morphine at a druggist's shop on South College Street, and later purchased paregoric. A nurse friend took her to the Tyson Sanitarium and Dr. Zarecor and Dr. Douglas soon arrived. Both physicians tried to restore her to consciousness, but she died at 2:00 p.m., a casualty of "the deadly blight of the awful morphine habit."[35]

Help was available at various sanitariums. Using capitalist free market theory, one can clearly perceive that there was business enough to sustain these early private sector drug rehabilitation centers in Nashville. And since the Tyson and Douglas sanitariums were a profitable concern, it follows that there was a larger population of drug addicts than might not once have warranted recognition. The Douglas and Tyson institutes were only two of such establishments in Tennessee. In 1911, the James Sanitorium (*sic*) in Memphis claimed it was "the only sanitorium" (*sic*) with a 90 percent cure rate. The institute had cured drug addictions, alcoholism, and cigarette and tobacco habits for more than ten years. One testimonial claimed that "after using forty grains of morphine a day for twenty years an addict had been cured at the James Sanitorium [*sic*]." If the afflicted could not get to the institute, which operated under a state license, the institute would come to the addict by way of mail order sales of cures for tobacco and alcohol abusers as well as "hypodermic or internal" drug cures.[36]

Drug abuse was a problem in late nineteenth-century Knoxville also. The city had its own district, the "Bowery," catering to bohemian appetites. In 1900, the *Journal and Tribune* carried a story entitled "A Night on the Bowery." According to the article, nine-tenths of the criminal element were residents, and "the color line is very lightly regarded … and all men are equal so long as they have the price of a drink about them." In addition to cheap restaurants, bordellos, cheap lodging houses, stables, saloons, and a profusion of second-hand stores there were also two or three small drugstores. Their "principal business at night seems to be the sale of morphine and cocaine, the twin fiends of the district which are sending many of its inhabitants, especially women and girls, to their graves." At these drugstores "all night long, pale-faced women, or girls, or boys scarcely out of their teens, with blood-shot eyes and bloated features showing long dissipation, come slipping in and go out with the tell-tale little round box of powdered cocaine, or morphine."[37] Thus young people of both genders were abusing addictive drugs, at least in Knoxville.

Suicides that resulted from overdoses of opiates were not uncommon.[38] In Chattanooga, for example, a former railroad fireman committed suicide by drinking laudanum in August 1911. His wife was suing for divorce because of his drinking problem. He went to his mother's residence after purchasing the narcotic, went to lie down for a few moments, and took the lethal dose. A similar incident occurred in 1889 when a furniture factory worker killed himself with laudanum.[39] In early June 1874, a Memphis newspaper article tellingly entitled "The Old, Old Story" explained how Ms. Willie Melrose, a prostitute, had killed herself with an overdose of morphine. Two heartbroken courtesans committed a dual suicide in Nashville in 1867, while eighteen years later, Annie McCreary, a passenger from Helena, Arkansas, arrived in Memphis. She attempted suicide by jumping off the transfer steamer. An officer took her to the stationhouse and it was there that she was interviewed. She confided with the reporter saying: "Yes, I took morphine, but I take morphine all the time. I have used it for three years."[40] George Wade, aged thirty-two, it was reported, died suddenly in Murfreesboro on August 20, 1874. He "had for some time been on a spree, and had become nervously prostrated." He then took some morphine to settle his nerves. He was found dead the next morning.[41] In Nashville, the story of Mary Buffington, known to the police as "Morphine Mary," was revealed in a newspaper report in 1878. She became addicted to opium and soon took up the morphine habit. She "would do anything—beg or steal—to get either laudanum or morphine." According to Nashville police Captain Yatter, "Morphine Mary" could "drink a pint of laudanum—ten times as much as would kill ten people." She was a pathetic case, "whom only death could cure."[42]

An *exposé* in the *Nashville American* in 1889 uncovered an opium den. It was located on the topmost floor of a pretentious brick structure on Broad Street and did not suffer for patronage. The establishment's operators had no fear of a police raid because there was no law banning opium smoking dens in the city. Yet they kept an eye out in case "some spying traitor will learn their unholy secrets and publish its horrors to the world." Prostitutes from bagnios on Front Street (today First Avenue) were discovered by the police "reveling in the fumes of opium." To enter the "Nashville Joint," the reporter tapped on the opaque glass of a side door. A woman answered and he was admitted. According to the report in the *American*:

> She then guides him through a room which generally several men and women are lolling. After leaving the room she takes him up several flights of stairs, and finally ushers him into a room almost suffocating of the smoke of that weed, whose slaves are seen stretched about the floor, in attitudes so indecent as to forbid description. These depraved and soundly slumbering wretches the fair attendant passes with a kick if they happen to obstruct her pathway. She leads them into other apartments … where men and women are languidly smoking long pipes of Chinese manufacture.

He declined to "hit the pipe" and was left in a room with fumes were so thick that he retreated downstairs and spoke with the cook, asking who frequented the opium den. "Everybody" was the response, which meant "upstanding citizens, men who are apparently above suspicion." He learned there were other "Chinamen" who operated opium dens in other parts of Nashville. The reporter claimed that the City Council would soon pass an ordinance outlawing opium dens.[43] That proposed law was, however, never established.

These substances continued to be used, even though smoking opium was outlawed in the United States in 1909.[44] The variety of abused drugs increased with the gradual introduction of cocaine starting in the 1880s.[45]

Opiates were not the only class of drugs subject to abuse. During the Creek Indian War (1813–1814) soldiers imbibed the "black drink" before mutinying and marching out of Fort Jackson in the Mississippi Territory. This Native American concoction stimulated the central nervous system with a cornucopian dose of caffeine, and was used to strengthen one's resolve to march and keep awake while on guard duty.[46] About 1885, cocaine was popularized soon after the death of President Ulysses S. Grant, whose doctor utilized it to ease the pain of the ex-president's throat cancer. At first, it became wildly popular among those rich who could afford this panacea's price. As production increased due to demand, the price plummeted. It was soon bowdlerized and became commonplace and used as a recreational drug.[47] In 1903, Memphis Police Captain Perry recalled the presence of cocaine among the city's poor and criminal elements in the 1880s.[48] In addition, cocaine was thought to be the cure for morphine, heroin, alcoholism, and opium addictions. Moreover, and even more astonishing, cocaine's exhilarating properties made the white powder a preferred component not only of medicines, bur for wines and even soda pop. An advertisement in the *Daily Memphis Avalanche* in December 1885 extolled the virtues of J. S. Pemberton's tonic, "French Wine of Coca." Laced heavily with cocaine, it was the "ideal Nerve Tonic and 'Intellectual Beverage'" that would cure numerous diseases as well as boost one's mood by ridding the consumer of "tired and good for nothing feelings."[49] Large drug houses provided cocaine at high cost that declined as early as 1886 when production caught up with an incredible demand.[50] As demand spurred productivity, firms such as the Parke Davis Company became an especially ardent producer of cocaine and cocaine products, selling coca cheroots, coca-leaf cigarettes along with their other products providing cocaine such as Coca Cordial, pills, ointments, sprays, and, of course, hypodermic injections.[51] Even Sears and Roebuck offered "Peruvian Wine of Coca." According to the 1897 Sears Catalog: "If you wish to accomplish double the amount of work or have to undergo an unusual amount of hardship, always keep a bottle of our Peruvian Wine of Coca near you. Its sustaining powers are remarkable." Because the management of Sears expected "a large demand for this wine, we have made arrangements for an extra-large shipment...." The cocaine solution sold for $10 for a dozen bottles.[52] In 1910, a U.S. Senate Document asserted that 15,000 ounces of cocaine were sufficient for medicinal and surgical uses, but over 150,000 ounces were produced in America. According to the report, cocaine ruined lives and led to robbery, rape, and murder.[53] Free market demand led to increased production and occasion for many Americans to become drug addicts. So did some physicians. In 1900, Dr. T. D. Crothers made a study of drug addiction among physicians and concluded that 6–10 percent of American physicians were addicted to cocaine, morphine, and other drugs. The public viewed addiction as a moral lapse, the then-current opinion being "that the victims in all cases are weak and vicious, giving way to low impulses, and lacking the morale which should be common among educated men. Never was there a greater mistake." Medical schools must, it was recommended, teach more about "morphisms" and the addictive properties of other drugs.[54]

Cocaine became a problem near the turn of the century when its use reached epidemic proportions. While the drug was closely associated with black men, its use was not circumscribed to them. One headline in a Chattanooga newspaper in June 1914 claimed "Negro Cocaine Fiends, New Southern Menace." The article, by New York City physician Edward H. Williams, contended that cocaine drove black men to rape and kill. In Tennessee, one in seventy-four African Americans were cocaine addicts—perhaps because, as they themselves said: "'Cause I couldn't git nothin' else, boss." In Knoxville, when the police made efforts to stop the cocaine traffic the use the drug increased, while in Memphis "where half the population is colored, but where no attempt is made to prevent the sale of liquor, the drug habit is increasing slowly, if at all." Anecdotal information held that black men used more cocaine than white men, and were motivated thus to commit more crimes. Particularly frightening was the bogus belief that cocaine improved an African American's pistol marksmanship. Yet another myth was that cocaine made blacks almost unaffected by mere .32-caliber bullets, which led southern urban police departments to use .38-caliber revolvers. Such delusions characterized white fear, not the authentic consequences of cocaine's use.[55]

A government report concluded that "the use of cocaine by the negroes [*sic*] is one of the most elusive and troublesome questions which confront the enforcement of law in the Southern States...." It was current knowledge, the report claimed, that, "throughout the South that on many public works, levee and railroad construction, and in other working camps where large numbers of negroes [*sic*] congregate, cocaine is handled among them by some method largely obscure." There was also evidence that contractors forced African American workers to become cocaine addicts "under the impression that they can get more and better work from their employees." Cocaine was also utilized in the white slavery traffic, corrupting "young girls, and ... when the habit of using the drug has been established it is but a short time before the latter fall to the ranks of prostitution."[56]

In Chattanooga, in late October 1899, it was reported police activity in Chattanooga had escalated because cocaine use was rampant "among the lower classes of negroes and whites." Authorities vouched that "the habit has become alarming and the people are demanding a rigid enforcement of the law restraining druggists from the sale of the poison."[57] The only problem was that there was no law specifically restricting cocaine sales. The summer of 1900 was a time of more widespread public anxiety about cocaine, and attempts were made to control the traffic in Chattanooga and Memphis. Chattanooga was alarmed by the spread of drug habits, and the local clergy demanded action. But many times those who used cocaine did not do so in a recreational sense, but became addicts because many patent medicines contained cocaine "masquerading as headache powders, and remedies for hay fever and catarrh. The state law banning the sale of such drugs was too lax, and the city should act itself to end the menace."[58] On June 6, the Chattanooga city council, alarmed at the use of cocaine and morphine had spread to an alarming extent, passed Tennessee's first drug control ordinance. The law made it a misdemeanor for anyone to sell or give cocaine to anyone who did not have a physician's prescription, even if it was for a pound. Only disreputable drugstores would lose business as a result. On East Ninth Street, in "Darktown" and "Cocaine Alley" small drugstores where business was once brisk "remained closed all during the night, for the first time in over a year."[59]

The ordinance was proclaimed effective a few days later; a headline in the *Chattanooga Daily Times* for June 8 triumphantly declared "Fiends in Cocaine Alley Are Experiencing Trouble in Securing Their Favorite Stimulant." The ordinance had cut off addicts "giving them a chance to recover and reform."[60] Yet, there were no facilities available to help addicts in their withdrawal, recovery, and reform. The Chattanooga ordinance then aimed at the result not the cause of drug abuse. Yet cocaine addicts skirted requirement that it required a physician's prescription to obtain the drug. Many drugstores, it so happened, had their own "doctors" who wrote prescriptions for eager addicts. Those drugstores had secured the services of medical doctors, "whose only claim to being a physician lay in their having secured a physician's license to practice," were ensconced in a small office in the rear of the drugstores and wrote prescriptions for any sort of drug an addict craved. The city attorney declared that such operations were a violation of the recent law. Some of these prescriptions were for a pound of cocaine that the addict could draw upon until the limit had been exhausted. Police Chief Hill vowed to crack down on these kinds of operations.[61] Regardless of the offensive against cocaine in Chattanooga, its use was not curbed. In November 1903, cocaine use had reached such high levels that Sheriff Hays initiated a "systematic war against the doctors in this city implicated in the sale of cocaine." African Americans' use of the banned drug had reached alarming proportions, claimed Hays, resulting in the doubling of prosecutions. Four physicians and three druggists on Ninth Street were "seriously implicated and that several arrests will be made soon."[62] The war against cocaine, while ostensibly virtuous, had hardly been victorious.

In Memphis, "Cocaine Joe" and "Sallie the Sniff" would find life more difficult if the city council passed an ordinance similar to that of Chattanooga's. The sale of cocaine had reached such heights that the police were unable to cope with the problem. According to the police, there was a time when only a handful of people were addicted to the drug, but "now 80 per cent of the colored population ... are using it in quantities that support about a dozen small drug stores and also contribute to the volume of business of a few corner groceries." The use of cocaine was not limited to the black population, "but whites are also using it in large quantities." As a result, crime had increased. Statistics showed that the percentages of criminals using cocaine was nearly treble that of criminals not addicted. A vacant house had become a rendezvous for addicts. A sanitary officer went through the place collecting a bushel basket of empty cocaine boxes, all sold by one drugstore. "In the basement, where it was damp and dark, a negro woman was found. She had been there for seven days and was rolled up in a worn-out blanket. About her were scattered empty boxes." One tenderloin district drugstore stayed open all night, selling small packages of cocaine for 5 or 10 cents each. Average Saturday night sales of cocaine in two retail drugstores ran from $25 to $100 a night and the business was growing. A 5-cent package of cocaine furnished a five-hour high. The problem was serious, and the city government enlisted the cooperation of the Chattanooga Retail Druggists' Association, which collaborated in curbing indiscriminate sales of cocaine. After the passage of the law, every addict would be forced to name his source.[63]

Under the new law, no one was "allowed to give or sell cocaine in amounts less than one pound except on a certificate from a physician, and this certificate must be filed and open to the inspection of the police at any time." A pound of cocaine in 1900 sold for about $35, an amount that was well beyond the average addict's means. The penalty was not less than $5 and not more than $20. "There was no discussion at all ... and the ordinance was passed on a unanimous vote."[64] As in Chattanooga, there was no thought about providing aid to addicts. It was a simple matter of making drug use and sale a misdemeanor rather than a felony, to control addicts and addiction, some of which occurred as a result of the unregulated access to the dangerous drug.

Patterns of cocaine addiction seemed to be different in Knoxville, where, claimed the *Journal and Tribune*, "Only the Poorer Classes of the City Are Addicted." As late as 1899, the use of cocaine was virtually unknown in Knoxville, but by 1900, it was commonly available in every city drugstore. It sold in packages of three grains for a dime, which at that rate would bring the enormous price of $256 per pound. A year earlier, only a dollar's worth was sold in Knoxville, and by 1900, it jumped to an average of $50. According to the report, the "first genuine cocaine 'sniffers' that made their appearance in Knoxville were half a dozen negro women from Middlesboro [Kentucky]." These sable cocaine sirens arrived about August, 1899, and introduced its use on Central Avenue, Knoxville's red-light district.[65] From there, the habit spread to both races and both genders. Many bar patrons salted their beers with cocaine, but this was not as economical as hypodermic injection. Yet only the rich could afford syringes so the poor resorted to sniffing the drug. An ordinary dose was one and one-half grains. [66] The city council weighed the matter duplicating the Chattanooga and Memphis examples, enacting an ordinance in July.[67, 68] By 1904–05, the practice evidently had not been eradicated as the city council enacted further legislation regulating the sale of cocaine, opium, and morphine.[69]

It would appear then that by 1900 three of Tennessee's cities experienced serious drug addiction problems and seemed on their way to controlling and even eradicating the use of cocaine, morphine and other opiates. Such conviction was not justified.

Only three years after the Memphis city council passed its ordinance, Memphis had become a "'COKE' CENTER." A reputable physician held that there were more cocaine addicts in the Bluff City than before the passage of the anti-drug ordinance. The doctor held also that the "number of users of this drug is monthly increasing among negroes." Cocaine's effects were even more horrible to contemplate than those of morphine. Disreputable physicians provided prescriptions to addicts. The letter of the law was observed but its spirit was not. Memphis Police Captain Perry declared that cocaine addicts were "the worst class if degraded criminals.... They howl and talk to themselves hoarse and do all sorts of queer things." Addicts in Memphis's "Tin Can Alley" or "Jay Bird Alley" also had "coke parties." "Livid eyed negresses [*sic*] and negroes congregate[d] on stools at an early hour of the evening. They pass the usual compliments ... at the appointed hour the sniffing commences." The group then formed into couples until one individual was left. It was this person's job to dispense the cocaine. "The actual partaking is generally preceded by a sort of lullaby.... And the fun commences. Each one of the guests pulls out his box and each in turn is sampled by everybody present. Often thereafter one of the group might perform some antic causing the assembled to laugh hysterically." Such "coke parties" lasted until midnight, and the police were often called to quiet the noise. Cocaine, according to one black addict, gave him a sense of power: "You feels you is more powerful den white folks and figger [*sic*] you can lick four perlicemens."[70] It was also commonly believed that many black on white rapes were directly the result of cocaine use.[71] Thus a white supremacist fear surfaced, namely that cocaine could upset the existing racial order, giving black men a sense of racial superiority and great, although short-lived, physical strength. It was obviously a dangerous substance, but existing ordinances and police enforcement had not done a good job since 1900, explaining the increase of cocaine abuse. Opium was also a drug of choice in Memphis among the white population by 1905.[72]

In Chattanooga, law enforcement was not apparently strict. Few arrests were made for cocaine possession, but by early July 1911, police arrested Pat Lowry, an African American, near East Ninth Street. His was evidently the first arrest for cocaine pandering in many months.[73] More alarming was the news about Dr. J. L. Jackson. The physician sold prescriptions for cocaine, and had been in trouble with the law before. The constabulary had cleansed East Ninth and "Darktown" of pushers. In fact, they had broken up a gang of cocaine pushers that had been working secretly for ten years. Dr. Jackson and an African American associate, Will Ross, were the wholesalers of the operation. Jackson received the cocaine by express train with no known origination point. He gave Ross a portion of the drug, while Jackson sold it from his "own rooms on King Street, in the heart of the lowest section of the city." In other days, Jackson was a respected doctor in Chattanooga and had a profitable practice. While he dabbled with cocaine, he discovered there was a great deal of money to be made selling the drug, and so he began his "cocaine trust." Many cases were brought against him in the lower courts, but there was never enough evidence when the grand jury deliberated, or in criminal court. It appeared as if Jackson would once again escape the law.[74]

An article in the *Nashville American* of October 23, 1899, was headlined "COCAINE FIENDS OF NASHVILLE." The drug was in such high demand that its wholesale price of $6.30 per ounce had increased by a dollar since April. The drug had become so popular since 1896 that drugstores provided convenient "handy packages for sale." Like any other city in the nation, the City of Rocks was populated by cocaine fiends, and "their name is legion." Addicts were most commonly said to be African Americans, although to be certain this was not a universal truth. The relatively low retail price of cocaine had largely driven morphine out of the market. According to the report in the *American*:

> [Moreover] The local demand is so great that drug firms in this city are now constantly prepared for the run that comes in day and night. The cocaine is put up in approximately 2 grain paper envelopes and kept in the vicinity of the cigar stand, where it can be handed out without delay. The 2-grain packages sell for five cents, and the first class fiend will buy and use from seven to ten packages a day.

Each Saturday night, one drugstore in the notorious "Black Bottom" section of the city that prepared for the nightly rush by making eighty packages readily available to addicts. One pharmacist on Broad Street bought cocaine in bulk putting it up in lots of 1,000 packages in a "good size box which is well filled all the time." It was estimated that the retail profits from cocaine sales amounted to an astounding $100 per day in Nashville.

Typically, the drug was sniffed, and when combined with whisky made "a fiend a hard man to handle when he runs amuck of the law. Among the regular fiends the drug is known as 'coke.'" The high demand for the drug led to larger wholesale purchases by druggists seeking an adequate reserve to provide higher profits.[75]

Even though a state law restricting cocaine sales had been passed in Nashville in 1901, by 1903 very little had changed in the State Capital. Cocaine, or "croke," as it was called on the street, was even more insidious than before, allowing dealers to make higher profits. Whether it was sniffed or injected was "remarkable for producing insensibility to pain and all surroundings, as well as the complete loss of all sensibility as to honesty." The report in the *American* of June 29, 1903 continued:

> The wonderful quality of the powder for producing insensibility probably accounts for its popularity among the ignorant and lower class. Some time ago one of the

local officers was called to take into custody a negress [*sic*] who was the victim of "croke" and was making some remarks to her in regard to the habit.

"Why do you like to sniff cocaine?" the officer asked.

"Well do you see that long row of houses?" the victim said, pointing to the many pretentious buildings lining the street?

"Yes" was the reply. "Well when I take the croke I feel just like I owned all of them buildings and was about to start out to collect the rent."

One highly educated young white addict was arrested for stealing his friend's watch. Other similar thefts were traced to him by detectives, and it was established that he stole in order to pay for his cocaine habit. He was jailed for six weeks and under the care of a physician he was released "looking bright and healthy." Within twenty four hours, however, he was seen "leaving a drug store with the old glassy look in his eyes." The penalty for selling cocaine, as established by the General Assembly of Tennessee in 1901, was a fine of not less than $100 and no more than $500, or imprisonment for thirty to sixty days, or both depending on the discretion of the court.[76] The law had little effect due to lax enforcement.

It was evident that drug abuse had become a very serious social problem in Tennessee, a fact that did not go unnoticed by Dr. Lucius Polk Brown, Tennessee's Food and Drugs Commissioner. Largely upon his insistence the Tennessee General Assembly passed an Act to control addictive drugs.[77] It went into effect on January 1, 1914. The Tennessee statute went further than the already existing national law, the Harrison Act, in that it limited dispensing or distribution of drugs to veterinary surgeons, dentists, registered physicians, and to pharmacists. One regulation was unique to Tennessee's efforts, namely that those then currently addicted could, after registering with the Food and Drugs Commission as addicts, obtain a permit which allowed them to continue their habits. This provision, according to Brown, was "in order to minimize the suffering among this unfortunate class, and to keep the traffic in the drug from getting underground and hidden channels." The permit system was strictly enforced. The abrupt suspension of the sale of addictive drugs would, claimed the Commissioner, "certainly result in great suffering to the indigent class of addicts, possibly in many deaths, and certainly in driving the traffic outside the law." Tennessee's permit system did not include cocaine because Dr. Brown believed use of it was habitual, not addictive and did not "produce such toxemias as are consequent on the use of morphine; therefore its abrupt withdrawal results in no such untoward consequences as with the latter drug. No provision, therefore, need be made for the relief of persons addicted to it."[78] According to Brown's figures that within the first year of the Tennessee anti-narcotics law operation, there were a total of 2,370 addicts using state registration figures, of which fully two thirds were women, the actual figures being 1,586 females to 784 males.[79] Addicts were of all colors and genders. Women were especially prone to laudanum addiction but men used heroin more frequently. However, "ordinarily men seem to use more of the drugs than women, the only exception to this being laudanum."[80] A total 63.5 percent of women between the ages of twenty-two and fifty-five years were addicts, as opposed to 59.6 percent of men in the same age bracket. Tennessee's Food and Drugs Commissioner believed this gender difference was mainly due the onset of menopause. Among men the doctor attributed addiction as a factor of the first ten years in the life period (twenty-five to thirty-five) to "the fact that it is seems that is about the age when dissipations are commonly taken up, these being more distinctively a male attribute."[81] Thus, in Tennessee at least, the majority of women became addicts due to their gender's biological predilections, while most men were addicts as a result of intemperance and debauchery.

Surprisingly, Commissioner Brown indicated that well over half of the active cases of narcotic addiction were due "to the indiscreet administration of drugs by physicians."[82] Blacks, he believed, used fewer narcotics and more cocaine than white men. In East Tennessee the ratio of addicts to non-addicts in the population was figured at one addict in every 1,359 persons, while in West Tennessee the ratio was one in only 928 (he presented no figures for Middle Tennessee). The difference in the ratios was due to the rich lowlands of the South, which were "credited with having an unusually large proportion of addicts, and these figures are in accord with that reputation." Brown reckoned that there were in the neighborhood of 5,000 addicts in Tennessee out of a national population he calculated at 269,000, a figure that did not jibe with the accounts of "sensational writers." Additionally, the annual cost of the drugs used in Tennessee by addicts was placed at $145,000, out of a total of $14,038,000 spent on illicit drug use nationally, "a sheer waste of money, to say nothing of the damage to the community ... which is appalling."[83] Addiction spread sometimes from one family member to another, and from physicians' careless prescription of narcotics to which they themselves were addicted. Heroin was then a drug of recent introduction and its use was nearly confined to boys and men as a means of dissipation. Instead of being injected it was inhaled. Heroin use began when the subject took it for a toothache, headaches, or some similar minor trouble. In the end, the heroin addict became "a salesman of the product." The Commissioner also believed that "in every place where a number of boys and young men are employed together there will be a certain amount of heroin addiction." Recognizing that it was a very difficult habit to cure, Brown advised that "the sale of this drug ought to be hedged about with just as rigid and drastic restrictions as are possible to enact into law."[84] Striking a humanitarian note Dr. Brown believed:

> The drug addict is ... more to be pitied than censured, and every effort should be made to help him attain a fulfillment of the desire, which is almost universally present, to get rid of the disease.... The drug addict is a sick man both physically and mentally, and should be studied and treated as a sick man and not as one always willfully delinquent.[85]

The problem of enforcing the Harrison Act and combating drug addiction took a back seat to other concerns as the United States drifted toward involvement in local anti-drug efforts. For example, in October, 1915, Assistant United States District Attorney W. D. Kyser addressed the Memphis and Shelby County Medical Society on the need for the physicians' help in enforcing the Harrison Act (1914), which governed interstate traffic in narcotics. Kyser especially wanted their help in purging from their professional ranks doctors who willfully disobeyed the law by giving prescriptions for opiates and associated drugs. The society acted with alacrity and called its board of censors to wait upon the assistant district attorney, investigate and provide the names of all offending physicians. There were no doctors known to be violating the Harrison Act in either Shelby County or Memphis.

In fact, E. V. Sheely, president of the Memphis Drug Club, indicated that since March 1915, there had been a 32 percent drop in narcotic prescriptions in the Bluff City. That the Harrison Act was having its desired effect, at least in Memphis, was reinforced by Dr. W.R. Wallace of the Petty & Wallace Sanitarium. He revealed that since March 1, the "number of patients had increased from 75, ordinarily, to ... 200, but since that time the sanitarium was reaching normal again." Since the Harrison Act went into effect, according to Wallace, "we have received patients of all kinds from many of the adjoining towns in Tennessee, Mississippi, and Arkansas. From 200 from which statistics have been gathered, we found that 35 of them were over 60 years old. One was a veteran of the Civil War and had been using drugs [*sic*] since he was wounded during a battle back in the war." Wallace believed that it "is worth mentioning too, that of these 200, 37 of them were physicians, or about 12 percent." Wallace urged the physicians to be more careful and scrutinize cases before prescribing narcotics

Assistant District Attorney Kyser admonished the physicians to be certain of their diagnoses and prescribe narcotics only when absolutely necessary. Any lapses would be prosecuted to the fullest extent of the law. Moreover, Kyser said: "It is a crime, gentlemen, not only in law, but in morals, for a man calling himself a doctor willfully and maliciously to violate [the Harrison Act]."[86] Thus drug addiction was, in the eyes of federal law enforcement, a moral crime, a position contrary to that of Dr. L. P. Brown, who held that drug addicts were "more to be pitied than censured ... every effort should be made to help him attain a fulfillment of the desire...."[87] Thus the permit system codified in the 1913 law was contrary to federal belief and policy. (After Dr. Brown took on public employment in New York City in 1915, the novel Tennessee permit system languished into oblivion.)

The extent to which Tennessee physicians served as informers on their kind is unknown, but the traffic and abuse of drugs did not cease. As the United States entered the war in Europe, many cities anxiously looked forward to having a training camp nearby. Camps would boost local economies. However, Secretary of War Newton D. Baker—a former Cleveland, Ohio, mayor with a track record of strong anti-vice activity—had much to say about where a military camp would be located. Together with the wartime Commission on Training Camp Activities, he made certain the character in a perspective city would not work to dissipate the recruits. In Chattanooga, this took the form largely of ridding the city of prostitutes, but the problem of drug traffic and use was also a target for their activities. In late June 1917, Chattanooga police and military police from Fort Oglethorpe raided a room in the Southern hotel annex which was used "by a group of dope fiends." Four men were found with morphine and paraphernalia in the raid led by the chief of military police.[88]

"Headaches Are Higher," proclaimed a headline in a Chattanooga newspaper in 1915, the result of the Harrison Act and the demand for narcotics in war-torn Europe. The article purported that codeine "that old reliable that used to be put up in headache pills at 10 cents a dozen has advanced to the aristocratic figure of $6.80 an ounce, with indication that it will go even higher."[89] "DOPE FIENDS DISAPPEARING" read another reassuring headline in the *Chattanooga Daily Times*. The city had more strictly enforced the Harrison Act and the city's own anti-drug law with intended effect. Will Ross, continued the newspaper story, the "colored 'King Bee' of the dope fiends, who is now serving a sentence in the federal prison in Atlanta, and other followers of his nefarious trade … [sold] small packets of morphine and cocaine from their pockets to men and women who were alive and yet dead.…" Ross not only sold his drugs but also established a recruiting system to gain more customers. According to Chattanooga druggists, the number of prescriptions for narcotics had dropped off substantially since Ross was convicted under the city and federal laws. Physicians also worked to decrease the number of prescriptions by weaning addicts with a lower does each time an addict requested another prescription.

The once common phenomenon of the travelling addict was seldom seen anymore claimed one Chattanooga druggist. "Dozens of them used to come in our store every week. I think that they have all decided that the best thing to do is to stay where one physician can give them all of their prescriptions and gradually cut them down. No matter what their condition is they find it mighty hard to get prescriptions, especially in small towns."[90]

Memphis drug-addict entrepreneurs had made the city a base of morphine supply for the New Orleans underworld by August 1917. Deputy federal collector of internal revenue Larry A. Douglas arrested Ms. Maxine Campbell and confiscated 1,800 morphine tablets. Campbell averred that she had purchased the illegal pills from a Memphis physician, Dr. Ben Fiedman, and J. M. and Leon Thompson druggists. All three were arrested and were released on bail.[91]

Whether from its medicinal and nontherapeutic applications addiction was caused by using opiates as pain killing medicines. The difficulties we face today with controlled substances and a largely ineffective "war on drugs" are but reflections of the Tennessee past. The presence of the abuse of cocaine, morphine, heroin, laudanum and opium in the cities appears to be a function of growing urbanization with is attendant concentrations of people of differing races, creeds, and attitudes. Tennessee's anti-narcotic act of 1913 seemed humane, allowing addicts legal access to their drugs. The federal Harrison Act (1914), forced addicts into the underworld for their supplies. It was in itself recognition of the dimensions of the problem, and was aimed at punishing suppliers and addicts. It made drug use a moral perplexity that could only be altered or ended through tough law enforcement. Unhappily, the drug problem is still with us in the early twenty-first century, and it appears as incapable of solving with aggressive law enforcement today as in the last two centuries. We might do well to heed the words of L. P. Brown, Tennessee's first Food and Drug Commisioner: "The drug addict is a sick man, both physically and mentally, and should be studied and treated as a sick man and not as one always willfully delinquent."[92] The history of the presence of narcotics in Tennessee fails to foster belief in a simple solution to a long-standing social problem. The same history, however, works to absolve our times from the aspersions cast upon them by dewy-eyed and nostalgic comparisons to a past thought to be devoid of such ongoing social problems.[93]

2

The Management of
Prostitution in Tennessee's Past

The management of prostitution is seldom recognized as having much place in Tennessee's history. Nevertheless, in the last two centuries, Tennessee's municipal governments were compelled to deal with controlling prostitution. As a genuine urban social phenomenon, prostitution presented dilemmas the solutions to which were both novel and familiar. Evidence shows that in the nineteenth and early twentieth centuries, prostitution in Nashville, Chattanooga, Knoxville, and Memphis was tolerated and regulated by municipal authorities, while at other times it was the object of dramatic reform.

One of the earliest documented municipal attempts to control prostitution in Tennessee's history was in Nashville in 1854. In early November that year, the Board of Alderman passed on first reading an ordinance requiring two weeks' notice to be given "to occupants of houses of ill fame" prior to their removal.[1] This law led to the "expelling [of] the prostitutes from the lower part of the city..." The law did no more than evict the prostitutes, leading the editor of the Nashville *Union* humanely to criticize:

> It is very easy for the *board* to get together and pass an ordinance to eject an unfortunate class, who are under the ban of respectable society, from the city ... and it is not quite so easy to provide a means for their reformation and existence, after they have passed and put into execution such an ordinance.... If these beings are to be turned out, which may be all proper and right, to make room for "progress," in humanity's name provide some means for their shelter and subsistence until they can do something for themselves.[2]

Apparently there was no such rehabilitation effort made, but judging from the Minutes of Nashville Board Alderman, the hard line against prostitution did not lose any of its vigor.[3] In January 1855, for example, the board passed what could be called an anti-prostitution-advertisement-ordinance, making it "a penal offense for Lewd Women to expose at their front doors or to use vulgar language to persons passing by."[4] Later, in 1856, city authorities sent the police to crack-down on "Bawdy Houses."[5]

Yet, as relentless as these measures appeared to have been, six years after the initial aldermanic effort, prostitution had not been eliminated. Indeed, by late March 1860, the Nashville *Republican Banner* began an editorial, entitled "A Needed Reform." It read, in part: "Mayor McGavock last year said that in the city of Nashville there were *fifteen hundred prostitutes* [sic]. Few and scattering efforts are being made for their reformation. The preaching and religious services at the work house did some good; at least it revealed the extent of the evil."

Memphis, admittedly, had a similar problem. Nevertheless, reform was needed in both Memphis and in Nashville. The *Republican Banner* suggested:

> [A religious mission established in] the disreputable quarter of this city known as "Smoky Row," might have a sanitary effect in that locality. It is true that the fallen nymphs do not … venture into the heart of the city, with their broils, their tournaments, and their quaint language … but if anyone doubts that Nashville has her full share of the pestilence, let him visit our police courts … any morning of the week and satisfy himself with "the ocular demonstration and the proof" in the flocks of leer-eyed, unshod and half-calicoed [sic] unfortunates who come there to confessional. We see none of that "bud-bustiness of bosom" either … but … a waste of deformity and scantiness of covering, shocking to moral vision.

These "wretched … abandoned … [and] depraved" young women had been tricked into leaving their happy homes "for the attractions of the city by some unprincipled serpent in human guise has painted too glowingly for virtuous resolution to withstand." Numerous police court cases involving prostitutes revealed the breadth of the problem. Apparently the Sunday preaching at the workhouse had either not been effective, or had stopped all together. It was time to consider a mission in the heart of Smoky Row to help end the enigma. "No harm will be done if nothing is effected, and there is certainly a prospect of doing the most good where the most evil exists."[6]

The suggestion was never implemented and the evils of Smoky Row continued, even expanded, with the occupation of Nashville by the Union army during the Civil War.

Thus, on the eve of the Civil War Nashville's red-light district was thriving. Because of an eccentricity in the method in which occupations were listed in the 1860 U.S. Census for Nashville, it is possible to identify the number and locations of prostitutes in the capitol city. According to one study, a total of 207 women were listed as prostitutes in Nashville that census year. This is at variance with the figure of 1,500 prostitutes in the capital city. Nevertheless, a section of the city, close to the riverboat trade, two blocks wide and four blocks long, being the first block south and the first block north of what is today Church Street, on First, Second, Third, and Fourth Avenues was the area of heaviest concentration. "Other houses were clustered in the vicinity." Despite the sensational crackdowns on prostitution in the 1850s, the practice flourished, so much so that by 1860, a number of entrepreneurially skilled madams ran houses and owned property valued at anywhere from $15,000 to $24,000.[7] Thus, despite apparent strong legal and enforcement measures, prostitution was managed largely by municipal neglect in antebellum Nashville.

During the Civil War, the arrival of increasingly large numbers of Federal soldiers in Nashville in late February 1862 was followed by a related enlargement of prostitutes in "Smoky Row." Their presence in the occupied city was tolerated by army commanders until the summer of 1863. By that time, Brigadier General R. S. Granger, in command of occupied Nashville, was "daily and almost hourly beset" by Army surgeons and regimental commanders to "save the army from a fate worse … than to perish on the battlefield." The remedy for the problem was to rid the city of prostitutes who were sapping not just the soldiers' physical strength but were also "annoying and destructive to the morals of the army." The prostitutes living and working on "Smoky Row" were a moral threat and a physical impediment to the conduct of the war.

In a move reminiscent of the 1854 municipal action, a martial and summary round-up of all prostitutes were sent north. In the meantime, as a result of the influx of contraband into the city, black prostitutes soon took the place of expatriated white "Cyprians." Within a few weeks, it was reported that the prostitutes aboard the steamboat *Idahoe* were on their way back to Nashville because there was no city that would accept the vessel's singular cargo. Indeed, news of the military operation had reached the secretary of war, who was by no means pleased. By August 4, nearly a month's cruise on the Cumberland, Tennessee, and Ohio rivers, the vessel returned with its singular lading to Nashville "to resume their former modes of life."[8]

Realizing the futility of exile, the provost marshal conceived a method of routine medical inspection and licensed prostitution. The management plan for legalized prostitution consisted of four parts. First, a license would be issued to each prostitute by the provost marshal's office, and her address recorded. Second, a weekly medical examination of each registered prostitute would be conducted by an army surgeon; those who were deemed healthy received a certificate while unhealthy women were to be sent to a hospital for ailing prostitutes, paid for out of the weekly 50-cent tax charged all registered prostitutes for its upkeep. Fourth, any prostitute "found plying her trade without a license and health certificate" would be incarcerated for thirty days at the city work house. A soldiers' "Syphilitic Hospital" would be established later. According to one army doctor, "this is the first time and place that anything of this kind had been [established] in our country." The hospital for the soldiers was at the Hynes High School, located at the contemporary intersection of Fifth and Jo Johnston, while the infirmary for prostitutes was located on Second Avenue.[9] The results of this social management experiment demonstrated that the number of reported cases of venereal disease increased as did the number of registered prostitutes. In April 1864, the total number of reported cases of venereal disease treated at the female hospital was placed at ninety-two. Six months later, the aggregate for treated cases of venereal disease was 994. The total number of registered prostitutes, 352 in April 1864, had grown to 506, 456 white and fifty black a year later. The soldiers' facility "was so full … that the other [military] hospitals had to retain that class of patients instead of transferring them." Thus the system managed prostitution but did not stop the spread of venereal disease.

This unprecedented managerial experiment had both social and medical consequences. The number of prostitutes in Nashville grew at least partially because of what can be termed a better working environment. Many of them had been "drawn to Nashville from northern cities by the comparative protection from venereal disease which its license system afforded." The prostitutes happily showed their certificates to patrons, while the weekly inspection system by army surgeons protected the women from quacks and charlatans. Additionally, once the system was initiated, there was an improvement in the deportment of the prostitutes. Before management they "were exceedingly filthy in their persons and apparel and obscene and coarse in their language," a posture that "soon gave place to cleanliness and propriety." Ignorant of the germ theory of disease, regimental surgeons indicated that while the system of medical inspection and licensing of prostitutes had not eliminated sexually-transmitted diseases, it had controlled their spread. "Additionally, once the system was initiated there was an improvement in the deportment of the prostitutes." Before management they "were exceedingly filthy in their persons and apparel and obscene and coarse in their language," a posture that "soon gave place to cleanliness and propriety." While the system of inspection and licensing of prostitutes had not eliminated sexually-transmitted diseases, it had controlled their spread.[10]

In August, 1861, while under Confederate authority, the Memphis City Council established a system in which a "policeman for every bawdy house in ... the city" was appointed. His job was to maintain order and more importantly, to collect a tax levied by the city upon each and every bordello. For reasons never explained, the ordinance was summarily repealed three months later.[11]

Things hardly improved after Memphis fell to Union forces in 1862. By April 1863, prostitution had grown so rampant that the military police issued Special Order No. 13 on April 29. According to the Provost Marshal: "Scarcely a steamboat but brings an addition to our already large population of lewd women, who make exhibitions of themselves upon our streets, and, for the time, seem to have taken possession of the city." Drastic action was called for, and all houses of ill fame were ordered closed and all prostitutes were to be shipped to other cities. The gambit, however, failed as it had in Nashville.[12]

Consequently, a system was established in Memphis that was similar to the Nashville management system. The Memphis experiment began on September 30, 1864. Prostitutes or mistresses were now required to take out a $10 license and a weekly health certificate after a medical examination. Fees provided the wherewithal for treating only certified prostitutes at one of the "private female wards" in the City Hospital.

An overt spirit of regulation prevailed in Memphis and a number of restrictions not known to be part of the Nashville plan were enacted by the martial authorities. For example, all public women in Memphis were forbidden from "street walking, soliciting, stopping, or talking with men on the streets; buggy or horseback riding for pleasure through the city in daylight; wearing a showy, flash [sic] or immodest dress in public; any language or conduct in public which attracts attention; visiting the public squares, the theatre, or other resorts of LADIES."

The City Hospital administrator reported in February 1865 that twenty-eight women had remained in the hospital since January, while fifteen were admitted since the first of the month. The martial mayor of Memphis, also reported in

February 1865, that 134 women had registered as prostitutes, kept mistresses, and housekeepers. He also reported an overage of $3,893.49 in certificate and medical inspection fees. As in Nashville, while venereal diseases had not been eliminated, at least prostitution was controlled.[13]

As the armies left Memphis and Nashville the number of prostitutes likewise dwindled, and the novel nineteenth-century experiments in managing prostitution faded as well. In an era in which the germ theory of disease was unknown, the first response of the U.S. Army Medical Department was to control venereal diseases through the dramatic forced exile of public women. In the end, however, the management, taxation, and legalization of prostitution in both cities, while perhaps unsettling to morals, had shown itself a much more effective method of controlling this urban prostitution within certain physical limits, that is, within what would come to be called a "red-light district." The U.S. Army's inclination for dramatic raids followed by managed tolerance helped reinforce a pattern of cultural behavior responses to urban vice, which would persist throughout the nineteenth and early twentieth centuries in these Tennessee urban centers.

According to moral reformer George H. Napheys' 1873 text *The Transmission of Life*, prostitution in American cities had evolved into a hierarchical organization. At the top were the "houses of assignation," followed by the "house of prostitution," under which were saloons, where only "the lowest class of depraved women are found…" In the house of assignation, the "mistress of the house furnished room and board to her inmates, and sometimes clothing, for which articles she takes care to keep them in debt to her." In the house of prostitution, the inmates were boarders only, and "they remain within, and await the chance comers, and are called 'parlor boarders.'" The life of a prostitute was a mobile one in which they "go from house to house … city to city, driven by an aimless restlessness."[14] It is most likely that commercialized prostitution found in Tennessee's cities did not vary much from the norm described by Napheys.[14]

Napheys' approach to reforming prostitution by means of moral change in New York was emulated in Nashville in June 1886. An itinerant evangelist, Rev. J. A. Munday, met a group of six well-heeled gentlemen, including a well-known Nashville preacher to rid the city of vice by confronting it head on with religion. Along with a reporter for the *Daily American*, Munday would lead these distinguished men (who were anxious "that their names not be published") on a visit to various Nashville brothels. Their mission was to rescue the prostitutes from their lives of sin and misery. He assured them: "I'm going to work among those poor women on North College Street, brethren, if every man in town deserts me … brethren, I want to save souls."

He seized his Bible and led his reformist team to its first destination in the red-light district on College Street. Ringing the doorbell of Madame Mag Seats' bagnio, Munday announced they wanted to "pray, sing and talk with the inmates." Incredulous, Madame Seats told the evangelist that all the girls were absent just then. Undaunted, they briskly walked to the back porch. Although there were few women available the stubborn minister demanded: "Tell them a man wants to talk to them about their souls."

Two girls descended the stair case. Flabbergasted, Munday asked: "Are these all I can get?" The minister led the group in singing "What a Friend We Have in

Jesus" with gusto; others clustered on the porch for the remainder of the service. "Occasionally, a slight titter could be heard.... The inmates regarded the preacher as a crank, and were no more moved ... to mend the error of their way than had his word had been merely the rustling of the wind." Impervious, Munday went next to Emma Wilson's brothel. Madame Wilson told Munday he was not welcome, and she tellingly asked: "Why should you come here to save us? Who would help us if we wished to change our lives?" Staggered, Munday assured her that accommodations would be made for all those who desired to abandon their errant lives. Wilson consented. The reformers met the same result as they had previously. The answer to Madame Wilson's query, however, revealed the fatal flaw in the reformists' plans.

Still unfazed, Munday led his group next door to the house of Nettie Moore. They stood in the parlor and robustly sang "Rock of Ages" as women gathered in the parlor, but gave no sign of being moved. Munday then appealed to them to remember their "pure mothers, some of whom might now be in heaven, to turn from their ways of sin ... several broke down utterly and ... wept as if their hearts would break." Seizing his opportunity, Munday prayed for them to turn to the Christians of Nashville who would aid them in coming to Christ. His prayer was effective. There followed a homily with Revelation ii: 7 as the text. He continued: "Notwithstanding your wickedness your acquiescence to the sin of adultery and fornication, God has provided mansions in heaven for every one of you who will who will come and be saved."

"God," Munday proclaimed, "was anxious and able to make you pure as snow." His assurances "touched the heart of every woman ... not an eye was dry...." Munday asked those who desired salvation to stand up and "every one of them, with tears in their eyes, arose." After he invited them to attend the afternoon prayer meeting, the band of reformers left the brothel, their day's work done.[15]

At a meeting at the German Lutheran Church, twenty-two prostitutes asked for the prayers of the congregation; five were converted professing they "would not go back to their dens of sin even to get their finery." A man and his wife stood and proclaimed they would take two of the five converts to the Nashville Woman's Mission Home. It was the consensus among the congregation that the women could live exemplary chaste lives "if they could only be given homes." Herein lay the crux of the problem. The prostitutes were poor and unable to leave the bagnios unless "the good people of the city" would assist them. Reverend Munday echoed these sentiments saying: "They can and will be saved ... if only they can have the support of the Christian people. Homes must be prepared for them."[16]

Munday continued his efforts but recognized the courtesans were "contemptuously treated by heartless church members [so] that in many places ... they are afraid to go to church."[17]

Munday wholeheartedly endorsed the Woman's Mission Home and declared that it was fundamentally essential for "the Christians of this city ... to run their hands down in their pockets and turn loose a few of those almighty dollars and enlarge the ... Woman's Mission Home, so that those who are anxious to abandon sin can have a place of refuge ... and rescue the fallen who are on the road to hell."[18]

The Woman's Mission Home charity, founded in 1874, was scarcely adequate to meet the needs required to offer prostitutes an opportunity to reform their lives and find a means of making an honest living. It simply did not have enough support from the Christian community in Nashville.[19]

The evangelist was asked if he intended to continue his moral reformation efforts. He was unsure, as he had "other engagements which are pressing me.... Look here, my good brother, business is business, and I have some to transact for the Lord; so, good bye."[20] There is no evidence that Munday returned to Nashville to continue his business of soul saving and reforming prostitutes.

The community of the prostitutes in Nashville continued thereafter to intermingle with the general public in the streets along a block bounded by Market, Broad, Front and Church. The brothels of Black Bottom shared notoriety with those of "Hell's Half Acre," on the western inclines of Capitol Hill. Along what is now Jo Johnston Avenue were so-called "fancy houses" catering to a racially mixed clientele, while another center for prostitution developed on Criddle Street in North Nashville. The incidence of prostitution in the so-called "Men's Quarter," located on Cherry (now Fourth), between Church and Union Streets, was more discreet.[21]

There seems to have been little problem with prostitution in the city until November 1915, when it was suddenly reported with mixed metaphors in the *Nashville Banner* that: "Nashville's red light district received a black eye when the city commission ... unanimously adopted a resolution directing the chief of police ... to close up all the houses of ill fame in the City of Nashville."

The hasty resolution by the City Council was stimulated by a communication from the Centennial Club, a civic organization "comprised of some of the best women of the city." Former Mayor E. H. Crump of Memphis had apparently sent out an embarrassing circular all over the state "calling attention to the fact that the governor was almost living in the midst of houses of ill fame." Certainly the mayor of Nashville, who "lived closer to the dead line" (the border of the segregated district) than any member of the council, would appreciate the need for action.

During the debate on the resolution, one commissioner announced that while he had been a member of the Board of Public Health he had taken it upon himself to investigate "one house of seven inmates, and found that every one of them was badly infected." He claimed all of the segregated district's prostitutes were infected with venereal disease. Furthermore, he had it on very good authority that "eight out of ten men at one time have gonorrhea ... [t]he chances of being cured are only 80 percent, the rest remaining infected for life." Clearly segregation did not confine disease to a given section of the urban landscape. "The segregated district is a lawless center," he said. Recognizing that the proposed ordinance would not eradicate prostitution, he argued: "No one with a grain of gumption supposes that it will, but it will be fighting the evil and not merely trying to manage it." The resolution to summarily close the red-light district was adopted by a unanimous vote. Centennial Club women, however, wished action to be delayed until steps had been taken "to perfectly provide for the unfortunate inmates." Commissioner J. O. Tankard, accordingly offered another resolution that would soften the blow to the prostitutes.

[In essence] since the beginning of time lewd and licentious women have dwelt among men ... [it is necessary] to devise plans for uplifting ... this unfortunate class

... to offer ways and means by which they may be enabled to make an honest and upright living, and not become a parasite on society and a menace to our homes ... therefore ... by this revolution we invite the Ministers' Alliance, civic organizations, and all Christian people interested in the upbuilding of our city and the uplifting of these unfortunate women ... to meet with this board....[22]

The police chief stated that no attempt had yet been made by the mayor to follow through with the action against the red-light district. There were, the chief had calculated, some sixty-five houses of assignation in Nashville, each sheltering an average of three women. When he became chief of police, houses of ill repute, saloons, and similar places ran openly with no real effort by municipal authorities to close them. When asked for his opinion of the order closing the red-light district, the chief, clearly a management proponent, according to the *Nashville Banner* newspaper report of November 12, 1915, responded:

I think it is the most disastrous thing that was ever perpetrated on a community. I have visited cities where this action was tried, and have letters from the chiefs of police of those places and other cities telling me how such a plan has worked out. The women are scattered, broadcast over [the] town, fill the hotels and apartment houses and residence sections, and walk the streets dressed like other women. It is impossible then to control the evil in any way.

One judge was of the opinion that while city ordinances allowed the regulation and/ or suppression of houses of prostitution, there was nothing in any law that required suppression. While the magistrate was not convinced that the state's nuisance law of 1913 militated against houses of prostitution, Nashville did have an ordinance making them illegal, and until the commissioners repealed it, the statute would uphold the suppression of the resorts.

Notwithstanding his management biases, the chief followed the orders, and, on the morning of November 12, 1915, sixty-one years since the similar incident in antebellum Nashville, issued closing edicts affecting over 200 women on the dozen streets over which the district stretched westward from the Cumberland River. "The women, many of whom were without funds, home or friends, were not expecting the action ... and it came as a shock to them." Variations in condition existed among the prostitutes, as some of those living in the more pretentious houses nearest and north of the capitol, on Seventh, Eighth, Ninth, and Tenth Avenues had saved money and many wore diamonds, while those in the district that stretched from First to Fifth Avenue faced more serious consequences. They were behind in their rent and weekly board to local merchants and their plight was judged "pitiful." Some wept, while there was one apparently brought on by the eviction notices.

In the meantime, as a local manifestation of the national campaign against "white slavery," the local vice commission tried to raise money to assist the prostitutes. At its meeting in the First Presbyterian Church on November 11, an appeal for $5,000 was made and as a result of the conference between the mayor and the management of the Florence Crittendon Home and the Door of Hope, space was found to accommodate some of the women. According to the vice commission, it was a question of efficiency and charity: "The enforcement of this order ... means that the women who have been following prostitution for a living will be thrown out. What can they do? They are helpless and inefficient, but they are human beings.... They should be given every chance to reform and until the way opens for their earning a livelihood they should be cared for..."[23]

The editor of the *Nashville Banner* echoed prevailing reformist opinion, writing that and must be closed, there should likewise be a means of helping the wayward sisters of the bordellos because "they are still women." Humane instincts and Christian charity spoke "in their behalf against too severe treatment." The editorial warned that "prostitution cannot be suppressed while woman are weak and wicked and men are still viler..." Segregated districts only produced crime and disease and once established the "red-light" district in Nashville had attracted lawless elements from New York and New Orleans. Attempts by owners of houses in the closed red-light district along Capitol Avenue and Berryhill Street to secure an injunction against the city were initially successful, but in the end was dissolved.[24]

Thus, houses of prostitution were eliminated from Nashville as part of what has been called a "Great Coercive Campaign" typical of the progressive era. The "prostitution evil" was "widely perceived as ... [a] ... great bastion ... of urban vice. So long as ... [it] ... stood, the dream of an urban moral awakening would be no more than that: if ... [it] ... could be subdued, the purified, morally homogenous city might at last become a reality."[25] In the reformist climate of the times, management of this vice was therefore morally repugnant. Prostitution had to be eradicated, not managed. Dramatic moves, not against individuals, but against segregated red-light districts, were a hallmark of the urban anti-prostitution movement, which was given even more moral, credibility as a battle against "white slavery." Indeed, the campaign against "white slavery," in addition to providing lurid newspaper copy, was a hallmark of early twentieth-century American urban reform. Although no consensus has been reached, some historians have convincingly shown a connection between such moral-control movements were a genuine expression of and motivation for the larger Progressive impulse.[26]

The anti-vice reformers of the Progressive Era were not only motivated by class bias, ethnic, and racial prejudices but also by the commercialized social order into which prostitutes had been so completely blended. According to historian Ruth Rosen: "Whether they looked forward to a social order free from male domination and the commercial exploitation of women or backward to an idealized vision of traditional rural life based on religious values, they were profoundly dissatisfied with the present."[27] The character of the national crusade against prostitution during the Progressive Era was shaped by social anxieties resulting from new commercial/industrial America. Indeed, as one historian puts it, "the most salient characteristics of the response to prostitution were confusion and bewilderment; it was an American expression of modernization and its discontents."[28]

The Nashville vice commission was contemporary with similar groups nationwide. It, like its counterparts, was composed of clerics, professional men and women representing such local groups as the Board of City Missions, the Centennial Club, the Women's Federation of South Nashville, the Christian Women's Federation of South Nashville, the Christian Woman's Board of Missions, the Women's Christian

Temperance Union, the Y. W. C. A., King's Daughters, Council of Jewish Women, and the Parent Teachers' Organization. Teaching personal morality, part of women's domestic sphere, was linked to issues of Progressive reform, and the "white slavery" reform was a means by which social-control could be legitimated politically. Vice commissions aimed at controlling sexual freedom. Moreover, as the Chairman of the Nashville vice commission and pastor at the First Presbyterian Church sermonized: "Not one, but scores like the girl dragged by the scribes and Pharisees into Christ's presence are waiting to see what the virtuous people of this community propose to do with them."[29]

While he did not dwell upon the practical aspects of the problem in his sermon, the actions of the vice commission would squarely address them. In his homily, he suggested that if prostitutes were treated "right, and not as ... cattle or hogs ... the goodness in them will respond." "It is the duty of the people to give them a chance," he intoned. He characterized the prostitute, "[o]nce ... somebody's little daughter" as "defective, with mind undeveloped [sic] and resisting power low. It is said that fifty percent of such women are noticeably subnormal, and seventy-five percent mentally deficient."[30] Such terms as "mentally deficient" were used because they "described inappropriate gender and class conduct. By labeling such women feeble-minded, reformers could defend against, as well as condemn, poor women's sexual aggressiveness, social boldness, impatience with delayed gratification, and disregard for the future."[31] The executive board of the vice commission decided to place its headquarters in the former red-light district.[32]

Soon the vice commission announced that a "Friendly Aid Center" would be established "for the benefit of women in the segregated district." According to one veteran social worker: "All Women in the district who desire to make a fight for respectability will be taken into the home, and any who are addicted to alcoholism or drug habits will be given treatment. The women will be fitted to make an honest living in business houses by being given business training in the center."

In the meantime, Ms. Kate Adams of Chicago, "one of the best known social workers in America," and members of the vice commission visiting committee, had conducted a surveillance of seventy-six of the ninety-four (80 percent) brothels in the red-light district announcing to the occupants the existence of the center. They left cards reading: "When in need of a friend for any reason, phone or write Friendly Aid Center, 422 North Sixth Avenue, telephone Main 2843." Additionally, Ms. Adams believed the district, "an allurement to the students who come to this city," would soon be a thing of the past.[33] While the vice commission did not manage to secure a house in the red-light district, the aid center apparently did operate successfully and a new and distinct red-light district in Nashville did not develop again at least until the 1920s. Thus, in Nashville the forced elimination of organized brothel-prostitution combined with private attempts to provide and alternative moral norm and vocational education to erstwhile prostitutes proved more effective than decades of management by salutary neglect. The role of women's organizations and the question of morality in the elimination of prostitution is likewise typical of similar reforms in other states and cities during the Progressive Era.[34] While there is no indication prostitution was eradicated from Nashville after 1915, the red-light district was, at least temporarily.

Memphis was renowned for its red-light district on or near Beal and Gayoso Streets. After the Civil War experiment, the city managed prostitution by carrying out raids. According to the Memphis *Public Ledger* in late February, 1874:

> Police raids on disreputable houses ... are all the rage at present. The unfortunates are driven through the streets to the station-house like a herd of wild Texas cattle, but they are released on *payment of ten dollars, which is ruled to be the exact value of the crime supposed to have been committed.*[35] [Emphasis added.]

The round up and fining management ploy served as a means to admonish prostitutes and ease local anxiety regarding the practice. More importantly, the fines served to unofficially license prostitution and to fill the city coffers.

A newspaper account in 1885 provided some continuity with the documented activity during the Civil War. Kate Hannigan, "a bright but vicious girl," left her home and had taken up residence at a local bordello. She was removed from the brothel after the police had received a letter beseeching the constabulary to save her. The eighteen-year-old Katie was staying in the Madame Lou Scholls' bordello at 99 Market Street. The police acted accordingly and arrested Katie on the night of September 30. After spending a night in jail, it was believed by a newspaper reporter that she would soon "be sent to the house of the Good Shepherd..."[36] Madame Scholls was not charged with contributing to the delinquency of a minor. The story demonstrates, like the 1874 round up, a degree of cooperative-management between madams, prostitutes, and the Memphis government.

A 1907 editorial in the Memphis *Commercial Appeal* stated: "Dives have been flourishing as they have never before. Hundreds of lewd women, equipped with vials of chloral and knock-out drops, have been imported. Street walkers have been as thick as wasps in the summer time." Houses of prostitution were located on Main, Third, Fourth, and Mulberry Streets. The red-light district proper could be found centered on Gayoso Street. The famous "Stanley Club" was located at 12 Gayoso Street, where "the affront of the commercial spirit was eased by expensive furnishings and a proper regard for the amenities." The African American owner and madam, Mrs. Grace Stanley, was one of the most garish and wealthy women in the city.[37]

W. C. Handy's song "The Beale Street Blues" has it that "If Beale Street could talk, married men would have to take their beds up and walk."[38] One historian explained that prostitution supplemented the Bluff City's reputation for immorality but that it "is, of course, impossible to know its extent, but those who remember Memphis during the years before the First World War agree that it was widespread."[39] Early in the twentieth century, city officials had made attempts to enforce municipal nuisance laws in Memphis. For example, in 1903, it was reported in the city's annual police report that only ten persons were listed as having been arrested for maintaining houses of prostitution. In 1906, some ninety-eight cases dealing with the same offense were prosecuted.[40] Nonetheless, there was not yet an organized move to eliminate prostitution in Memphis as in Nashville. This was most likely because "prostitution, like dives, were necessary features of a man's world, the kind of world the old South believed in."[41] Yet, even in Memphis, organized prostitution could not escape the spasms of the coercive moral rehabilitation impulse of Progressive reform.

In the midst of the summer's heat and war-time excitement on July 14, 1917, the red-light district in Memphis was subjected to the same pattern of coercion validated by the passion of moral reform as had been witnessed in Nashville two years earlier. "Pandemonium broke loose.... Women ran from house to house" as the Memphis Police Chief abruptly and summarily served notice on all houses of assignation that the red-light district was closed.

The entire operation took but half an hour, and it clearly indicated that the district would no longer be tolerated. For example, about a year prior to the raid, the council forbade the playing of pianos, Victrolas, and even dancing in all houses of assignation. This action had placed nearly three-fourths of the houses out of business. Madams were, therefore, fatalistic about the action, knowing it was the "finale to the slow but sure policy of this administration to completely wipe out the underworld." It was estimated that nearly 1,000 women would be forced to leave.[42] It is not surprising, however, to once again consider the stimulus provided by the U.S. Army in the expulsion of prostitutes from Memphis in 1917. Memphis business and civic leaders, like those in other cities in the U.S., wished to have a military training camp located nearby. This would be a positive mark of patriotism as well as an opportunity for local merchants to profit from the soldiers' pay. Secretary of War Newton D. Baker had much to say about where a military camp would be located, together with the wartime Commission on Training Camp Activities, and worked to close to a number of urban red-light districts as measures to protect the health of recruits.[43] Just a few days before the sudden closing of the segregated district, C.P. J. Mooney, the editor of the *Commercial Appeal*, concerned that Secretary Baker would give no indication as to why a military training camp might not be located near Memphis, wrote "we should know ... in order that we might consider them."[44]

Promptly after the suppression of the segregated district in Memphis, an unforeseen problem arose—that of providing for a new class of unemployed. While the newspapers might headline stories with titles such as "City's Underworld Wiped Out for Good," it became evident that a large majority of the former prostitutes were now without a means of support. In short order, in a pattern seen in Nashville, the local Protestant Pastor's Association formed a collections committee to ease the "pitiable plight" of the "Prodigal Daughters." The work of the committee and the class cohesiveness of the prostitutes themselves was all that had kept them from sleeping on bare floors. Donations came from as far away as West Virginia. Many of the women opted to take advantage of the association's offer for transportation to leave Memphis rather than remain and be reformed by the city's religious community.[45] The campaign against the prostitutes was soon forgotten, "as crusading zeal was channeled into a more momentous issue, that of meeting the threat of German militarism."[46] Given the district's long and celebrated history in Memphis, it is also possible that the elimination of the segregated district was motivated less by moral courage than because of the health requirements of the U.S. Army. If hygienic standards could be raised by eliminating the red-light district Memphis would stand a better chance of attracting a major military training camp. Local merchants would profit from soldiers' pay, and prostitutes represented too much competition for the doughboy-dollar. Happily for the merchants, removal of this source of economic competition was a patriotic and moral act. The removal of a segregated vice district was less an indictment of traditional method of management of organized prostitution or an outraged sense of morality as a reaction to the U.S. Army's health standards. The segregated district had been eliminated, but the vice would continue in another more integrated, subtle form.

Chattanooga and Knoxville, 1838–1917

Chattanooga experienced dilemmas with prostitution and as in Nashville and Memphis, organized prostitution would be dramatically expelled. The kernels of an identifiable red-light district had been established in Chattanooga soon after the Civil War.[47] The district's growth was stimulated and sustained by local demand, the transient nature of railroad employees' lives, and tolerant management characterized by *de facto* taxation by municipal administrations, and later by the presence of large numbers of soldiers training at Fort Oglethorpe, Georgia, but nine miles from the city, during and after the Spanish-American War.[48]

The first conflict between the city officials and the prostitutes occurred in 1885. In 1908, according to the testimony of one sixty-six-year-old long-time resident of Chattanooga, J. L. Whiteside, the red-light district's development in the Third Ward began in the Florence and Helen-Street area in the late 1860s:

> Gradually those white sporting women began to move into that district by first renting property and then buying a little piece of property, and putting up a little shanty of their own, until they have quite a settlement of sporting persons, and during the administration of [James A.] Allen, Chief of Police [1882–1887], he cleaned up the whole neighborhood, and scattered them all over town … till the administration of Mr. [John B.] Nicklin, as Mayor, [1887–1889] when they were all moved back by his order.[49]

A system had developed whereby the prostitutes were summarily and periodically rounded up under the direction of Chief Allen, fined, and released to later be subjected to the same process. The money from the fines helped enrich the city treasury when the prostitutes were taken to the Mayor's Court, serving thus a *de facto* municipal tax and licensing of bawdy houses. Difficulties arose in June 1885, when, after the "periodical raid of the police on the fallen women of the city," it became apparent that Chief Allen, contrary to the order of Mayor Hugh Whiteside, had been taking the prostitutes to State Magistrates where "the humiliating spectacle of our State receiving blood tribute from the harlots was again presented." According to one report, "the State will receive the fines and the police receive two or three dollars in each case, while the city loses from $100 to $150."[50] A crisis in municipal government ensued in which the mayor accused the chief of "attempting to utilize the women to make money for himself," while Allen accused the mayor of refusing to swear out warrants for the "arrest of lewd women and other."[51, 52] The prolonged investigation on the matter resulted in Allen's exoneration and the expulsion of prostitutes from the city.[53] Thus the management of prostitution in Chattanooga was characterized by a policy of "occasional raids [which] was virtually licensing the prostitutes, an outrage of public decency and a great error in public policy." Mayor Whiteside stated he did "not approve of taxing these women to carry on their business and cannot too severely condemn the practice of arresting them once in six or eight weeks, no matter how quiet they are, and following full license in the interim."

A new management policy was forged in which a roster of prostitutes was drawn up and orders given to Chief Allen to launch "a series of systematic raids to drive the women out of the city or force them to retire to the most remote sections." These raids were to be daily in their frequency until prostitutes were eliminated from the populated regions of the city.[54] By July, public women were to be notified to close up their establishment in five days. Some houses were already uninhabited, their residents having left for other cities. Yet even in the face of such concerted opposition, according to the *Times*:

> It is understood that the majority will submit quietly, saying that the matter will blow over in a few days and they can reopen without interference. One Madame, however, is quite indignant and declares she will fight it until she expends her last dollar. She states that she will receive a full complement of boarders this week and prepare for a systematic contest.... Whether or not the movement will be successful remains to be seen.[55]

Chattanooga's clergy was not silent on the matter. Reverend G. C. Rankin of the Methodist-Episcopal Church was most outspoken. In one "very sensational sermon ... [he gave] the most direct exposition of the vices of city of society ever delivered in the city...." The clergyman recognized the *de facto* nature of tax on prostitutes, blasted the concept of prostitution as a "necessary evil," which made sin "respectable at the expense of virtue." He asked the city's newspapers to print the names of the landlords renting to the madams. The answer, he said, was the formation of an organized reform movement to be led by the women of Chattanooga with the support of law enforcement.[56] Yet another sermon by Rankin, "For Men Only" spelled out the consequences of prostitution as police corruption, red-light districts, venereal diseases, moral depravity, blackmail, as well as crimes against society and humanity.[57]

The prostitutes, however, were resilient in their resistance to the municipal round up and preaching, and in only two years, tumescent municipal revenues were reported by the Mayor's Court, a result of increased arrests for "lewdness." According to Mayor A. G. Sharp (1885–1887): "Lewdness ... will present a problem for the consideration of moralists, and the solution to the problem will be hailed with pleasure by the authorities."[58] Raids were frequent in 1888, and by 1889, little had changed, and raids fining of the "inmates" of houses of prostitution were carried out under the guise of regulation. If law enforcement officials "wanted to break up these houses," wrote a reporter for the *Times*, "it would be an easy matter for them to pull them frequently enough to accomplish this result, but from the infrequency with which the arrests were made it appears evident that the only purpose [for them] is to make money out of them in the way of cost and fees." Such sporadic midnight raids continued into 1900.[59]

After the initial diaspora and homecoming, the district grew more stable and settled in a two-block area bounded by Florence Street on the west, Ninth Street on the north, the back end of Carter Street on the east, and Tenth Street on the south. Apparently there was no ordinance passed as in New Orleans to establish a red-light district. Instead, in a familiar Tennessee urban pattern, organized-commercial prostitution was kept sequestered and supervised by municipal police and tolerated by city officials and local clergy. As one local butcher would put it: "There has been a Red light district ever since know the town [*sic*], and it always [will] be and nobody else wants it, [want to do] nothing there to bother it."[60]

The district remained permanently and prosperously ensconced in the Third Ward except for an occasional police raid. It would be fully thirty years until "the problem" would find any semblance of a solution. Thus, management of the municipal vice in nineteenth-century Chattanooga consisted of a system whereby, notwithstanding any moral outrage, the organized business of prostitution served as a source of revenue for the city and as an outlet for the satisfaction of the prurient interests of a substantial community of Chattanooga men, including at least some of Chattanooga's officials. In the nineteenth century, it was not uncommon, according to Ruth Rosen, that within red-light districts, prostitutes "were quietly allowed to carry out their business, except when they failed to pay off local police or when the political climate demanded a raid to demonstrate elected officials' implacable hostility to vice. When arrested, prostitutes generally received fines rather than jail sentences."[61]

For some twenty years then, there seems to have been very little conflict with respect to Chattanooga's red-light district until 1908 when the Third Ward Business League and some neighboring property owners, in the case *M. G. Weidner et al. v. Irene Friedman et al.* won a court injunction barring the presence of houses of prostitution in the Third Ward. This did not exterminate prostitution in Chattanooga, but did cause it to vacate to other environs. "When the original injunction was issued in the case it resulted in general exodus from the district." Unfortunately for the prostitutes, however, "citizens of the river district objected to the houses being located in that portion of the city, and so another injunction was issued in the case it resulted in a general exodus from the district and the occupancy of the river district." Soon afterwards, however, the old Third Ward district was again populated by prostitutes.

Several of the original complaints withdrew from the case, especially the Third Ward Business League members, together with "several members of the City Council," persuaded the judge to allow a consent decree to be put on the records so the prostitutes were allowed to move back into the district. A complication arose when others, also parties to the original suit, had citations for contempt of court issue.[62]

Then-City Councilman James J. McMahan's complaint in the case powerfully illustrates life in and about the red-light district in Chattanooga in the early twentieth century:

> The houses do their business thru [*sic*] all hours of the night; and loud cursing and vulgarity come from the men and women gathered at these houses at all hours of the night. Lewd and lascivious music is constantly heard at all of them; and these noises plainly reach the house where … [McMahan] … lived, and constantly disturbed his family. Drunken men were constantly going to and from these houses, and

constantly using loud and vulgar language and oaths unfit to be heard by decent people. The women themselves constantly appeared, day and night, on the streets in front of these houses in a partially disrobed condition, constantly using vulgar language and oaths, smoking cigarettes and otherwise misbehaving themselves.... Men would come [mistakenly] to the complainant's house, at night frequently, and ask to see "the girls"—often calling the name of some prostitute...[63]

Even though the police had cracked down the business of prostitution continued. Black cabmen offered a means to the illicit business of prostitution as they would solicit passers-by. "If the men are afraid to go in the houses, the cabmen offer to call the woman and take them in their cabs of some place of assignation with the men." Thus the same prostitutes stayed in Chattanooga's Third Ward "with the negro cabmen making assignations and going in and out of these houses."[64]

Attitudes toward prostitution in Chattanooga were ambiguous. Some, such as Councilman McMahan, deplored it absolutely, while others, perhaps typified by one witness at trial, were more philosophical: "It is not right, it is an evil necessity, they had them before we came, and they will have them after we are gone, and it has happened before our fathers, and [will continue] after they are gone."[65] Part of the problem revolved less around outraged moral sensibilities as fluctuating property values. Some of the madams had made profit enough to have substantial brick houses built, while landlords found that their rents decreased after the prostitutes were banned from their Third Ward warrens. Once the prostitutes left, it was difficult to sell or rent their holdings, because of the reputation associated with the properties, to any but blacks. One complainant declared: "I would rather have the white women, I consider the property more valuable with the white women there than with the negroes [sic]."[66] The use of the phrase "an evil necessity" to excuse the presence of prostitution is interesting in that it hints to a contradictory attitude prevailing among many men that sex within the bounds of matrimony was not as fulfilling as sex with prostitutes.

Captain Will Burk of the Chattanooga Police Department agreed, observing that the vacuum created by the sudden exit of the prostitutes from the Third Ward resulting in the influx of African Americans and a general worsening of conditions in the erstwhile vice-district. Moreover, he believed prostitution was excusable as long as it was not disorderly. The venerable J. L. Whiteside was of the same opinion, and favored a segregated district because when "[t]hey were under the immediate supervision of the police and well-regulated [there was no trouble], and where an evil cannot be suppressed that is the best policy." Another witness with property interests in the district called for the sequestering of the white prostitutes to "keep them in those 2 half blocks ... it would not affect me at all..."[67]

Irene Freidman, a veteran Chattanooga madam of long standing, and one of the litigants in this case, testified through her 1911 deposition:

It seemed to be the policy of the statesmen of Chattanooga to recognize *bawdy houses as a social evil, which should be regulated by confining their operations to a given district in the city, and pursuing that policy more than 30 years* the district which is now known as *the red light district was selected as the proper place for* *carrying on and indulging in this social, <u>necessary evil</u>.* The land embraced in this district is hardly fit for anything else.[68] [emphasis added.]

Another senior Chattanooga madam, Nellie Hood, put it quite plainly. Her revealing testimony illustrates both social hypocrisy and how the management system worked:

*Some of the complainants in this bill were liberal patrons of the bawdy houses while they were in full operation...*The truth is that this district and the houses situated in it, have been under strict police surveillance, all the time, and no persons are permitted to visit these houses in the day time, except clerks with bills to collect and persons having business transactions with the owners or occupants of the houses permitted to do so.[69] [emphasis added.]

In the end, the Tennessee Supreme Court decided that "disobedience to a valid order, while subsisting, though erroneous, is a contempt of court" and therefore that the prostitutes must cease and desist, obey the original injunction and otherwise vacate the Third Ward. Inasmuch as the court had not ruled directly upon the question of the legality or illegality of prostitution, and given the districts continuity over forty years, it is no surprise that the scarlet domain flourished from 1912–1917. This boom was in keeping with the notion that prostitution was neither legal nor illegal, but fell under a prevalent Victorian male-oriented carnal convention that it was "a necessary social evil."[70]

The district continued to prosper, indeed, to prevail over the original injunction's intent. By a remarkable happenstance, available *Chattanooga City Directories* for 1907–1917 list various women whose names appear in court transcripts as prostitutes at addresses in the red-light district as "Mad," most certainly an abbreviation for "Madam." In 1907, a total of four women, all on Helen Street, share that designation. A year later, the list included three on Florence, and five on Helen Street. A year after the first injunction a total of fifteen women share the designation "Mad," an increase of nearly 50 percent. Business had increased, and one can gauge the impact of the injunction in the 1910 directory as only three madams remained in the red-light district. Five other women, however, still listed as "Mad" had taken up residence at various other locations in the city, at Foster, Pine, Chestnut, Foundry, and Douglas Streets. Prostitution, much less the red-light district, had not been destroyed in Chattanooga.

Two years later, in 1912, a total of thirteen women on Florence and Helen Streets, in the heart of red-light district, were specified as "Mad," while two others had locations in Foundry Alley and Clift Street. Consequently, the injunction was honored more in the breach than the observance. It is possible also to see in this the persistence of established nineteenth-century male sexual attitudes and behavior patterns, not to mention the dominant double standard, after a pretense at regulation. There might be lewd women but never lewd men. Prostitution was, after all, considered a "necessary social evil." Figures in the directory for 1913 show fourteen listings of "Mad" in the red-light district; consequently, there were as many houses of ill-fame. By 1917, however, the flush times had ended, and there were no listings for "Mad" on Helen Street, and only one woman on Florence was listed with the title, a fact consistent through 1920.[71]

Chattanooga greeted American entrance into the First World War with great enthusiasm. Fort Oglethorpe, Georgia, a permanent army fixture since 1904, became a training center for nearly 24,000 conscripts, a fact not unhappily noticed by area merchants eager to profit from the swollen ranks of the new soldiers. Secretary of War Baker, however, issued his famous letter on May 24, 1917 to the governors of all the states calling for cooperation in keeping the army mobilization camps free from promiscuous influences. He threatened that he "proposed to move the camps from those neighborhoods where clean conditions cannot be secured."[72]

Obviously the red-light district posed a threat to the health of inductees, and the profits of local merchants and landlords. No doubt they were spurred by the "American Plan," under which the military had authority to arrest any woman caught within 5 miles of a military cantonment. The city authorities wasted no time in acting. Indeed, Chattanooga and Hamilton County officials, with a hitherto unknown sense of urgency, had by the next day thrown down the gauntlet and inaugurated a strict eradication of prostitution. "Underworld women-characters always undesirable and particularly so as military camp followers-will very shortly find themselves *persona non grata* in Chattanooga." Reacting before "conditions actually present themselves" orders were to be issued to prostitutes to either leave the city immediately or face arrest and trial in criminal court. Moreover, city commissioners decided against a clear history to the contrary that "there should be no restricted district-no plan whatever of segregation, but that on the contrary, the wisest policy to pursue was the complete eradication of immoral houses and banishment of immoral women." While some had initially expressed themselves in favor of establishing a segregated district—which, according to Police Chief William H. Hackett had been resorted to during the Spanish-American War—they refused to stand in the way of the majority opinion.[73] Officials in nearby Rossville, Georgia, agreed to cooperate with the effort and keep soldiers in the company of women "whose character is not approved by the town's authorities" off the streets. The *Times* reporter wrote further that of the initial arrests: "Every type of woman could be found among the lot. They were white, black, a few well dressed, some thinly clad, others who bore the indelible marks of their life, and a few who seemed mere girls not yet out of grammar school." In a column entitled "Order to Clean Up," the editor asked his readers to inform on any known prostitutes.[74] It was total war:

> No exemption of any kind are to be made, and those who are of the "marked" class would save themselves trouble and serious discomfort if they voluntarily leave.... It is the intention of the authorities to prove that a determined effort to stop prostitution can be made effective and that it is possible in any great emergency to stop commercialized vice....
>
> And now ... it becomes the duty of the public to assist in ... enforcement in every possible way. Information filed with the police department of the presence of suspected persons will receive prompt attention ... with the proper aid from citizens [army officials] will be able very shortly to present the army officers with Chattanooga's clean bill of health.[75]

In a move reminiscent of the crackdown of 1885, it was soon reported that twenty-four women were "placed on the list of undesirable citizens in Chattanooga," and given their day in court and "told to move on." It was hoped this would be the beginning of a general housecleaning. These first twenty-four "were in the main 'old timers,' well-known to the police" and were given two or three days to leave, according to their circumstances. "The crusade will continue," the *Times* quoted the city judge as declaring, "until all those arrested by the orders were rounded up." Characteristically, only women, and not their male customers, were prosecuted. Police Chief Hackett, in a dissenting voice, "said that, regardless of his personal views as to how best handle the situation, he and the men under him would extend themselves in an effort to gain the desired end."[76]

The effort to rid Chattanooga of prostitution, as it existed in the Third Ward red-light district, was at least initially successful. The city directory for 1917 shows a definite decline in the number of houses of assignation, as does the edition of 1920. Five months after the initial campaign against prostitution in the segregated district was initiated, the *Times* editor protested "that vice has not yet been controlled and that vicious men and women are still plying their trades in the city." It was to be expected, much as the Nashville chief of police stated in 1915, that "when the segregated district was abolished, there would be a general scattering [of] ... immorality and the constant spread of disease..." Realizing the limited size of the Chattanooga police force, the commanders of Fort Oglethorpe had organized military police to aid in the suppression of vice. The two constabulary forces were reported to have been working "in perfect harmony" and had "succeeded in making the city fairly clean and safe."

Expressing continuity with a report in the *Times* of 1889, it was stated twenty-eight years later that these "professionals in vice and immorality" repeatedly appeared in police court with the result of being a mere fine, suggesting the collusion of municipal authorities and the prostitutes.[77] Repeat offenders, suggested the editor of the *Times*, ought to be subjected to stiffer, sterner, severer punishment, even though this suggestion would be a break with historical continuity. If the vice could not be eradicated in or out of a segregated district, then, "we at least ought to be able to rid ourselves of the brazen kind who flaunt their iniquities not only where they become scandals to the community where they reside, *but under the very nose of the judge himself*. It is this brazen kind ... whence comes the disease and moral demoralization [*sic*] against which the government has declared the soldiers of the mobilizing armies must be protected."[78] (emphasis added.)

Knoxville likewise had to confront the challenge of managing prostitution early in its history. Perhaps the earliest anti-vice legislation in Tennessee is manifest in section 2 of the 1838 Knoxville ordinance outlawing "misconduct." According to city minute books, all bawdy houses—defined by the ordinance as those "to which men resort for the purpose of having illicit intercourse with lewd woman" were prohibited in the city limits. Fines of $50 and/or three months' incarceration were prescribed as punishment.[79] The city continued throughout the nineteenth century to periodically pass similar laws, indicating that law enforcement was lax at best and subject to spasmodic reactions and transitory flare-ups of moral outrage. For example, in 1867, the city again made houses of ill fame illegal and likewise provided fines for those renting property used for purposes of prostitution. Again, in 1868, it was declared "unlawful for any female of known bad repute to walk the streets of the city of Knoxville for the purposes of soliciting or with intention of attracting attention or notice from the opposite sex after seven o'clock P.M."[80] A year later, this overseeing strategy was fortified when it was made unlawful for any male, sixteen years of age or older, to accompany a prostitute through the streets or in a carriage. Additionally, the 1869 ordinance extended the management of prostitution by determining:

> ... it shall not be lawful for any woman or girl ... to stand upon the sidewalk in front of the premises occupied by her or at the alley way door or gate of such premises, or sit up on the steps thereof in an indecent posture, or accost, call, or stop any person passing by, or walk up and down the sidewalk or strole [sic] about the ... city indecently attired.[81]

With such legal management measures as these, it would seem evident that Knoxville had firm control over the threat of prostitution. By 1885, however, the city was, according to the *Daily Chronicle* "Again Overrun With Bawdy Houses." A campaign of what can be called press management of prostitution began. Respectable family men, it was reported, frequented these houses of ill-repute. Police knew of them but had orders not to interfere. In one case there was a house of ill-repute where two women "who move in good society, and are well thought of in community ... who go to market in day light, stop at this place and fill engagements with men who have families at home." Women in brothels lounged about in "Mother Hubbard dresses" fanning themselves and soliciting customers who sipped whiskey. The only way to end the evil was to publish the names of property owners renting to prostitutes and habitués of the brothels.[82]

Further reports by the *Chronicle* revealed that Knoxville's bordellos were located at scattered locations on Hardee, Vine, and Crozier (Central), Main, Gay, Patton, Temperance, Clinch, Church, Cumberland, and Henley Streets, near the National Cemetery, in Branner's Addition, Marble Alley, Gunter's Bottom, and Hill Street. They were found likewise near the corner of Clinch Street, near the "colored Presbyterian Church," while there was "one just back of Barrett's saloon." According to one policeman: "In fact they are pretty well scattered all over the town. There was a time when they were confined to Crozier Street, but since the town has grown and property owners [are] not so conscientious about renting these people find no trouble in locating over the city." Indeed, a new brothel was said to be opening on Crozier Street, managed by a prostitute lately expelled from Chattanooga, while brothels were said to be found in Mechanicsville, Park Street, and North Knoxville.[83] As one citizen stated: "The public, if they understood the true situation, would not be surprised at the failure of the police to enforce the law. The keepers of these houses could make it very embarrassing for some members of the force if they chose to."[84]

Thus the 1867 ordinances prohibiting renting property for purposes of prostitution had fallen into disuse, allowing the practice to enlarge and flourish in Knoxville. An "experienced member of the police force" was interviewed on the "necessary evil" question and expressed the opinion that the only real answer was licensing. Citing the examples in Paris and Vienna, the constable acknowledged the system did not "stop the business, but it regulates it in such a way as to prevent public annoyance. In my opinion," he said, "they should be licensed and placed in a distant part of the city under constant police surveillance." Only segregation would prevent depreciating real estate values and public outrage. A "prominent citizen," however, took a stiffer stance and wanted "the business entirely broke up, and an example made of some of them that would be remembered."[85]

Knoxville Police Chief Atkin, however, bluntly stated: "I am going to let them run as long as they behave themselves." Others spoke out for segregation, such as a "practical business man" who wanted the prostitutes either removed or a segregated district established in "an isolated part of town." As might be expected, ministers decried prostitution calling it an evil that had to be ended in Knoxville.[86]

The *Chronicle* printed what might be termed social control fables in an effort to stop solicitation of prostitutes. In one tale a respectable family man was harried by a prostitute's extortion. In another melodramatic tale, a wife followed her husband to the very doors of a brothel, and "with tears streaming down her face, she begged him to remember the little innocent children at home.... Raising his fist he struck the devoted mother ... a brutal blow, and leaving her on the ground went in to join his vile associates." In another narrative, said to be "no fiction," one married man had forsaken his ailing wife and family for the bagnio, forcing his daughter to seek him out and beg him to come home, which he did.[87] By the middle of August, the *Chronicle* reported that the anti-prostitution ordinances in Knoxville were to be enforced. The chief of police had been ordered by his superiors to close all bawdy houses. The editor, somewhat self-assuredly, announced: "It is [our] duty as a newspaper, not to regulate the morals of a town, but to support the law abiding in regulating, and to point out where they need correction."[88]

Yet the *Chronicle*'s apparent success in controlling Knoxville's sexual morals and eradicating prostitution was not enduring. By 1890, the chief of police submitted an incomplete report to the Common Council specifying the names and addresses of all known prostitutes, madams, and houses of prostitution in Knoxville. Five years after the *Chronicle*'s campaign against lewd women, there were at least a total of sixteen houses of prostitution in the city, with a total of sixty prostitutes. Two were located on Cumberland Street, ten on Crozier, and one each on Marble Alley, Gay, and Clinch. Most likely out of feigned ignorance of the existing 1867 ordinance to the same effect, a statute was introduced to make the rental of any property to known women of ill repute a misdemeanor, punishable by a $50 fine.[89] Management of prostitution in Knoxville was thus more a matter of haphazard tolerance than sincere effort as prostitution was not isolated in a red-light district but scattered throughout the city. This state of affairs would change beginning in 1900.

That year, Samuel Gordon Heiskell, a progressive Democrat, was elected to his second of five terms as mayor of Knoxville.[90] Heiskell, a proponent of rational management, was faced with a demoralized public generally unhappy with the unregulated growth of prostitution. This was made even more urgent by Rosa Scott, madam at a bagnio on Clinch Street. Because her brothel was located on a main thoroughfare between West Knoxville and Knoxville, thousands of people passed it daily. Attempts to fine Scott out of business failed because "[s]he always had money to pay the fines, and persuasion to get her to move away availed nothing." In Heiskell's second administration (1900–1902), it was determined to make a test case of the issue to ascertain whether or not the municipal government had the right to force Madame Scott to relocate. The case, *The Mayor and Alderman vs. Rosa Scott*, was finally decided by the Tennessee Supreme Court. The court held that while the city had the right to fine Rosa Scott for keeping a bawdy house, she could not be forced to move "because she was a human being and had the right to live somewhere." A criminal judge could levy fines and sentence her to the workhouse, but the city had no such authority. The idea of a segregated district developed within the Heiskell administration as the best policy to manage the "social evil." Although the idea was deliberate, it was not a matter for legislation, but an administrative policy decision.

Houses of prostitution were then scattered throughout the city and had to be concentrated. According to Heiskell, "from time to time, women were induced to move" until the red-light district emerged.[91] At first it was "sparsely built up, by degree, and under pressure, the women were notified that they must move there, until ... a very large majority of the sporting women of the town lived there."[92] The Knoxville red-light district was located on Central (formerly Crozier), running from the 400 to 700 blocks, always on the south side of the street. Knoxville City Directories for 1910–1913 are quite explicit about identifying madams, much as in the case of Chattanooga, giving the Central Avenue address of each "Mad." The number of bordellos in the red-light district fluctuated from ten in 1910, fifteen in 1911, ten in 1912, and fourteen in 1913.[93] According to Heiskell: "Nobody attempted to abolish it."[94] Nobody, that is, until the local moral reformist movement, armed with the Tennessee Nuisance Act, declared war upon prostitution in Knoxville starting in 1913.

A battle of the most adverse kind raged in this moral reformist offensive. Soon after the passage of the Nuisance Act in 1913, the Anti-Vice Commission appointed by the Knoxville Federation of Churches sought the help of the city administration in ridding the city of the red-light district.[95] Mayor Heiskell refused to have a part in the abolition of the district, an action that caused local clergymen to brand his attitude as "outrageous." The mayor called the request by the Anti-Vice Commission "unmitigated humbuggery." According to his honor:

> You or other citizens have the right to go before any justice of the peace, grand jury or any criminal judge and swear out warrants against any sporting woman in the city and against every woman in the city who enters a house of prostitution, but you have done nothing but to make political capitol ... until you have taken out warrants against inmates of houses of prostitution you have no right to make any complaint against any citizen or official of the city.... When you take prostitutes into your homes and care for them as you said you would do in published statements you will show that your efforts are bona fide and every man in the city will rally to your support.[96]

Disappointed but taking the mayor at his word, the Anti-Vice Commission began a crusade that ultimately resulted in the destruction of Knoxville's segregated district.[97] By March 1914, after the district had been eliminated, the anti-vice forces noted that the scourge against which they had crusaded had not ended at all; prostitutes were now dissipated throughout Knoxville, and the Anti-Vice Commission wanted the city's police force to institute a policy of arresting them. This was more than Mayor Heiskell could bear.

At the City Council Meeting of March 27, 1914, he denied the request of the moral crusaders and went one further. According to the city's chief executive, unless a prostitute was engaged in some independent violation of the law, such as drunkenness, profanity, or any felony, the police were forbidden to pursue or prosecute them as a group or as individuals. Heiskell did this in a deliberate effort, he said, "to put the full solution of this social evil in Knoxville upon those who have been the cause of breaking up of the segregated district ... those who are responsible for the break up of that district must bear the responsibility of prostitutes being scattered over the city in easy reach of men and boys and carrying with them diseases which always accompany prostitution." A resolution to this effect was unanimously adopted by the Board of City Commissioners.[98]

A mass meeting of women and clergy protesting the order was held shortly thereafter. Declaring the "fight against vice is a good one," Reverend J. J. E. White expansively continued that it was "the cause of the home, the heart of our civilization, manhood and womanhood, the boys and the girls of the kingdom of God. It is the cause of purity, patriotism, and the cause of law and order." Mrs. L. Crozier-French introduced a resolution demanding the enforcement of the law by city officials.[99]

The mayor and council were just as adamant that the segregated district was the means of managing prostitution. For example, they twice showed their unanimous support of the mayor by reaffirming the resolution of March 27 forbidding policemen from cracking down on prostitutes, with the Mayor at one point calling the moral reformers "political blatherskates, agitators and bogus reformers."[100, 101] According to Heiskell: "They have brought about this woeful condition of affairs and they must bear the burden of condemnation on the part of the people for so doing." With the abolition of the district, he claimed:

> [Prostitutes] are living in all parts of the city, and the men and boys have easy access to them and in quiet ways and quiet places they can attract a larger number of customers then they could possibly have attracted in a public bawdy house; because young men and full grown men and even boys will visit these women when they can do so without being discovered, who would not visit them in a public bawdy house; and the result is that there is more illegal sexual intercourse going on in Knoxville today than there has been since 1900.[102]

No, he would not as mayor swear out petitions under the Nuisance Law against them, but invited the members of the Anti-Vice Commission to do so. Moreover, the city attorney had issued an opinion that because the Nuisance Act was not a city law and because it did not stipulate that the Knoxville City Commissioners had the responsibility to execute it, the mayor would not do so unless citizens swore out a warrant.[103] Regardless of Mayor Heiskell's management bias, the forces of moral reform in Knoxville carried the day and by the mayor's admission of May 4, 1914: "We no longer have a red-light district; but we still have the prostitutes everywhere…"[104] The reform was thus largely symbolic, serving more as a token for the anxious forces of social control in Knoxville than the beginning of a moral millennium. Moral reform required the liquidation of prostitution, which was in keeping with the larger social-control impetus of the "Great Coercive Campaign" of the Progressive movement.[105]

The first known urban experience in Tennessee history directed toward managing organized commercial prostitution before the Civil War saw the establishment of an ordinance to legislate morality in Knoxville. There followed in all four cities a pattern of banishment and then control and tolerance under a policy of benign neglect that resulted in a *de facto* legalization of prostitution. During the Civil War, there were stricter guidelines enforced by the U.S. Army in Nashville and Memphis. In these cities prostitution was policed and regulated by occupation forces in attempts, at least ostensibly, to protect the health of the soldiers. The martial model was one that promoted organized prostitution. Certainly the army did not encourage its outright legalization, but the system of medical examinations and license fees gave prostitutes at least an ambiguous legal status. Red-light districts would evolve in these four Tennessee cities loosely based upon the Civil War model, except that the system of medical inspection would lapse. Adding to ambiguity was a double standard that excused the exploitation of women as instruments for the expression of male lascivious interests—it was a "necessary social evil." As current wisdom in another yet related context has it, it wasn't so much a problem of supply as it was one of demand.

The relative entrepreneurial success of the red-light district indicates the business acumen of some of the women in the red-light districts, such as Mrs. Grace Stanley in Memphis. The segregated district in Nashville on Seventh, Eighth, Ninth, and Tenth Avenues was "where organized vice maintain[ed] its most pretentious dwellings." At times, prostitutes demonstrated their resilience and business acumen after leaving one city only to establish a bagnio in another municipality. Chattanooga prostitutes seemed especially capable of such action. For example, Lizzie Donney, "a notorious prostitute," established a house of prostitution in Nashville after leaving Chattanooga in 1885. That same year, Ms. Lee Tumlin established a bordello in Knoxville shortly after having been arrested and expelled from Chattanooga. The red-light district in Chattanooga contained "houses … as fine as the majority of residences in [the city]." At other times, as in the pre-red-light district era in Knoxville, convenience and secrecy were the rules; one house was described as being "so constructed as to have several entrances, that is, by going in at a side door, and unless you are acquainted with the house, nothing would be thought of it." In 1888, a sense of community was evident, as manifest in the Chattanooga funeral of Rosa Walker "the proprietor of the bagnio on Florence Street." The hearse was attended by twelve carriages filled with women "all the inmates of houses of similar character in the city." She had inherited the house from her mother and perpetuating her heritage and "maintained it as her mother had done … in order to gain … a livelihood." Funeral services were brief and were "attended only by women who display their devotion one to another even until death."[106] Newspaper reports of the closing of the red-light district in Memphis also spoke of solidarity among the prostitutes, crediting their "spirit of 'stand together'" in the face of expulsion. A report in Chattanooga spoke of one determined madam who had elected to stay open regardless of the campaign against her business. These women formed a separate urban community of their own hitherto known but not acknowledged. Ruth Rosen suggests that "women living together could under certain conditions, create a surrogate family life ... which ... bonded the entire group together."[107] In an age when woman's place was in the home, the organized business and sub-culture of prostitution thrived despite periodic raids and an adverse decision by the Tennessee Supreme Court. It serves also as an example of successful (even if quasi-criminal) feminine enterprise in a male dominated society which defined and defended woman's sphere as strictly in the home. It may indicate also a bifurcated male attitude, separating as it did "home" and "house," concerning the enjoyment of sex. Further demonstrating this double standard is the fact that when the red-light districts were eliminated in three of the four cities, each municipality's chief of police openly disagreed with the policy but acquiesced in carrying out orders. In Knoxville, the municipal government had followed a policy of promoting a segregated district and later adamantly defended the practice, but it was no match for the fervor of the anti-prostitution crusade galvanized by the forces of moral reform and social control.

Prostitution had evolved into an organized business in its own sequestered sections and, despite periodic raids, was tolerated in all four Tennessee cities throughout the nineteenth century. A combination of heightened social anxieties and moral sensibilities stimulated by changes triggering rapid commercialization and fear of hygienic disaster worked to provoke drastic and quick action in the second decade of the twentieth century. In all four cities, action stimulated by moral reform or martial authority would result in the destruction of organized prostitution and its concomitant the red-light district, but not certainly of prostitution. In Nashville and Knoxville, the demands of local vice commissions composed of ladies' clubs, local professionals and clergymen, resulted in the banishment of prostitutes and the eradication of the red-light districts, even if the city administrators were to varying degrees opposed to their abolition. In Memphis and Chattanooga, after decades of tolerance and municipal management by neglect, the destruction of segregated districts became a prerequisite for having U.S. Army troops stationed nearby at training camps in 1917. In both cases, the local constabulary carried out the work, although in Chattanooga the provost marshal at Fort Oglethorpe augmented the local police in the suppression of vice.

Events in Chattanooga, Nashville, Knoxville, and Memphis were not isolated phenomena but part of a wider national context of moral reform manifest as anti-prostitution activity. The Tennessee House of Representatives passed a draconian bill in March 1917 that would have resulted in the arrest of any woman found working in a brothel. A fine and sentence of sixty days in a city's work house were prescribed as punishment. The Senate, however, after three readings, failed to approve the measure.[108] There is no record of any debate by the Senate on this measure. Regardless, the intolerant wartime mood of 1917–1918 served only as a climax to two decades of similar activity, which was an "anti-prostitution crusade" in urban American.[109] There is no record of any debate by the Senate on this measure. The bordello, wrote John C. Burnham, "was only one among many noxious social institutions fought by the progressives ... [and] the most striking tangible alteration in American social life in the Progressive era was the decline of the traditional red-light segregated district in American cities."[110] According to one authority, however "the effects of such moral reforms were social repression and social control of the laboring poor."[111]

Nevertheless, what some scholars have characterized as the "Golden Age of the Brothel in America" had come to an end in Tennessee as it had in the nation by 1920.[112]

Prostitution, nevertheless was not eradicated, it merely changed form after the decline of segregated districts.[113] Thus the noble victory sought by moral reformers was short-lived at best, and was less a matter of substantive reform than one of the appearance of correction.[114]

3

Editorial Disputes

In Tennessee's journalistic history, acrimony and homicides between editors in the streets were not everyday occurrences, but common enough to occasionally garner the attention of the nation.[1] Yet they did not conform to the rules of the Code Duello. Mark Twain, in his *Journalism in Tennessee*, related how a friend went to the Volunteer State for his health and sought a position at a newspaper office. His interview with the editor of the paper at whose office he applied was several times interrupted. First came a shot through the open window. Denouncing "that Scoundrel Smith, of the *Morning Volcano*, the editor snatched a handy revolver from his belt and fired, dropping Smith with a bullet in the thigh." A little later, while the editor was looking the applicant's trial copy, a hand-grenade came down the stove pipe and played havoc in the room. Next came Col. Blatherskite Tecumseh, who, calling for "the poltroon who edits this mangy sheet, forthwith engaged in a revolver duel with the object of his wrath...." The applicant decided he might do better to seek employment in some other state.[2]

Editorial homicides, shootouts, or, as Twain called them, "revolver duels,' were not really duels, but were often called such. One editor might insult another, a rebuttal and/or a challenge would be printed—or in rare cases an apology—but the fighting took place in the streets or sometimes, more peaceably, entirely in the columns of the newspapers. The following narrative will help in the understanding of these "affairs of honor" thought of as typical of the character of ante and post bellum Southern newspaper editors. Ironically, freedom of the press seems to have been less important than issues of personal antipathy which were aired as a result of the exercise of that liberty. Freedom of expression could lead to serious consequences.

After William G. Brownlow resigned as a Methodist circuit rider in 1828, he moved to Elizabethton, Tennessee, and founded the *Whig*. It was there that he made his first editorial enemy, Landon Carter Haynes, editor of the *Tennessee Sentinel*.

During the period when the two lived in Elizabethton, they exchanged editorial attacks. Haynes tried to ignore insults by Brownlow who taunted him as a "young puppy, because ... the ... unprincipled scoundrel, does not possess the nerve to assail me."[3] These were serious fighting words in the nineteenth-century South.

Such insults could not be ignored, and on the evening of March 2, 1840, two shots were fired at Brownlow at his home. The shots missed by inches. Haynes denied responsibility and suggested Brownlow staged the incident attempting character assassination.[3] Two months later, after Haynes had made remarks questioning the ancestry of Brownlow's mother, the two met in Elizabethton. The upshot was Brownlow caned Haynes who in turn shot Brownlow in the thigh. Brownlow characterized Haynes as "the prince of villains, hypocrites, and political prostitutes."[4]

At a Methodist camp-meeting in the summer of 1842, Brownlow's enemies attacked him with clubs. The parson pulled a derringer, which misfired, and he was beaten, as he said, receiving nine blows that "failed to hit me on the right arm, the hand I use when I write out the history of rogues, perjured villains, stealers of TOLLS, of HOGS, and all other like measures."[5] He continued to bait Haynes and was himself the object of retaliatory slander and suffered another clubbing in 1848, which left his health physically and arguably mentally for the worse. Rather than quit the newspaper business, he decided to move to Knoxville and established the *Knoxville Whig* on May 19, 1849.[6] A confrontation came in the early 1850s, when William G. Swan established a Democratic paper in Knoxville. After some editorial sparring, Brownlow arrived at Swan's house brandishing a pistol, challenging him to a duel. Swan declined, and Brownlow publicly accused him of cowardice. Regardless of such vituperative language, no duel took place. There were no politics underlying the affair between the two editors.[7]

According to the recollections of Nashville Judge T. Bell in an 1887 interview, the first editorial difficulties in Nashville took place in 1835, between General R. C. Foster and Jeremiah Harris. Harris was the editor of the *Nashville Union*. Initial remarks made by Harris provoking an assault with a pistol on Harris at the *Union* office. Foster wounded him, but bystanders interceded. Many feared the shooting would lead to further difficulties. It did not, but according to the Judge: "Shooting ... was ... common ... in those day ... men of different opinions would get into discussions, and the first thing one knew pistols were popping." It is not surprising that other editorial mêlées could occur.

Another newspaper pseudo-duel, about 1847 recalled Judge Bell, was that between William High Smith and Billings, one of the editors of the *Patriot*. Ignominious words led Smith to assault Billings who stabbed him with a knife, wounding him superficially. It might have ended there, but Edward Zane Carroll Judson (a.k.a. "Ned Buntline") fanned the flames, writing in his magazine *Ned Buntline's Own* about the matter in a provocative style, goading the two men to fight what was essentially a pseudo-duel in the streets of Nashville. Neither was hurt in the confrontation, although Buntline nearly lost his life to a mob incited by his having made one Nashville man a cuckold. Judson, a womanizer and a lothario, had compromised another man's spouse; details are scarce, but Judson had an affair with the teenaged wife of Robert Porterfield in Nashville in 1846. On March 14, 1846, Porterfield challenged Judson to a duel in the city cemetery at dawn; Judson was killed. At Judson's murder trial, Porterfield's brother shot and wounded Judson, allowing him to escape in the chaos. He was subsequently captured by a lynch mob and hanged from a hotel awning on the square. He was rescued by friends who cut the rope, or the rope broke, no one seems to know for certain. He moved to New York where he continued a successful literary career writing "dime novels."[8]

A shooting incident in Nashville occurred on March 13, 1852. After making disparaging remarks about newspaper editors in general, Reece B. Brabson, member of the state legislature met Felix Zollicoffer, the editor of the Nashville *Republican Banner* near the City Hotel. Zollicoffer insulted Brabson who slapped Zollicoffer's face. The editor drew a pistol and shot at the unarmed politician. A bystander hit Zollicoffer's arm and the ball lodged in a door. Neither the editor nor the politician was hurt. Zollicoffer would shortly be involved in a more serious affair.[9]

In 1852, the presidential election was a contest between General Winfield Scott, the Whig candidate, and Democrat Franklin Pierce. Zollicoffer was still editor of the *Banner*. John Marling was the editor of the Whig *Union*. Political rhetoric spurred hostility, but the issue that divided the men was the question of where to place a bridge across the Cumberland River. Marling accused Zollicoffer of being mercenary in his motives to place the bridge at the foot of Church Street. On August 20, the two met in the street in front of the *Union* office. Zollicoffer loudly denounced Marling who drew his pistol, and fired wide of the mark. Zollicoffer took aim, his pistol misfiring. One witness said he took the cap off his pistol in a gesture of conciliation, but it was to no avail. He replaced the cap while Marling fired, hitting Zollicoffer's right hand. Zollicoffer shot back, hitting Marling in the head, resulting in a serious but not fatal wound.[10] According to the *Union*: "The bullet entered his face a little to the right of his nose, passed immediately above the throat, and was found lodged in the back part of the neck, about two inches behind the ear, near the base of the skull."[11]

Marling, after making a less than complete recovery, would be appointed American ambassador to Guatemala.[12] The pseudo-duel received national press attention.[13]

On or about October 6, 1857, John M. Fleming, editor of the *Knoxville Register* clashed with Irish Patriot John Mitchel, who was spending time in Knoxville while in exile and befriended the city's Democrats. Mitchel confronted Fleming in front of the Lamar House Hotel concerning a *Knoxville Register* column that had ridiculed the Irishman. Words were exchanged and Mitchel struck Fleming with a cane. The incident led to a street brawl. The police soon intervened and dispersed the crowd that had gathered. After an hour had passed, Fleming returned to the street and challenged Mitchel, though accounts differ as to what happened next. Fleming claimed he challenged Mitchel to a duel.

According to Fleming, Mitchel "stood at the distance of six to eight paces, with his hand on the cock [hammer] of a partially concealed pistol. Yet he ingloriously withdrew from my presence while shouts of "coward!" "sneak!" "dastard!" "coward!" broke forth spontaneously from the crowd from his shameful exit. Fleming cursed Mitchel as "a miserable scoundrel" and a "white livered coward." Mitchel, however, responded only by withdrawing from the crowd, thereby averting a street brawl or a pseudo-duel. Mitchel, later denied that Fleming made any challenge, stating that Fleming was at a loss for words in this second encounter, so he merely dismissed Fleming as a "whipped man" and left the scene.

The Register was an American (or "Know-Nothing") Party newspaper. The "Know-Nothing Party," strong in the 1850s, was a xenophobic nativist political organization that opposed immigration of foreigners, especially the Irish Catholics, into the United States. As its editor, Fleming demonstrated his approval of Know-Nothing policies. The presence of Mitchel, a Democratic party favorite and a fiery political activist, was enough to get Fleming's "Irish up."[14]

On November 18, 1859, after months of editorial warfare between editors George G. Poindexter of the *Nashville Union* and Allen A. Hall of the *Nashville News*, political controversy became personal. The trouble stemmed from Poindexter's charge that Hall, as editor of the *Nashville Republican* in 1834, favored a proposal for gradual abolition of slavery. Insults led the Poindexter to reply: "[I am] fully able and prepared to protect my person against assault and to punish the assailant."

The editorial feud culminated on a damp and drizzly morning, as Poindexter carried an umbrella concealing a Navy colt pistol, and walked toward the offices of the *News*. According to a contemporary account: "Mr. Hall ... took position in front of his door, and as Mr. P. advanced, he commanded him twice to stop ... at the second command [Mr. P.] ... made a movement as if to draw a weapon.... Hall leveled a double barrel shot gun and fired. Mr. P. fell upon the pavement about fifty feet from Mr. Hall, and died.... His pistol fell by his side ....Mr. Hall ... delivered himself into ... custody..."[15]

A grand jury found no true bill, exonerating Hall of Poindexter's murder.[17]

The shoot-out did not go unnoticed by *The New York Times*, which editorialized against the ridiculous absurdity of the Southern code of honor.

> In order that nobody else may hereafter be surprised in a state of mental perplexity on such a subject, we cordially recommend Southern gentlemen to ... solemnly decide ... whether it be more advisable to "slap with the open palm," or "thwack with an umbrella." Honor and chivalry and buncombe alike demand that so knotty a point be no longer left *in dubio*.[18]

In neither the Marlin-Zollicoffer nor the Hall-Poindexter case was the assailant tried. Such brawls were considered *de rigueur*, unavoidable in antebellum Tennessee, and the public generally sympathized with the victor. "If it was a drawn battle sentiment was curbed until one or the other went down."[19]

In 1860, a young attorney, Henderson M. Somerville, accepted the editorship of the *Memphis Appeal*, then Tennessee's leading Democratic paper. The *Appeal* supported Stephen A. Douglas. Dr. Jeptha Fowlkes, editor of the *Avalanche*, severely criticized Somerville. A challenge was made but Fowlkes begged off saying he was a family man. He apologized and the matter was settled. In a 1903 interview, then Judge Somerville confessed that he did not "believe Fowlkes' family was any more relieved than I was."[20]

While the Confederacy was destroyed, the Southern code of honor as it related to editorial quarrels was not dead. In July 1866, an editorial dispute erupted between the editor of the *Memphis Appeal*, General Thomas Jordan, and Colonel Matthew Galloway, editor of the *Memphis Avalanche*.[21] The challenge originated from Galloway's writing a severe attack against Jordan for his authorship of an article published in *Harper's Weekly*, blaming Jefferson Davis for the failure of the Confederacy. Because dueling of any sort was illegal in Tennessee, the two editors agreed to meet in Arkansas. Before they could make their rendezvous, both were arrested in Memphis. The mediation of a third party, J. H. McMahon editor of the *Memphis Enquirer*, soothed tempers and there was no excursion across the river, and a duel was never consummated.[22]

An editorial appeared in the May 16, 1883 issue of the Memphis *Commercial Appeal* written by Colonel Galloway, the editor of the paper depicting ex-Confederate General James R. Chalmers, then representative of the Second Congressional District of Mississippi, as a Republican, "a political ingrate and traitor, and a hired persecutor of old friends."

The general responded with alacrity to the insult, and telegraphed to the *Avalanche*: "... I will prove that he is not only a liar but a literary thief." Galloway fired back that Chalmers was "...the dirtiest beast in the filthy den of the Republican party ... whose touch is ... pollution." The two plotted a rendezvous in Mississippi; however, they were arrested in Memphis and placed under a bond of $1,000 each. Thereafter, they limited their quarrel to journalistic sniping.[23] The outcome was admirable, wrote the editor of the *St. Louis Globe-Democrat*:

> When a man thinks another is likely to assault him, the Southern way—the way of those who appear to control public opinion in the South—is to shoot the suspected person in his tracks. The better Northern way is to have him put under bonds to keep the peace. This plan is much more conducive to public order than the other.[24]

In Nashville, in late December 1887, John J. Littleton, editor of the *National Review*, secretary of the State Republican Executive Committee, and vice president for Tennessee's branch of the National Republican League of Clubs was cold bloodily shot down in the street. His assailant, son of a prominent family and a locally important Republican, was Joseph B. Banks, twenty-six years old and regarded as one of the foremost young businessmen in the city. Banks was involved in local politics and moved in the best social circles. Littleton had established a career as a journalist in Kingston and Chattanooga before moving to Nashville. Both men were well known in Nashville. The cause for the urban ambush was an editorial in the *National Review* in which Littleton had denounced Banks, "charging him with nameless acts of total depravity." It was on all sides agreed that Banks had been insulted and that he would assume the initiative.[25] Rumors spread that "the matter would result in shot-guns. No challenge was issued."

Shortly before ten o'clock on the morning of December 27, on High Street near the Watkins Institute, Banks, hidden in a nearby house, emptied a double-barreled shotgun into Littleton.

Littleton claimed to be walking up the street to his office when Banks fired the shotgun. He tried to defend himself but Banks fired another load into his legs and he collapsed. According to Littleton's later death-bed statement:

> ... suddenly I heard a shot fired from behind me.... That shot felled me to the ground, and suddenly ... I was on the ground, I raised my head. I had a revolver....

My arm was filled with shot, so that I could not use it.... I looked and saw a man standing in the door on the opposite side of the street with a gun sighted at me.... I said "That is enough; don't fire again." He fired two more loads into my legs.... I raised up and saw Joe Banks. He broke and ran.... He gave me no warning; he fired twice.... I did not use my revolver. I did not have time to get it out.[26]

Littleton bled to death. Banks, on the other hand, surrendered to authorities and was put in a furnished room on the second floor above the city prison. He received an estimated 500 visitors in the apartment in the jail. Banks spoke very little about the shooting and appeared calm, even serene. He ate supper sent from a nearby restaurant and retired at about eleven o'clock.[27] Finally, after four years of trials, appeals, and delays, on April 8, 1892, Banks was acquitted of homicide charges.[28] He had gotten away with cold blooded murder.

Knoxville was no stranger to editorial squabbles.[29] William Rule, editor of the Republican *Knoxville Chronicle*, was accosted in the streets on the evening of March 11, 1882 by the editor of the Democratic *Knoxville Tribune*, James W. Wallace. That morning's *Chronicle* contained an article in which the youthful Wallace found offense. The trouble stemmed from intense political enmity but was sparked by an apolitical article in the *Chronicle* charging that the *Tribune* was guilty of unfair and even salacious advertising. According to Rule, "a few Sundays ago ... after advertising that it would not do so, [the *Tribune*] published a sensational romance, and then, in order to escape punishment, lied out of it, and begged and whined like the cowardly puppies that they are." It was a variety of journalism the *Chronicle* would never engage in and "which no gentleman could take pride. But the *Tribune* boasts of its enterprise."[30]

Wallace met Rule on the street that evening and demanded a retraction. Rule refused and according to his account:

> ... the irate young man ... writhing under some irrepressible grievance, hoarse ... trembling with excitement, commenced some sort of formal denunciation, which he had evidently been practicing.... In order to assist the young man in his explosion, we struck him a blow with a small cane ... whereupon he drew a revolver and commenced firing. He fired two shots, the first at such close range that one side of our face was slightly burned with powder. We retreated ... he fired again and then ... went in a dog trot across Gay Street into the *Tribune* office, and thus the curtain dropped on ... a thrilling tragedy.[31]

Wallace had acted entirely in self-defense, claimed the *Tribune*, and Rule was not hurt. Wallace turned himself in to authorities. The reason for the altercation claimed the *Tribune*'s editor paper was simply that "... we have advocated unswervingly the success of the Democratic party ... and.... Our efforts to show the thievery and rottenness of some of our local politicians have no doubt won us the bitter hatred of the *Chronicle* and the Republican leaders in Knoxville."[32]

Rule's Republican friends and colleagues surprised him the next evening with the presentation of a brand new cane, the one used in the altercation having been broken over Wallace's head.[33] Apparently no legal action was taken.

Six years after William Rule's affair, his brother, James, editor of the *Knoxville Journal*, faced a more serious challenge. As services at St. John's Episcopal Church began on Sunday, January 29, 1888, a street brawl occurred leaving one man dead and two wounded. Just minutes before the ruckus, James Rule, on his way to church, was advised that three men on the opposite side of the street wished to speak with him. Rule walked across the street to meet with the angry John and William West. Rule had been warned of a possible attack and carried a concealed revolver.[34]

The cause of the enmity was a letter from "XYZ" in the *Journal* in which a doctor complained that the current city physician was unqualified. In 1886, the city passed an ordinance requiring the city physician have a medical degree. The law had not been enforced and now the Board of Aldermen had "reappointed the notoriously incompetent individual ... and at a salary increased from six hundred to one thousand dollars!"

Dr. A. T. West was the city physician to whom the letter from "XYZ" referred. Dr. West and his sons John and William called at the offices of the *Journal* insisting they be given the name of the letter writer. He was told that he would have his answer on Monday morning. Dr. West replied "This thing has gone far enough, and has got to be settled now, To-day."

West's sons waited to confront James Rule. They met him across the street from the church.

They demanded to know XYZ's identity but Rule declined, promising to act on Monday. "[T]hey said it must be done at once." Rule insisted it was impossible at that time for him to discuss the matter further as he was on his way to worship services.

John West then drew a long knife and William a pistol. Rule backed down the street until he stumbled and fell. As the choir began to sing "O come let us sing unto the Lord," the West brothers overwhelmed him, beating Rule over the head with a pistol and stabbing him in the back.

Rule drew his revolver and fired blindly at his attackers, mortally wounding John West. Rule was taken home and his wounds attended to. The Wests left the scene thinking they had killed Rule. William West was found by the constabulary to be tried the next day

John West was taken to his father's residence, wounded in the abdomen. In his deathbed confession, he contended he was unarmed, his behavior polite and that Rule would not reveal the letter writer, stepped back, drew his pistol, and fired.[35] Evidently, there were no prosecutions.

In 1890, thirty-three years after his dramatic incident with Mitchel, another controversy developed in Knoxville between the bellicose John M. Fleming, now editor of the *Knoxville Sentinel* and another antagonist, James Phelan, owner of the *Memphis Avalanche* and Congressman of the 10th District (Memphis) over the official textbook *History of Tennessee* published two years earlier.[36] When publicity reached Fleming of its pending publication the Knoxville editor wrote to Phelan asking for an advance copy and "took occasion to be very complimentary to Mr. Phelan. Phelan replied that he had no advance copies and thanked Fleming for his kind remarks."[37]

But when the State Legislature considered a bill making Phelan's state history an official text for the public school system, editor Fleming became incensed, accusing

Phelan of using his influence as a congressman to gain the contract.[38] Phelan wrote an apology, which Fleming refused.[39] Phelan then denounced Fleming as "a liar, a coward and a scoundrel," and issued a challenge.[40] The accusation by Phelan, however, had put him "outside the code (Duello) limit," and could not therefore fight him honorably. It is one of the requirements of the code, stated Col. Matthew Galloway, himself no stranger to editorial spats and the Code Duello, "that all communications looking to a hostile meeting must be concluded in the most polite and courteous language; and a gentleman cannot consistently fight with a man whom he considers a liar, a coward and a scoundrel. The code ... is for the settling of disagreements among gentlemen, and the combatants must treat each other as gentlemen."[41] Fleming reminded Phelan: "As a historian in the public schools you ought to know ... the constitutional and legal penalties against the 'giving, sending or accepting of a challenge to fight a duel.'"[42] Phelan had "made an egregious ass of himself."[43]

In a letter to the editors of *The New York Times*, Phelan explained Fleming's animosities were "founded on the fact that I had not supplied an advance copy of a book I had written and because he had 'been shut out.'"[44] In the end, the challenge was denied.[45] Fleming attempted suicide in late 1890; the newspaper account claimed he "had not been himself since his famous controversy with Congressman Phelan." Soon thereafter, Phelan died in Nassau, Bermuda, where he had retreated for his nerves after the prolix dispute with Fleming.[46]

A pseudo-duel developed in Memphis on February 17, 1893. Mike Connolly editor of the *Appeal-Avalanche*, and Edward Ward Carmack, editor of the *Commercial* were at odds. The dispute arose over a war of words about gambling in Memphis. The two editors were arrested and were released on their own recognizance and ordered to appear for examination in court on the charge of preparing a duel. Tempers were "amicably adjusted" by the editor of the *Memphis Scimitar*, and the duel was called off.[47]

It was only four months later that Carmack took offense at remarks made by W. A. Collier, one of the owners of the *Appeal-Avalanche*, in early May 1893. Carmack answered:

> It is not the slander of such tongues as that of the person who owns and controls the *Appeal Avalanche*, or those who do its dirty work, that can defame the *Commercial*. He has indeed succeeded in debauching a once honored newspaper until it has sunk to the level of a night-strolling trollop, plying its trade in the back alleys of the town, dealing in shame for a morsel of bread and selling its soul to whomsoever may buy.[48]

News spread of a plan to fight in Holly Springs, Mississippi, at 1:30 p.m. On the morning of May 4 bench warrants were issued, charging them with an attempt to fight a duel. Deputies were sent to arrest the editors.

At eight o'clock, Carmack was seen in front of the Peabody Hotel; he went into the saloon and took a stiff drink, went to the street where he jumped into a hack and arrived at the railroad depot. Carmack and his second, W. J. Crawford, found a seat in a smoking car. Before the train left the station, they were discovered, arrested, and taken to the courthouse.

The authorities were also looking for Collier, who slipped through the constabulary's cordon. As their hack started toward the depot, a deputy sheriff emerged and notified Collier that he was under arrest. Collier and his cohorts "quick as lightning" yanked the deputy into the carriage, physically restraining him. They made it to the train and after a scuffle with police, occupied a sleeper car and headed for Holly Springs.

One duelist was on board while the other was headed to the courtroom in a streetcar. Carmack entered the packed courthouse and spoke to the judge. He was allowed to leave on his own recognizance. In the meantime, Carmack's associates commissioned a train that left for Holly Springs about two o'clock. A telegram informed Collier that Carmack, although late, was coming on the special train to fight the duel. To complicate matters, Carmack's train was sidetracked, delaying its arrival until 3:30 p.m.

Crawford boarded the train saying Carmack was ready to meet Collier, who claimed that the hour for meeting had passed. Then Crawford offered Carmack's train to Collier, agreeing to stop anywhere between Holly Springs and the Tennessee State line. This was also declined; shortly thereafter the two trains returned to Memphis.[49] For all the bluster, the editors' honor was plainly upheld by a convenient technicality in the Code Duello.

The nineteenth-century history of newspaper-related shootouts extended into the twentieth century and pseudo-duels found its culmination in the November 8, 1908, street shootout in Nashville when Edward W. Carmack, editorial journalist, erstwhile U.S. Senator, failed candidate for governor, prohibition advocate, and then editor of the *Nashville American*, found himself suddenly confronted by erstwhile friends and then political enemies Duncan Cooper and his son, Robin. Shots were exchanged and Carmack, twice involved in pseudo-duels, was instantly killed, and Robin Cooper was wounded.[50] It was the culmination of a history of editorial skirmishes, pseudo-duels, violence, shootouts, and plain murder associated with Tennessee journalism beginning at least in 1835.

4

Dueling and the Code Duello

If your superior forgets what he owes you & his station, & attempts to insult you ... put him to instant death.... Never ... outlive your honour.

Andrew Jackson, December 28, 1818.

Tell my father that I die as I lived—a gentleman.

Edward Hamlin, August 27, 1870.

When the topic of dueling comes to mind people usually think of antebellum days of the old South when rich gentlemen planters played poker, sipped whiskey, and discussed politics, or the market price of slaves and cotton. Inevitably the topic of conversation would turn to news of the latest duel. Dueling was beyond politics and concerned those issues of "honor," which they firmly believed could only be equitably resolved by resort to murder as justified by their belief in the creed of honor and the Code Duello. The code ritualized how such murders were to take place. Rules governing the selection of seconds, proper wording, and delivery of a challenge, the manner in which it should be presented to the one whose conduct rendered defense of one's honor necessary and the weapons of choice. Certainly they were aware that killing by dueling was both murder and illegal, but considered such deaths less than homicide and more proof of their manhood on the "field of honor." News of the latest duels were known to the men of their social standing. Just as a lawyer or businessman keeps abreast of changes in politics, interest rates, law and market fluctuations, so gentlemen of the antebellum South kept pace with the dueling world.

It is important at the outset to recognize that "gentlemen" were central to the practice of dueling in the antebellum South. Duels were not fought by skilled tradesmen, the so-called "mechanics" of the era. In practice, only gentlemen—

businessmen, lawyers, merchants, bankers, planters, editors, and politicians and military officers—fought over insults to their self-styled "sacred honor." A definite class distinction was at play in dueling confrontations. Dueling was an activity strictly limited by practice and class to the upper echelons of society. Shielding "honor" from insult was an obligatory prerogative of gentlemen of the antebellum South to maintain their manhood from slander. As Andrew Jackson wrote to his nephew, a cadet at West Point, about honor, discipline, and punishment: "If your superior forgets what he owes you & his station, & attempts to insult you ... put him to instant death.... Never ... outlive your honour."

Duels were deadly affairs conducted according to a standard set of rules found in the Code Duello, formally published in America in 1828. Duels had their origins in the Sicilian vendetta and the street fight. In its day, a duel was an accepted practice of gross disdain toward law and order. But insomuch as it was orderly and conducted under rules that developed into the Code Duello, it was popularly immune from censure. But dueling was illegal in the Volunteer State; as early as 1801, Tennessee's state constitution banned dueling. So duels took place out of state, often just across the Tennessee–Kentucky line, where, although dueling was likewise illegal, they were carried out avoiding the letter of Tennessee law. The conventions for dueling were formal and class oriented, to providing aristocratic gentlemen a means of defending their honor. The Code Duello determined how and when the one insulted was to behave in arranging a confrontation before a challenge could be sent; the designation of a second; the correct manner of responding to a carefully composed polite note declaring an offense to one's honor before a challenge; and issuing a challenge. The code included instructions on the duty of the challenger and his second before fighting, the duty of the challenger and his second after a challenge was sent, the venue for the combat, the duty and deportment of antagonists and seconds on the dueling ground, the manner in which weapons were chosen, loaded, and presented to the duelists, the manner in which firing would commence. And finally, the degrees of insult and the procedure in which insult could be compromised by gentlemen without dueling. The rules were precise and inflexible: above all, the parties of the duel were to remain cool, calm, and collected, and were forbidden to publicly accost an opponent once a challenge had been accepted.[1] One nearly ubiquitously cited example in Tennessee history is the famous Jackson-Dickinson duel of 1806, resulting in Dickinson's death and Jackson's serious though not fatal wound. In time, duels transformed into something other than gentlemanly murders, and so-called duels bore no resemblance to affairs governed by the Code Duello. They evolved into pseudo-duels or street shootouts having no relation to the affairs of honor in the pre-Civil War South. Perhaps the most famous and first example in Tennessee history was the Andrew Jackson, Thomas Hart, and Jesse Benton pseudo-duel, brawl, and shootout in the streets and hotel lobbies of Nashville in 1813. This chapter deals with both the formal duels, fought in accordance with the Code Duello, and with those instances when the code only nominally justified a fight. In the Volunteer State's history, "duels" between Tennessee newspaper editors occurred in the streets were not everyday incidents, but common enough to garner the attention of the nation before the Civil War, and even Mark Twain. In his *Journalism in Tennessee*, he satirically related how Southern newspaper editors often resorted to "revolver duels."[2]

Editorial homicides, or shootouts, were not really duels, but were often called such. One editor might insult another, a rebuttal and/or a challenge would be printed— or in rare cases an apology—but the deadly fighting took place in the streets or sometimes, exclusively yet harmlessly, in the columns of newspapers. The following narrative will shed light on the violence of "affairs of honor" governed by the Code Duello, those commonly thought of as typical of the spirit of antebellum aristocratic Southern virility. Formal dueling between citizens of more plebian distinctions were not common until the period after the Civil War and Reconstruction and garnered no attention, bolstering the notion that the lower class of tradesmen or yeomen farmers did not fight duels. Dueling was reserved for gentlemen.

Formal duels, as opposed to brawling, were thought of as the duty, if not sport, of gentlemen. They were deliberate rituals to keep society civilized and the women and children safe from violence, or at least that is what its advocates insisted. In these duels, a man demanded "satisfaction." Only one of the equal social status could give or take redress for an insult to one's reputation or character. However, under the Code Duello, getting satisfaction did not necessarily require a killing but could be won simply by showing up on the dueling grounds to harmlessly exchange shots. Once the antagonists mutually established they were satisfied, whether or not a killing or maiming had taken place, the affair was considered over. That is, antagonists might fire their guns in the air or purposely miss, showing courage and thereby safeguarding their honor. One such example was the duel between lawyers Waightshill Avery and Andrew Jackson in 1788. The dispute arose from a remark Avery, a more experienced attorney, made in court that stuck in Jackson's craw. Jackson, notoriously thin-skinned, made a challenge which was accepted. The two met on August 12, 1788 late in the evening behind the courthouse. Their seconds, however, persuaded both men to fire into the air, avoiding bloodshed and satisfying their honor and saving their reputations. The two remained on friendly terms thereafter.[3]

Jackson and John Sevier, the famous Indian fighter and first governor of Tennessee, fought a duel in 1803. In the aftermath, no one was shot and the two renewed their amity. Their dispute arose over gossip that circulated the autumn of 1803 that Governor Sevier was guilty of using his office for unwarranted personal benefit. Jackson was rumored to be the source of the accusation. On the other hand, Sevier was said to claim Jackson's election as general of the Tennessee militia, a position that was won by a thin margin of one vote was the result of voter fraud.

On October 1, 1803, Jackson, also a state judge, left his courtroom in Knoxville and was confronted by a large crowd and Governor Sevier. Wasting no time, Sevier attacked Jackson verbally. Coarse epithets and passions skyrocketed all too quickly with both men asserting a wish to kill the other. Ironically, although the two men affirmed a wish to duel, they could not agree on a time or a place. Letters with details and proposals were sent back and forth by way of seconds, with each man misunderstanding the proposals of the other. In accordance with the Code Duello, Jackson's first letter to Sevier, dated October 2, 1803, noted that Governor Sevier claimed Jackson's election to the position of general of the militia resulted from voter fraud:

The ungentlemanly Expressions, and gasconading conduct, of yours relative to me on yesterday was in true character of your self [*sic*], and unmask you to the world and plainly shews that they were the ebulations [*sic*] of a base mind goaded with stubborn prooffs [*sic*] of fraud, and flowing from a source devoid of every refined sentiment, or delicate sensation. But sir the Voice of the people has made you a Governor. This alone makes you worthy of my notice or the notice of any Gentleman. To the office I bear respect, to the Voice of the people who placed it on you I pay respect, and as such I only deign to notice you, and call upon you for that satisfaction and explanation that your ungentlemanly conduct & expressions require, for this purpose I request an interview, and my friend who will hand you this will point out the time and place, when and where I shall Expect to see you with your friend and no other person. My friend and myself will be armed with pistols.[4]

Sevier's response mocked Jackson's letter and challenge practically mimicking it word for word, but with much better spelling:

Your Ungentlemanly and Gasgonading conduct of yesterday, and indeed at all other times heretofore, have unmasked yourself to me and to the World. The Voice of the Assembly has made you a Judge, and this alone has made you has made Worthy of My notice.... I shall wait on you with pleasure at any time and place not within the State of Tennessee.[5]

Sevier accepted the challenge to meet Jackson on a dueling field any place or any time preferred by Jackson but outside the state of Tennessee—this because dueling was prohibited by the Tennessee Constitution and a state law of 1801.[6] They agreed to meet in Virginia. These notes and similar propositions passed between the two men for the next seven days. Jackson grew so unsatisfied with the failure to determine a venue and time to duel that he published the following public notice "To all whom Shall See these presents Greeting—Know yea that I Andrew Jackson, do pronounce, Publish, and declare to the world, that his Excellency John Sevier Esqr., Governor, Captain General and commander in chief, of the land and Naval forces of the State of Tennessee—is a base coward and poltroon. He will basely insult, but has not the courage to repair the wound."[7] Although this violated the unwritten rule of confidentiality, they concurred on a time and place. Jackson arrived to the hastily designated field of honor. Jackson had had to wait for Sevier who arrived late. As Jackson saw Sevier approaching, he sent his second to deliver a letter to the governor, enumerating every insult he had allegedly made against Jackson. Sevier, though, refused to accept the letter, which outraged Jackson, who mounted his horse and charged Sevier, brandishing his cane. Stunned by the onward rush of Jackson galloping toward him, Sevier fell off his horse, and fumbled while trying to draw his sword, which broke as he fell under his own horse. Satisfied, Jackson and Sevier considered the matter done, honor had been satisfied. The two men and their seconds then rode back into Knoxville, cheerful and friendly.[8]

Another example of a formal duel took place as a precursor to the infamous Jackson–Dickinson duel. It was a fight between John Coffee, a faithful friend and business partner of Jackson and Nathaniel A. McNairy. The incident evolved from an extremely tangled web of controversy over a bet on a horse race in which it was said Charles Dickinson, a *bon vivant* young aristocrat and lawyer, had insulted Andrew Jackson's wife, Rachel, and a challenge to fight a duel with Jackson by an immature young Nashville lawyer, Thomas Swann. Briefly, Swann had made himself quite meddlesome, and after the noted horse race between "Truxton" and "Ploughboy" busied himself by making statements, which he attributed to Jackson, concerning some bets that were made on the race. Jackson denounced Swann as "a damned liar" for which Swann expressed himself as determined to have satisfaction. Swann's challenge was not accepted by Jackson, who declared that Swann was not a gentleman and so beneath Jackson's contempt, and in his letter called Dickinson a "poltroon and a liar." Moreover, Jackson threatened if he were to meet Swann in public, he would cane him. As it turned out, Jackson did happen to meet Swann in a local tavern and assaulted him with blows from his cane. Jackson then verbally assaulted Swann's compatriot Nathaniel A. McNairy, who in turn then challenged Jackson. In the process of making his challenge, McNairy insulted Jackson's foremost friend and business partner, John Coffee. Jackson refused to meet McNairy on the basis that he was not a gentleman, and so would not condescend to fight with such a lower class "poltroon." Jackson was waiting to challenge Charles Dickinson, then on a business trip to New Orleans. Coffee, Jackson advised, would have to take up the difficulty and challenge McNairy to a duel.

The Coffee–McNairy duel was arranged precisely according to the Code Duello. Inasmuch as dueling was illegal, he two agreed to meet on the field of honor just above the Tennessee–Kentucky state line on March 1, 1806. After a distance of 30 feet was measured off, the two faced each other with loaded pistols at the ready. McNairy's second won the coin flip and instructed the duelists with the proper procedure for initiating the shooting, making certain they understood instructions: "'Make Ready;' at which time the parties were to raise their pistols; then, distinctly count, 'one, two, three,' and then the word 'Fire;' at which time the parties were to fire."

As it happened, McNairy fired prematurely on the count of two, shooting Coffee in the thigh. Realizing his blunder, or perhaps that he had not killed Coffee, McNairy offered to give his wounded antagonist a shot at him as stood he unarmed. "Mr. Coffee then advanced toward Mr. McNairy, and said to him, 'G-d D—n you, this is the second time you have been guilty of the same crime.'" Such words were not in accordance with the Code Duello, and Coffee's second reminded him that the field of honor "was an improper place to have words." A compromise of sorts was made in which McNairy agreed to print an accurate account of the duel, including his having prematurely fired, in the local press.[9] With Coffee's integrity upheld on the field of honor, it remained for Jackson to fight his deadly duel with Charles Dickinson.

Charles Dickinson arrived back in Nashville on May 20, 1806. He wasted no time in printing a scurrilous attack on Jackson in his father-in-law's newspaper *The Impartial Review*. Jackson's confidant John Overton rode out to the Hermitage and provided Jackson a copy of the article, which read in part: "I declare him, notwithstanding he is a Major General of the militia ... to be a worthless scorner, 'a poltroon and a coward'...." Overton advised Jackson that he must challenge Dickinson. An hour later, Overton delivered a letter from Jackson to Dickinson. He concluded the letter by writing: "I hope, sir, your courage will be an ample security to me that I will obtain speedily that satisfaction due me for the insults offered, and in the way my friend who hands you this will point out. He waits upon you for that purpose, and with your friend will enter in immediate arrangements for this purpose."

The challenge had been made. Seconds were immediately agreed upon, and it was mutually agreed that the two antagonists would meet at Harrison Mills, on the Red River in Logan County, Kentucky, at precisely 7 a.m. on May 30. Although Jackson wished to fight sooner, Dickinson refused upon the grounds that he did not have pistols to offer. Jackson acquiesced. The distance between the two duelists was set at 24 feet (eight paces), with both men facing each other, their pistols held down perpendicularly. It was agreed that when each man was ready they were to raise and aim their pistols at one another and await the command to fire when they were free to shoot as they saw fit. Interestingly, perhaps remembering McNairy's blunder in his duel with Coffee just a few months earlier, it was agreed that should either discharge their weapon before the word "fire" was given, the seconds pledged to shoot the offending party down "instantly."

Knowledge that the duel had been arranged, save for the place and date of its execution, buzzed throughout Nashville and environs. Bets were taken, the odds in Dickinson's favor. It was rumored that Dickinson wagered anywhere from $500 to $3,000 and that he would bring Jackson down at the first shot. Whether true or not, Dickinson was known to be a crack shot of the two and many expected Jackson to pay with his life.[10]

On Thursday May 29, Dickinson left for Kentucky, assuring his wife that he would return on Saturday night, after he had transacted business. He rendezvoused with his second and "half a dozen of the gay blades of Nashville. Away they rode in the highest spirits, as though they were on a party of pleasure." Where they stopped for refreshment, Dickinson regaled his friends with his skill with a pistol. At one point, at a distance of 24 feet, he fired four practice shots that produced a pattern as small as a silver dollar. Several other times, he expertly cut a string with a shot fired from the same distance. He is said to have bragged to a tavern keeper: "If General Jackson comes along this road, show him that!" The party went frisking and galloping along the lonely forest roads, making short cuts that cautious travelers never attempted, dashing across creeks and rivers, and making the woods ring and echo with their shouts and laughter.[11]

Jackson's entourage, however, was not so ebulliently characterized:

[For one thing, the] mode of fighting which had been agreed upon was somewhat peculiar. The pistols were to be held downward until the word was given to fire. And then each man was to fire *as soon as he pleased*. With such an arrangement it was scarcely possible that both the pistols would be discharged at the same moment. There was a chance that by some extreme quickness of movement, one man could bring down his antagonist without himself receiving a shot. The question anxiously discussed between Jackson and Overton was this: "Shall we try to get the first shot or shall we permit Dickinson to have it?" They agreed that it would be better to *let* Dickinson fire first ... Dickinson, like all miraculous shots, required no time to take aim and would have a far better chance than Jackson in a quick shot even if both fired at once. And in spite of anything Jackson could do Dickinson would almost sure to get the first fire. Moreover, Jackson was sure he would be hit; and he was unwilling to subject his own aim to the chance of being totally destroyed by the shock of the blow.... Jackson was resolved on hitting Dickinson. His feelings toward his adversary were embittered by what he had heard of his public practicing's and boastful wagers. "I should have hit him, if he had shot me through the brain," said Jackson.... In pleasant discourse of this kind the two men wiled away the hours of the long journey.[12]

The dueling parties arrived that evening, Jackson first; he took lodging in a tavern, while Dickinson's party arrived later but stayed the night at another "house of entertainment" a few miles down the road. As the morning of the duel arrived, the parties met in a level clearing near the river bottom, amid a poplar forest. The prescribed eight paces (24 feet) were marked off and pegs hammered into the ground delineating the duelists' positions. Jackson's second won the coin toss and so was to count to three and then utter the command to fire. Both Jackson and Dickinson were "perfectly collected. All the politeness of such occasions were very strictly and elegantly performed." Jackson wore a loose fitting overcoat that partially obscured his naturally thin frame As the two men faced each other, their weapons pointing toward the ground, Jackson's second issued to command to fire.

As expected, Dickinson raised his pistol and quickly fired first, hitting his opponent—a puff of dust flew from his coat; Jackson raised his left arm, wrapping it tightly across his chest. He had been hit but was not killed. The cloak had helped obscure Jackson's thin frame. Dickinson's shot that was aimed at the heart had hit Jackson in the ribs. At first thinking his aim was somehow off, Dickinson blanched and fell back a few feet and exclaimed: "Great God! have I missed him?" He was quickly admonished to return to his mark by Jackson's second who gripped his pistol should he need it to shoot Dickinson down for failing to follow the terms of the dueling arrangement.

Jackson raised his pistol slowly, pulled the trigger, but the weapon neither snapped nor discharged. In his anxiety, Jackson had placed his weapon at half cock. He pointed it downward, cocked it, and took deliberate aim and squeezed the trigger a second time, hitting Dickinson in the lower abdomen. It was a fatal wound. Dickinson would bleed to death, succumbing to his wound within hours, suffering an agonizingly painful death later that evening. Jackson admitted that Dickinson had "pinked me a little;" yet while his injury was much more severe than that, Jackson would not die from the dueling wound.[13] The results of the duel helped solidify Jackson's reputation as a man not to be trifled with, as subsequent events in 1813 would attest.

Another fight, this time between William Carroll, a Nashville industrialist and general of state militia (later sixth governor of Tennessee (1821–1835)), who had accompanied Jackson during the Creek Indian War (1811–1813), and Jesse Benton, a young militia officer, was yet another altercation carried out according to the Code Duello. Benton believed he had been insulted by Carroll, and when the two arrived in Nashville in 1813 difficulty ensued. Jesse, a resident of Nashville for many years, had a good deal of his brother's eloquence and spirit, but not much of his talent and judgment. When Carroll and Jesse were in Nashville—Thomas was away in Washington saving Jackson from bankruptcy—the duel was to be arranged. Carroll asked Jackson to be his second, but he refused, claiming he was too old. He relented, however, and the two made the trek to Nashville from the Hermitage. According to Jackson's biographer, James Patton, the "incidents of the duel were so ridiculous that they are still a standing joke in Tennessee. The men were placed back to back, as the usual distance apart. At the word, they were to wheel and fire. The General, on placing his man, said to Benton 'You needn't fear him, Carroll; he'd never hit you, if you were as broad as a barn-door.'" [14]

When the command to fire was given, Benton quickly turned and fired first, and then stooped to as Carroll fired. "The act of stooping caused a portion of his frame that was always prominent, to be more prominent still. Carroll fired and his bullet inflicted a long, raking wound on the part exposed, which would have been safe but for the unlucky stoop." Succinctly, Benton had been wounded on his backside, while Carroll had been shot on his left hand, losing a thumb. [15] In the words of one newspaper recounting of the duel, Jesse had been shot "in a part not generally exposed to hostile fire by brave men." Carroll was openly charged with being a coward, despite the fact that he had had Jackson as his second. [16]

Out of this affair developed the brawl—which could scarcely be termed a duel fought under the formal rules of the Code Duello—between Jesse and Thomas Hart Benton, Jesse's older brother, and Jackson on September 4, 1813. According to one historian:

> On the morning of September 4, 1813, the Benton brothers took their saddle-bags to the City Hotel, to avoid ... the possibility of unpleasantness, as Jackson and his friends were accustomed to make their headquarters at the Nashville Inn, diagonally across the Court-House Square. Each of the Bentons wore two pistols. At about the same time Jackson, [John] Coffee and Stockley Hays arrived at the Inn, all armed and Jackson carrying a riding whip, the news was all over town in a moment. Jackson and Coffee went to the post-office, a few doors beyond the City Hotel. They went the short way, crossing the Square and passing some distance in front of the other tavern where the Bentons were standing on the walk.
>
> Returning, Jackson and Coffee followed the walk. As they reached the hotel Jesse Benton stepped into the barroom. Thomas Benton was standing in the doorway of the hall that led to the rear porch overlooking the (Cumberland) river. Jackson started toward him brandishing his whip. "Now defend yourself you damned rascal!" Benton reached for a pistol but before he could draw Jackson's gun was at his breast. He backed slowly through the corridor, Jackson following, step for step. They had reached the porch, when, glancing beyond the muzzle of Jackson's pistol, Benton saw his brother slip through a doorway behind Jackson, raise his pistol and shoot. Jackson pitched forward, firing. His powder burned a sleeve of Tom Benton's coat. Thomas Benton fired twice at the falling form of Jackson and Jesse lunged forward to shoot again, but James Sitler, a bystander, shielded the prostrate man whose left side was gushing blood: The gigantic form of John Coffee strode through the smoke, firing over the heads of Sitler and Jackson at Thomas Benton. He missed but came on with clubbed pistol. Benton's guns were

empty. He fell backward down a flight of stairs. Young Stockley Hays, of Burr expedition memory, sprang at Jesse Benton with a sword cane and would have run him through had the blade not broken on a button. Jesse had a loaded pistol left. As Hays closed in with a dirk knife, Benton thrust the muzzle against his body, but the charge failed to explode,

General Jackson's wounds soaked two mattresses with blood at the Nashville Inn. He was nearly dead—his left shoulder shattered by a slug, and a ball embedded against the upper bone of that arm, both from Jesse Benton's pistol. While every physician in Nashville tried to stanch the flow of blood, Colonel Benton and his partizans gathered before the Inn shouting defiance. Benton broke a small-sword of Jackson's that he had found at the scene of conflict. All the doctors save one declared for the amputation of the arm. Jackson barely understood. "I'll keep my arm," he said.[17]

The Bentons thereafter left Nashville. Thomas Hart Benton later became a well-known U.S. senator from Missouri, and a close friend and political ally of Jackson.

The next duel of note in Nashville was between Thomas Yeatman and Robert Anderson, also in 1813. Thomas Yeatman relocated to Nashville when quite a young man and secured employment as a clerk in the general merchandise store of William Weatherall, one of the foremost merchants in Nashville. Weatherall was an old man and wanted someone to take over his business, so when Yeatman proved himself to be a smart, young business man, he was admitted to partnership with the firm, which was then called Weatherall and Yeatman.

The firm of Weatherall & Yeatman did a general merchandise business, but after Weatherall's death, Yeatman went into the dry goods business, and occupied a house on College Street. In the adjoining store, A. W. Johnson was clerking, and the house next to it was the property of another merchant, Robert Anderson. Yeatman and Anderson were both courting one the wealthiest young ladies in Nashville. She was said to have been perplexed at their competition for her hand. This competition became a contributing factor in the duel between the two young men. Another cause for their growing enmity was purely business-related. Yeatman went on for goods, and about the time of his return, Anderson went for his supply. The means of procuring new goods from Baltimore and Boston was to haul merchandise from these cities by wagon, canals, and rivers. Other goods were procured in New Orleans and hauled north to Nashville on the Natchez Trace. In either case, the journey took two to three months.

While Anderson was *en route* north, he claimed to have heard something negative that Yeatman had said about Johnson & Anderson's credit rating. The morning after Anderson's return, A. W. Johnson was opening his store, and saw Yeatman walking across the street and observed Anderson approach Yeatman with a cowhide in his hand saying: "I'll teach you, you rascal, to injure my character and standing as a merchant" and began lashing Yeatman with the cowhide. Yeatman was a small, slender man, while Anderson was "stout and able bodied." There was no time to think. While Johnson stopped Anderson, someone else seized Yeatman, but not before he had rushed forward and pelted Anderson with his fists. When they separated, Yeatman remarked to Anderson: "You shall hear from me," and the next day, a challenge came to Anderson and arrangements for a duel were soon made. Yeatman's second was the future Governor Carroll, soon to be involved in a duel.

Anderson had already left Nashville for the designated field of honor in Kentucky as soon as he knew the sheriff was after him for planning to break the 1801 state constitutional restraint against dueling. Carroll and Yeatman had a couple of good horses in the rear of the store waiting, and Carroll was watching out for the lawman and his entourage. The sheriff and officers came into the store and informed Yeatman that he was under arrest. He replied, "All right, Mr. Sheriff," and asked permission to change his coat, which was granted. He went to the rear of the store and changed his coat, and promptly left via the back door, locking it behind him. Once outside, he mounted his horse and with his second, Carroll, made a getaway before the sheriff knew what had happened. Details are scarce, but in the end, Yeatman killed Anderson. Yeatman returned without a scratch and, as was typical, was never prosecuted for murder. According to one account: "He had only done what almost every other man would at that time and under those circumstances have done. Being struck with a horse whip was considered the greatest disgrace that could have been put on him."[18]

On September 22, 1826, just after sunrise on a dueling field near Franklin, Kentucky, just 200 yards north of the Tennessee–Kentucky state line, U.S. Representative Samuel Houston of Tennessee, gravely wounded William A. White, a veteran of the Battle of New Orleans. Both men were generals in the Tennessee militia, and their pistol duel can validly be called the "Battle of the Generals." In a convoluted turn of events, White was the stand-in for Nashville Postmaster John P. Erwin. Patronage politics were at the root of this affair of honor. President-elect Andrew Jackson had promoted another candidate for Nashville postmaster against Erwin (the son-in-law of Jackson's political nemesis, Henry Clay of Kentucky). Jackson encouraged Houston to thwart Erwin's appointment. Houston wrote to President John Quincy Adams that Erwin "is not a man of fair and upright moral character." He also attacked Erwin in a speech on the House Floor. When Houston returned to Tennessee after the 19th Congress (1825–1827), Erwin dispatched Colonel John Smith, a professional duelist, to deliver a challenge to Houston for besmirching Erwin's character. That challenge was rejected, but General White then proceeded to challenge Houston, who reluctantly accepted. Houston prepared by practicing his marksmanship at Jackson's home, The Hermitage. Old Hickory advised him to bite on a bullet while dueling: "It will make you aim better," he said.

In the week preceding the duel, Houston stayed with a friend who lived just a short distance from the dueling grounds. Here he continued his target practice. At his friend's house, there were two belligerent puppies, whom Houston nicknamed Andrew Jackson and Thomas H. Benton. It seemed the pup named Jackson won most of their encounters, and Houston took a liking to the canine. Houston arose at 3:40 a.m. the morning of the duel to the sound of General Jackson barking at his window. He began the business of molding bullets for his encounter. As the first bullet fell from the mold, a rooster crowed at the break of dawn, which Houston took as a good omen. He then scored the bullet twice, on one side for the dog, on the other for the rooster. He decided to use that particular bullet to load his dueling pistol.

On the appointed morning in a field near Franklin, Kentucky, Houston and White squared off at fifteen paces. The word "fire!" was given and Houston emerged unscathed. White, struck in the groin, called out to Houston, "you have killed me." White survived, but in June 1827, a Kentucky grand jury delivered a felony indictment against Houston. Nevertheless, Houston had left the House of Representatives to campaign successfully for governor of Tennessee. The state's then sitting governor, William Carroll, refused to arrest or extradite Houston arguing that he had acted in self-defense. After the duel, Houston chose as his coat of arms a dog and rooster, with the motto "Try Me!" "Many were comments made by those unfamiliar with facts in after years, when, President of Texas and Senator in Congress, [Houston] ... sported such a crest."

Another duel was fought in the same area after the Houston–White clash by Calvin M. Smith and Robert M. Brank, two young Columbia attorneys, in March 1827. Very little is certain about this contest except that it was fought at the same venue as the Houston–White duel 1826. The spark that led to the challenge was stimulated by some ridiculous slight that resulted from the two neighbors' "contest over a hog." Brank challenged Smith, the challenge was summarily accepted, the state line crossed, and Smith killed Brank "which sad fact is demonstrated by his unkempt grave near where he fell." Smith was later dismissed from the Maury county bar as a result. Smith sued and appealed the case to the Tennessee Supreme Court in the case *Calvin M. Smith vs. State of Tennessee*, 1829, which, in a strong opinion made by Tennessee Chief Justice John Catron, upheld state's anti-dueling law. His opinion resulted in one of the most articulate statements against the "barbarism of dueling and the code of honor and the duelist's cartel" ever written. Although his opinion is extensive and involved, a few excerpts from it will demonstrate the illegal status of the practice of code of honor killings. Catron, according to a lengthy article on *Smith vs. State of Tennessee* in the Nashville *Republican Banner* of July 2, 1870, strictly admonished:

> Let it be understood that the bar of Tennessee *dare* not fight, and it will be deemed cowardly to challenge a member of it; and this Court solemnly warns every lawyer, that if he violates the laws made to suppress dueling, we will strike him from the rolls of the court.... The truth is that such men are too often insolent and impudent bullies, who tyrannize and impose upon all orderly men about them; who literally dragoon society, by fear of personal violence into silence and seeming acquiescence, with respect to their conduct. That such a counsellor is a disgrace and serious incumbrance to any court where he is permitted to practice, all will admit; those who engage in duels, the statutes deem, and we will treat, as of this description.

Catron continued with a unique sociological interpretation and condemnation of those who killed in the name of honor and the Code Duello:

> Another class accept challenges, and even challenge and fight, for every reason that they want true courage; they have not moral and independent firmness enough to disregard the giddy assertions of that idle part of the community, who say a man is a coward because he refuses to fight; not that such people have either belief or disbelief of what they say; they are too light minded to form any settled conclusion, and repeat idly, as the parrot, what some revengeful neighbor has before said, who

gratifies his malice by mixing gall in the cup of another. The pride, weak nerves, and morbid sensibility of such a man forces him to the pistol's mouth of a ruthless and unprincipled antagonist, as feeble trembling and unresisting as the lamb to the shambles, and with an almost equal certainty of destruction, because he still fears the detraction of the malicious and the gossip of the giddy. The same principle of human action often induces the delicate and sensitive female, with fear and trembling, to assent to see herself made a widow and her helpless infants orphans, by the butchery of her husband in a duel. Any who takes the life of another, under such circumstances, (forced upon him by wicked design,) can be truly said be said to "have a heart regardless of all social order, and fatally bent upon mischief;" *and he should suffer death for the crime, because he has bullied his antagonist into resistance, and then murdered him.* [Emphasis added.]

Chief Justice Catron concluded, not mincing words:

> We are told that this is only a kind of *honorable* homicide! The law knows it as a wicked and willful murder, and it is our duty to treat it as such—we are here to fearlessly and firmly to execute the laws of the land—not visionary codes of honor, framed to subserve the purposes of destruction.

Despite Chief Justice Catron's eloquent dialogue on the absolute evil and illegality of dueling, however, the practice continued with never a participant being indicted for murder in Tennessee. In the public mind, affairs of honor were above the law.

For example, at daybreak on May 11, 1835, two well-dressed gentlemen appeared in a small grove of trees, about two miles south of Nashville. They saluted each other with freezing politeness, as called for in the Code Duello. They were Dr. Bernards, a young physician, and Carlos DuPont, a lawyer from New Orleans.

The night before, they shared an animated conversation about a woman in a gambling den on Main Street. Talk soon resulted in a quarrel, during which DuPont spat in the face of Dr. Bernards. The physician promptly challenged the lawyer, and they met the next morning in the grove of trees. The seconds measured out the distance (10 feet) and ordered the two antagonists to fire. Both fell wounded to the ground. Bernards was not seriously wounded, but his shot went through DuPont's right lung; Bernards was helped into a carriage waiting close by, and DuPont's cries "became more and more heart-rending, as he expired a few minutes afterward in the most intense agony." No arrest was made as dueling, while illegal, "was at that time rather favorable to duelists." Many of the "more reckless young men of Nashville even made a sort of hero of Mr. Bernards." Only one person, however, hated him for the killing. She was the young widow, Mrs. Caroline Frick, whose most prominent suitor had been Dr. Bernards. Some three months prior to the duel, he informed Frick that his rich uncle was moribund, and asked her to administer a medicinal powder to him. The attractive widow, who had nearly made up her mind to become Bernards' wife consented and went to the house of the doctor's sick uncle. Unfortunately, Frick learned from Bernards' uncle that the doctor had tried on two other occasions to poison him. Bernards, soon thereafter, informed the widow that his uncle had died not a half hour before. She declared she would never marry him, that he was a murderer. An autopsy showed no trace of poison in the uncle's remains. Bernards then inherited his uncle's fortune. In the meantime, Mrs. Frick became enamored of DuPont and "gladly accepted his offer to marry her." Bernards became enraged when he heard this news, a duel was arranged, and Mrs. Frick's fiancé was murdered.

Mrs. Frick was given the bullet that killed DuPont and she noticed that it had an unusual white hue to it. She asked a physician acquaintance about this curiosity. The doctor "threw the bullet into a tumbler of water, and poured half a dozen drops of water into the mouth of a large frog. The frog was immediately taken with convulsions, and died in less than three minutes." The upshot was that Bernards had poisoned the bullet with arsenic, which caused the quick death of DuPont after the duel. When confronted with this information, Bernards "decamped from Nashville." Kismet prevailed, however, and he did not live to enjoy his inheritance, as the steamboat he had taken passage sank due to an exploded boiler. "Dr. Bernards was so frightfully scalded that he died two weeks later in the most horrible agony."[19]

Memphis likewise had its share of duels. One of the earliest recorded incidents was between William Gholson and Albert Jackson (no kin to Andrew Jackson.).

In Memphis, a contest was fought in May 1837, which was brought about by atypical circumstances. A few weeks before the duel, there was a controversy between two women. One of them was perplexed that her female slave was runaway. She and other women were attending a luncheon and in the course of conversation she discovered that the slave was hiding in the house of her next-door neighbor. News of this scandalous situation spread swiftly through the small city of Memphis. Eventually, the woman falsely implicated as having harbored the runaway slave was confronted by the owner of the slave in the public market. She reached into a sack she was carrying and pulled out a long whip. "With it she proceeded to pound at the widow's face and breast and back." Passersby halted the affair quickly, which, it was believed, ended the matter. That conclusion was far from correct.

Several days later, three gentlemen were sitting and conversing at the Union Inn. One, William Gohlson, from Virginia, had settled in Memphis a few years prior and had become a prosperous merchant. He was a stout man described as having "an emphatic manner and no hesitancy in expressing his opinion." This, of course, was dangerous behavior in the antebellum South.

With Gohlson sat Georg LaVance, "a genial Memphian with the rank of a great duelist." A third man approached them, Albert Jackson, a well-known Memphis lawyer. LaVance invited him to sit with them and enjoy a libation. Jackson shared Gholson's proclivity of freely expressing his opinions. Soon the topic turned to the lady-horsewhipping. Gholson expressed an unfavorable judgment about one of the ladies involved in the incident. Immediately Jackson pushed back his chair and demanded: "I ask for a retraction, Now!" It seemed that one of the women was Jackson's cousin. Gholson, instead of apologizing, mentioned that he must have confused her with someone else. But he would not apologize. He answered Jackson's demand, saying: "I won't change what I said."

LaVance tried to calm the situation but could not. Within a few hours, LaVance was approached by Jackson who asked him to deliver a message to Gholson, who flatly refused to retract his comment. Not only that, but he refused to meet Jackson on the dueling grounds because he did not consider him his equal, a prerequisite to engaging in a duel. In so saying, Gholson was implying that LaVance was also his inferior. According to the Code Duello, this meant that if Gholson continued to decline a fight with Jackson, then LaVance must necessarily duel with Gholson. Knowing Jackson was no expert with a dueling pistol, and that LaVance was a crack shot, Gholson was forced to make a choice. He chose to fight Jackson.

Seconds were chosen; the clash would take place at dawn on the morning of May 15. Gholson showed no apprehensions, and even attended a dinner party for the night before the duel, arranged by his second. The duel was to take place across the Mississippi river at Hopefield, Arkansas.

On the pre-dawn hour before the duel, Gholson was seen confidently striding up and down the dueling grounds, with his arms akimbo. His second informed Gholson that Jackson had never been in a duel, good news in this situation. Gholson said: "I'll hit the spine and he'll be dead in a minute or so!" His gasconading, as it turned out, was but partially true. Although he was a novice on the field of honor, Jackson arrived and appeared calm and collected. The 30 feet were marked off, and each man expected to kill the other. They faced one another, and prepared to shoot after the words "Fire! One, two, three, four, five!" On the count of three, both contestants fired simultaneously. Jackson grabbed his hip and dropped his pistol. Gholson's shot had passed through Jackson's body, and he was left standing. Shortly, however, Gholson turned to his surgeon, walked a few feet, and fell, twitching, to the ground. Jackson was dead, shot through the heart, and Gholson was dying. According to a story in the *Memphis Enquirer*, one witness claimed the combat "surpassed all description for bravery—each determined and satisfied that he should kill his antagonist, both having declared they would strike, the one exactly where he did, the other within an inch and a half." The *Enquirer* said that "the parties retired, satisfied that all had ended '*most* HONORABLY, [*sic*]—to the rules of genteel murder." The editor of the *Enquirer* claimed:

> [The details were given] not because the horriful [*sic*] detail is pleasant to us, nor to gratify public curiosity—but to correct a thousand mis-statements which we found pervading a mourning public. A general gloom fills our community, though no measures were taken to prevent the catastrophe. We even doubt the expediency of such a course having been taken. Neither bails nor bonds would have healed he animosities rankling in such a bosom. A street encounter would undoubtedly have been the result, in which probably would have fallen several of the friends of each party.[20]

In an ironic way, the duel, while tragic and dramatic, was justified not as an affair of honor carried out according to the Code Duello, but because it prevented a general brawl in the streets of Memphis.

Col. M. W. Lindsay and A. H. Davidson, former business partners in Memphis, fought a duel with pistols at fifteen paces on September 14, 1854. The two men who had been business partners squared off in Arkansas, a favorite spot from which Memphians escaped the prohibition placed upon dueling in Tennessee. The exact cause of the dispute was not recorded. They exchanged shots without either one being hit and then the dispute was settled amicably. Presumably, their honor had been satisfied and they continued in their business partnership. The conditions of the Code Duello had been fulfilled on the field of honor.[21]

An idiosyncratic duel took place on the right (eastern or Tennessee) bank of the Mississippi river, just north of Memphis. It occurred on October 15, 1856. According to a newspaper report in *The New York Times*, citing a story from a St. Louis newspaper:

> We learn by letter from Memphis, of the 16th inst.; that a duel was fought in the vicinity of that city the day previous, It seems that on the late trip of the steamer *North Star*, from New Orleans to this place, two of the passengers, Col. Charles Burgthap, from Philadelphia, and Major Riegler, of Boston, who had been South on an electioneering tour, and who were old friends, having both served in the European armies, got into a warm discussion, the one defending Democracy, and the other one Republicanista, [sic] which resulted in offensive language of a personal character, against Colonel Burgthap. In the presence of so many passengers the Colonel felt it incumbent on him to demand a retraction of the insulting matter, which being denied, a challenge and acceptance to fight were soon settled upon. Two Hungarian officers named S. Szalay and T. Shultez, lately in the service of Walker in Nicaragua, who were passengers on the boat, volunteered as seconds. Pistols at fifteen paces were the terms proposed, but strange to say, the seconds, the master of the boat and all the passengers, including many ladies, opposed the proposition, and contended that the fight should be had with swords. The Hungarians offered their sabres, and the next day upon reaching Memphis, the parties landed and procuring the attendance of a Dr. Hill, also a passenger on the boat, proceeded to some grounds adjoining the city, accompanied by many of the lady and gentleman passengers. The duel was then fought with great fierceness and resulted in the defeat of Major Reigler, who, by the superior skill of his adversary, received two terrible cuts, the one on his neck, the other on his chin, causing him to drop on the field. Returning to the boat, the wounds of the Major were dressed, and a reconciliation of the parties was effected.
>
> Colonel Burgthap shortly afterwards made a speech to the passengers, justifying his course and defending dueling on general principles, which was warmly received by those present. It is supposed that the wounded gentleman would have replied, but for the disabled condition of his chin. Both men displayed great gallantry in the field, and were triumphantly escorted back to the boat by the spectators.[22]

Another duel that took place in Memphis was reported two years later. The conflict took place on November 28, 1858, near the Bluff City and was between Mr. Watters, of Virginia, and Dr. Nagle, formerly from Pennsylvania. The cause for the duel, while not recorded, must certainly have been an insult and the duel was arranged according to the Code Duello. Upon the command "fire!" both men blazed away with derringers, each hitting the other twice in the exchange. By agreement, if neither had killed the other they were to upgrade to revolvers. This they did, and in the end Mr. Watters was riddled with bullets and died on the field of honor. Improvements in firearms technology had made their mark in a duel on the field of honor in Tennessee.

Dr. Nagle, on the other hand, suffered such serious wounds that it was assumed he would shortly die. No effort was made to arrest or charge Watters with murder.[23]

Near the end of the Brobdingnagian duel between the North and South, a matter of honor took place that was not of such an immense stature. On December 28, 1864, the principals met on the dueling field. They were two were "well known to our citizens as worthy gentlemen." According to the *Memphis Argus* newspaper: "Details were scarce, and the reason for the duel was not known [ahead of time]." The fight took place on the road to Randolph, 3 miles north of Memphis. According to the paper, they faced one another with pistols at twenty paces. The two men, James Simpkins and James Stutts, had been good neighbors for many years. In this duel, the weapons of choice were shotguns; they atypically stood back to back, stepped off twenty paces, turned, and opened fire, a maneuver not strictly sanctioned by the Code Duello. Their weapons loaded with buckshot. They fired simultaneously, Simpkins received four buckshot and Stutts an alarming twenty-four, causing the death of both almost instantaneously.[24] The superficially brave and romantic phrase "death before dishonor" had played itself out, at the cost of two neighbors' lives and their grieving families.

Another battle in the Bluff City arranged according to the rules of the Code Duello was fought between Alonzo Greenlaw and Henderson Taylor. According to the *Memphis Argus* of July 13, 1866, this duel was one "of the most melancholy affairs it has ever been our duty to record." The fight took place in Mississippi, just over the Tennessee state line. Particulars as to the cause of the challenge were sketchy at best. The newspaper report related that Taylor, the son of a well-known physician, and Greenlaw met on the street. After a few words, Greenlaw struck Taylor in the face "with his open hand." The matter went no further until a few days later when Greenlaw received the inevitable note from Taylor, bearing a challenge to a duel. The two agreed to meet at a point in Mississippi 6 miles below Memphis to settle their differences and uphold their honor or die trying.

The duel was fought on the Thursday the 12th. The distance was ten paces, and the weapons of choice were "navy repeaters," not single-shot pistols. The two were to fire at any time the words "Are you ready—fire!" were spoken; they were "to continue discharging their weapons until one of the two fell." Greenlaw and Taylor fired straightaway and Taylor fell, "mortally wounded in the bowels at first fire." Nothing was known about the difficulty between the two men which "resulted so tragically, and whose sad features are rendered doubly sad by the fact that both are gentlemen of fine social standing, and connected with two of or oldest, most esteemed families." Greenlaw, possibly distraught at his murder of Taylor, unsuccessfully attempted to commit suicide on October 6, 1866.[25]

While it cannot be considered a combat according to the Code Duello, a peculiarly romantic fight that took place during the latter part of the Civil War might still fall into that category of a duel. It occurred during the Confederate retreat from Nashville in December 1864. Miss Mattie Caldwell, from the hamlet of Lynnville, Tennessee, "a cultured and aristocratic little village," remembered that as the last of Nathan Bedford Forrest's cavalry carried out its rear guard withdrawal mission, with Federal cavalry in hot pursuit, "witnessed a scene, the sort of which has heretofore never been printed." When the last of the Confederate troopers were on the south side of the town, "a Confederate officer of remarkable appearance rode back, stopping in front of Miss Caldwell's residence, sporting a "long flowing moustache, with hair and eyes as black as midnight, ... in curls nearly to his shoulders, a soft Alpine hat with an ostrich plume and gold star rested jauntily on his head. Faultlessly dressed, with a form erect and powerful, something so unusual at that time, made him more noticeable. He sat [on] his magnificent horse (also as black as black could be) as only a born horseman can." The cavalryman and horse were in strange contrast to the rag tag Confederate army that had only recently passed. While standing intently watching the approaching Federals, Miss Caldwell observed our Federal horsemen far outstrip the others, and rode directly towards the "Black Knight." The latter moved not a muscle, only to draw his long, keen sabre, holding at a parre. The Federal horseman rode straight at him. The clash came, and with it a clash of steel. For some time their bright blades flashed in the morning sunlight. Then a quick succession of parries and thrusts. The clicking steel could be distinctly heard by Miss Caldwell, who stood in her own door not forty feet off, and in full view of the deadly combat.

Finally a quick wrist movement of the black horseman parried the general's blade. With a movement like the lightning's flash, he gave his a body thrust, and before his adversary could recover, with another stroke he laid bare his brain, unhorseing him. Quickly turning his great black steed, he had barely time to escape the body of Federal troopers and the volley sent after him.[26]

Yet another deadly altercation fought according to the Code Duello occurred after an insult between two Memphis druggists on February 18, 1868. The *Memphis Bulletin* tellingly introduced its story on the affair saying: "Although shooting affairs are of daily occurrence in the city of Memphis, still 'affairs of honor,' as they are called, have been of late like the proverbial visits of angels, few and far between." The duelists were John H. Taylor and W. J. Mimms, both druggists on Poplar Street. Shortly before the duel, Taylor had made remarks about Mimms, reflecting negatively upon the latter's character as a gentleman. Taylor refused to apologize or retract his statement and the usual challenge was made and a duel was set. The affair was to take place across the Mississippi River behind the hotel in Mound City, Arkansas; rifles were selected as weapons. The parries rowed across the river, reaching the dueling grounds at about eleven o'clock. The duelists marched to the rear of the hotel, and were placed at fifty paces from one another. The rifles had been previously loaded and Mimms' rifle accidently went off as the two men took their positions. Despite the confusion this caused, the rifle was quickly reloaded, with "both parties looking cool, and seemingly determined to 'do or die.'"

"Gentlemen are you ready?" Both replied in the affirmative, and raised their pieces. "Fire!" a pause, and the word "one" was given, while simultaneously both rifles were discharged. All rushed forward; the smoke cleared away, and it was then discovered that—nobody was hurt.... Both had fully shown their pluck and defended their honor, and at the earnest request of the seconds on both sides, the shook hands and became again friends. An adjournment was then made to the bar-room of the hotel, where all hands "smiled" frequently, and returned to the city in the afternoon, with full faith in the axiom "All's well that ends well."

According to the *Nashville Press and Times* of April 17, 1868:

From Overton County comes to us a strange story, which we suppose has few parallels in the annals of difficulties settled after the code. The affair happened two weeks ago [*c.* 13th]. Where the bold spurs of a wild range deflect a trifle as they the boundary line of Fentress and Overton, lived for many years two families named Waldron and Jarvis. A feud had marred their intercourse for time out of mind until about a year ago, when the head of the last-mentioned family died. After this occurrence old troubles were apparently buried, and a friendly intercourse was established. This continued for many months, and until one of the Jarvises, a young man of twenty-two, while intoxicated, made some sneering remarks about one of the Waldrons, impeaching his courage. Two days after the latter sent a friend to young Jarvis, that as he did not consider him a courageous man he might have the pleasure of testing his bravery with any weapon he might choose. Young Jarvis was too proud to retract the language which had been uttered while under the influence of liquor, and he accordingly sent back word to the other that he would meet him four days from that time in what is known as "the Run," where they could settle the matter with rifles at 150 yards. Both men had been in the rebel army, and were accounted splendid marksmen.

It was on a damp, cold, dreary morning that the two young men, each accompanied by a friend, on their way to "the Run." Drizzling rain had fallen for hours, and the scene through the valley was dismal with clinging mists and pattering precipitation. The seconds paced off the distance, and the two duelists were situated with their backs facing one another; at the customary shout of one, two three, they turned and fired. Jarvis was wounded through the fleshy part of the left arm, while his bullet whistled savagely just above his antagonist's head. "Are you satisfied," said Waldron's second. The answer was no, "Waldron wants another shot."

A stern savage smile lighted up the features of young Jarvis and his arm was bound to staunch the blood, but he said not a word. The rifles were loaded again, and once more the shouted signal two men wheeled and fired. The reports were almost simultaneous. Waldron ran forward a few steps, staggered, reeled, and fell into the arms of his friend bleeding and senseless. He was shot through the heart. Jarvis went slowly home, saddled his horse, and, telling his family that he left the country.[27]

Perhaps the last true affair of honor carried out in accordance with the code in Tennessee originated in Memphis in 1870, between James Brizzolara and George B. Phelan on June 28, 1870, on a sandbar in the Mississippi River, near Hopefield, Arkansas, opposite Memphis.[28] James Brizzolara of the Memphis Democratic Executive Committee was criticized by George R. Phalen, a prominent local Democratic Party politician. After words were exchanged and the proper communications made, according to the Code Duello, a duel on the field of honor was fixed. They agreed to face each other and to continue firing their weapons until one of them had fallen. Brizzolara was a veteran of Garibaldi's army during the Italian revolution of 1848 and a Confederate soldier in the Civil War. During that time and Reconstruction, he had successfully engaged in many duels. He had been insulted by Phelan, a prominent Memphis lawyer and politician, who demanded satisfaction. Knowledge of the challenge was made known to the Shelby County sheriff who arrested Brizzolara. Upon his release on bail, Brizzolara replied that he would accept Phelan's challenge. The weapons of choice were Navy Colt pistols. The duel was held outside the Volunteer State because the state constitution banned dueling—in Arkansas, they would be free from the interference of the Shelby County Sheriff's jurisdiction. The two gentleman were placed at the agreed upon distance of fifteen paces. The evening sun was at Phelan's back, obscuring his position. The question was asked: "Ready?" Phelan replied in the affirmative, while Brizzolara "cried 'not ready!'" and coolly putting the pistol between his knees, proceeded to turn up his shirt cuffs, which had gotten down over his hand and annoyed him. According to a story in the Memphis *Public Ledger*, and at the word "fire!" the first shots (one each) were harmless "but the second shot of Mr. Phalen took effect on Mr. Brizzolara entering near the left nipple over the heart, and passing through a portion of the body transversely, coming out under the left arm."

Brizzolara fell to the ground and firing ceased, as prescribed by the Code Duello. "The surgeons had the wounded man removed to the boat," and a quick trip was made to the city "where he was taken to the home of his sister attended only by his surgeon … who reported … that while serious and possibly dangerous, the wound, is not necessarily so and that with proper care and perfect quietude, Mr. Brizzolara will soon be well."

According the editor of the Memphis *Public Ledger*:

> We record with a degree of pleasure counter mingled with pain, that both combatants accord to each other the utmost coolness and bravery. Mr. Phelan desires us to say that Mr. Brizzolara showed himself to be a man of nerve, coolness, and desperate bravery. The same qualities were accorded to by Mr. Brizzolara and his friends to Mr. Phelan

Brizzolara survived. Both his and Phelan's honor had weathered the brutal test of the Code Duello. If there were further animosities between the two men, they were not recorded. Phelan's brother, James, challenged a Knoxville editor to a duel in 1895, but it was never consummated.[29]

Soon after the Phelan–Brizzolara fight, a novel duel took place just over 300 yards beyond the Mississippi line, on a field of honor "well known in the annals of Memphis dueling" south of Memphis. At sunrise on August 27, 1870, the contest between Major Edward Freeman, a young merchant, and Edward Hamlin, a young lawyer, both Memphians, took place. It, like its immediate predecessor in Hopefield, Arkansas, was arranged according to the code. They fired at fifteen paces with dueling pistols. Hamlin was shot through his liver and he died within ten minutes. The cause of the fight was said to be "strictly private and personal." Hamlin's last words were revealing of the pervasive hold of the concept of honor as expressed in the code: "Tell my father that I die as I lived—a gentleman."[30] As with all duels, there were no prosecutions for murder, despite the state law defining it as such.

The Hamlin–Freeman duel was for all intents and purposes the last such affair carried out according to the Code Duello in the Volunteer State. Yet as atavistically poignant as Hamlin's last words were of the romance of the code, another fight, just two weeks later, also in Memphis, was more of an impulsive pseudo-duel, or more directly, a double murder. It demonstrates the newer spontaneity of dueling heretofore forbidden by the strict rules of the Code Duello.

The Tennessee Constitution of 1796 forbade anyone who had participated in a duel from holding office; the 1870 Constitution did too, while the 1801 law likewise forbade the custom. Yet, in 1873 William Rule, the editor of the *Knoxville Chronicle*, was challenged to a duel. He took a stand different from all others in the history of dueling in Tennessee, a stand that marks a definite turning point in the use of the Code Duello and dueling.

The circumstances derived after a business trip Rule made to Memphis in late 1872. There he learned of the failure of a major Memphis bank and the apparent fraudulent activities designed to keep the Memphis and Charleston Railroad (M&C RR) from collapsing. Major J. D. Wicks, a Confederate veteran, was the president of the M&C RR and had recently relinquished his position. The new president of the railroad had sent a letter to M&C stockholders showing that the road was not in good financial condition. In fact, to make good a $200,000 shortfall and keep the business from falling into receivership, it was necessary for stockholders to make good on the huge liabilities. They were asked to contribute 10 percent of the value of their stock—in cash—to keep the railroad solvent. This was going to be a significant loss for stockholders, many of them widows and pensioners, when the stock did not amount to anything near its face value. As Rule wrote in a letter published in the *Knoxville Chronicle* of December 19, 1872: "To say that such a demand comes like a clap of thunder in a clear sky would be putting it very mildly."[31]

The letter continued by exposing the skullduggery of the Wicks' administration of the railroad. According to the letter:

> But a short time ago dividends were being declared, and it seems very strange that the road should become so seriously involved in so short a time. If the road was in debt then, were did the money come from to pay dividends? If the officers of the company were so flush them why is it so hopelessly involved now? Did its former managers borrow money to pay dividends in order to keep up appearances—to keep up the price of stock—or has the business of the company been so recklessly managed as to account for the present state of affairs? These are questions that come up very naturally and people *will talk.* [sic][32]

These questions were soon made known as a copy of the *Chronicle* and the letter in it were made public in Memphis a few days later. Infuriated at what he regarded as an insult to his reputation and honor, Major Wicks, in short, challenged Rule to a duel. He would be in Dalton, Georgia, on February 9, 1873, and he invited Rule to meet him there to "discuss" the matter. This was clearly a challenge straight from the pages of the Code Duello.

The Memphis contingent accompanying Wicks was comprised of old school dueling adherents, namely ex-Confederate General Nathan Bedford Forrest, ex-Gov. then U.S. Senator Isham G. Harris, Colonel. Sam Tate—one time president of the M&C—and W. B. Greenlaw, whose son had been killed in an affair of honor in 1866. They arrived in Dalton but did not find Rule. Instead they were presented with a copy of the *Knoxville Chronicle* with a message from Rule addressed to the gentlemen from Memphis: "I have no business to call me to Dalton ... and decline your invitation ... the time to 'discuss' the matter further, had passed." He continued at length:

I am not familiar with the so-called "code of honor," but I suppose your communication means, and was intended to lead to a challenge to me to fight a duel.

With such an affair I refuse to any connection. I recognize no heathenish so-called "code of honor." I am opposed to dueling, for the reason that it is contrary to the spirit of the enlightened age in which we live. I am opposed to it because it is contrary to laws of my country, the law of humanity, and the laws of God. You might take my life, or I might take yours, and yet not a single feature of the publication complained of would be changed by the result. If that publication were false, it would be false still. If it were true it would remain true. Hence nothing can be gained by either of us losing our lives in the manner proposed.

My friends who have been approached on this subject by your friends, have uniformly expressed it as their opinion that I would not fight you in this way. I have good reason to believe that you knew this fact before you sent your challenge.

*   *   *   *

You may, and perhaps will, "post" me as a coward, because I refuse to murder you or give you an opportunity to murder me. Really, I do not know whether I am a coward in the sense you may choose to apply the term or not.... I do not propose to leave the country, but will continue to pursue my legitimate business, going wherever and whenever that business calls me. While I do not recognize the so-called "code of *honor*" *I wish you distinctly to understand that I fully recognize the right of self-defense* [*sic*] I do not court, but ... avoid, personal difficulties with my fellows; but, when attacked, I shall not hesitate to defend myself as promptly and effectually as necessity may seem to require.... I do not propose to pander to the barbarous prejudices of depraved minds by setting myself up as a target, to give you the opportunity of a so-called vindication of your honor. I have no respect for any such foolish notions. They may be in accordance with your ideas of honor and courage, but they are not with mine. Words cannot express my contempt for such folly. It is not proof of courage, but of cowardice! It is not evidence of manliness, but of a weak concession to a heathenish and brutal custom. It is not the way to defend a gentleman's honor prescribed by an enlightened Christian sentiment and the laws of civilized people.[33]

Wicks and his entourage of erstwhile dueling advocates then headed back to Memphis, never having had a chance, in their estimation, to murder Rule under the sanction of the outdated Code Duello. Wicks, in order to save face, wrote in a statement published in the *Dalton Citizen* and *Atlanta Constitution*: "Feeling assured that no charge or statement hereafter emanating from William Rule can harm anyone, I leave him to such a position in the public esteem or contempt, as a just and enlightened people may consign him."[34] The matter was closed, honor protected without bloodshed or recourse to the Code Duello.

Rule's courage was applauded in other newspapers.[35] Later, in 1873, a joint resolution passed unanimously in the Tennessee legislature that condemned and called for the punishment of anyone resorting to an affair of honor on the dueling field. The Federal Grand Jury then meeting in Knoxville sanctioned Rule's bravery and stance. Ironically, a bill to make dueling a capital crime was defeated in the Tennessee legislature in 1873.[36]

There are other references to so-called duels in Tennessee history, none of them after 1873 were carried out to the by now antiquated and discredited Code Duello. In fact, they mostly were not duels at all, but shootouts that newspapers referred to as duels. The Code Duello was at times nominally used to justify a fight, but seldom, as exemplified by the farcical Collier-Carmack duel in Memphis of May 1893. We have seen how newspaper editors engaged in "fake" fights in the 19th and early twentieth century, but these were not in accordance with the code. Nevertheless, such "duels" should be examined here as they were a carry-over from the so-called code of honor. They may be thought of as abridged Code Duello killings or pseudo-duels.

Excluding the old Code Duello arrangements, confrontations were not carried out according to any rules but the rule of who shot first and straightest. Such was the case in a little reported pistol fight on November 4, 1850 on the Nashville public square possibly inspired by the Jackson–Benton brawl of 1813. The shootout "between two young men named Vaughn, and two others named Lawrence, growing out of family difficulties.... One of the Messrs. Lawrence was slightly hurt." It cannot be said to mark the transition to of the end of the Code Duello yet does indicate a disregard for the code.[37]

On September 13, 1870, at the Shelby Station, on the Memphis & Louisville railroad a disagreement stemming from a game of ten pins between Samuel Dickey, a planter, and George Fleming, who kept a livery stable, led to angry words. Friends of each of the men did manage to ameliorate the differences of opinion after fighting words were exchanged. However, Dickey went to an adjoining store saying he intended to go hunting. He returned to the bowling alley and shortly thereafter Fleming appeared with a double-barreled shotgun, and "taking skillful and deliberate aim," shot Dickey who fell to the floor. "Horribly wounded and in the agonies of death, Dickey yet had strength to raise up his own gun, and fire at his assailant in reply. Fleming instantly fell dead, and Dickey expired directly afterward."

The New York Times reported that the affair caused great excitement in Memphis, yet there "was certainly nothing uncommon about such an impromptu duel taking place or in the participants being butchered or maimed for life as a consequence." Dueling exaggerated offenses to honor but a "homicide for a misunderstanding over a game of ten-pins is a ghastly illustration of that disregard for the sacredness of human life which has gained the Southwest so much discredit and even led some Christian people to call us a nation of barbarians." Laws designed to eliminate such affrays were of little use in Tennessee where this sort of lawlessness was tolerated.[38]

"One of the Most Desperate Conflicts on Record" read the headline of the Nashville *Republican Banner* of May 26, 1874. According to one report, A. J. Sellers and J. N. Patterson "fought one of the most desperate duels on record" at Cotton Grove, some 8 miles east of Jackson, in Madison County. Yet, despite the newspaper reporting it as a duel, it did not qualify as a duel at all, but a shootout reminiscent of cinematic gunfights in the Wild West. Sellers, armed with a double-barreled shotgun and two single-shot pistols, met his antagonist Patterson, equipped with a "navy six" in the main street. "After several shots, Sellers fell, bleeding from three painful wounds, one in the right shoulder, one in the right temple and a third in the upper lip, and Patterson retired with a ball in his left side." The sanguine encounter developed over conflict over a new suit of clothes the murdered man had purchased the week before. Sellers wanted to wear the suit to church on Sunday. Sellers grabbed the clothing and Patterson "snatched the clothing from Sellers" and the two began fighting. The quarrel led Sellers, who suggested they take the fight outdoors. Patterson, who had a crippled hand, was aware that Sellers had the physical advantage, remarked that he was no gentleman to behave as he did. Sellers proposed then that they settle the matter in some other manner, with firearms the following Monday. Sellers, without a second, called Patterson out asking "are you ready?" No, Patterson was not prepared, but stated he would be the next evening at 5 p.m. In the meantime, Patterson went to Jackson and "purchased a navy six, had it carefully loaded" and returned to Cotton Grove remaining silent about his intentions. The people of Cotton Grove thought the quarrel was "a piece of braggadocio that would end in the wind."

> But promptly to the hour on Tuesday [26th] evening Patterson and Sellers were observed approaching each other from opposite directions armed.... When within thirty yards of each other both came to a halt-Sellers leveling his gun ordering Patterson to throw down his pistol. Patterson refused to obey, saying that Sellers had him at a disadvantage but fired on Sellers with effect. Sellers then attempted to shoot but both barrels of his gun snapped. Patterson fired again. Sellers steadily advancing, having thrown down his gun and resorted to his pistols, fired once the shot taking effect on Patterson's right side. Patterson opened again rapidly, striking Sellers twice-three times in all. About this time Sellers fell from lack of blood, and Patterson, concluding he had killed his man, turned and walked off....

Patterson's whereabouts were not known, although Sellers was "in a critical condition."[39]

The term "duel" now had a less formal meaning that transcended the Code Duello. It at this point was replaced with a definition that meant any gunfight between two or more armed antagonists was a duel. In this, we can see the change in the perception of the custom of defending one's honor as the exclusive domain of the privileged of the aristocratic planters, bankers, merchants, and lawyers of the antebellum era. This would persist into the early twentieth century when the conclusion of the shootout/pseudo-duel would finally be achieved in Tennessee.

Another street duel, reminiscent of popularized "gunfights" in the old west, was a fight at Rockwood. It was reported on January 1, 1885 that two men, W. F. De Rossett and Nathan Pass "engaged in a street duel here yesterday" (December 31,

1884). They shared a difficulty of some kind and each "swore vengeance." The two men met on the street of Rockwood. Rossett and Pass "began firing at each other with shotguns." De Rossett was hit once in the face and in the arm. Pass was shot in the forehead and neck.[40] It is not known if either combatant survived.

Another altercation referred to as a duel was so only inasmuch as both parties shot at one another over a contested financial matter. Such events can only be called shootouts regardless of whether or not they were called duels. The Code Duello had no bearing on these "duels."

One such fight is worthy of identification. It was the Hamilton–McCary fight in Union County, Tennessee. The headline and the interdictory paragraph in *The New York Times* article read:

TWENTY-SIX SHOTS FIRED. Columbus–Hamilton and Frank Hamilton fought a duel on horseback at short range with Henry and John McCrary yesterday afternoon. [3rd] Twenty-six shots were fired. All parties except Henry McCray were injured. Columbus Hamilton will die. The affray occurred in Union county just over the border in Tennessee.

This "duel" on horseback had its beginnings in Maynardville, Union County, Tennessee. The Hamilton brothers were in Middlesboro, Kentucky, where they had a business dispute with Henry and John McCray also from Union County, Tennessee. The question was not resolved; words were exchanged, and failing to agree, they "coolly decided among themselves to settle the matter by the code duello." After remaining in Middlesboro for some hours and spending time in a local saloon, the Hamilton and McCrary brothers took a train and started to return to their homes in Union County. When the train slowed up at Liberty Hall, a whistle stop, all four men detrained. The Hamiltons walked to a friend's house where their horses were tended, saddled up, and started down the road. The McCrarys, with two cohorts, stopped temporarily to eat.

After the Hamiltons had secured their horses and had traveled about 4 miles, they were suddenly overtaken by the McCrarys coming up the road in a gallop. The Hamiltons wheeled around, and, drawing their horses to a halt, began firing at the advancing McCrary party; the McCrarys shot back. The firing continued for some minutes, there being some twenty-six shots fired. Columbus Hamilton received a dangerous wound in the side and fell from his horse. Frank Hamilton caught a bullet in his hip and his horse was also shot.

In the skirmish that followed, John McCrary was shot through his right arm but deftly changed his pistol to his left hand, continuing to fire. His hat was pierced with several bullets. Henry McCrary was uninjured, and with the assistance of his two friends carried his wounded brother from the field. "The Hamiltons were unable to continue their journey home Frank," according to the article, "being scarcely able to walk, while Columbus cannot live."

The authorities were notified and a posse was soon in pursuit of the McCrarys. A feud rivaling the "famous French–Eversole vendetta of Kentucky" was expected. It was up to the Union County constabulary to take decisive steps to quell any disturbance. Here the tale ends for lack of further documentation.[41] Once again, the term Code Duello was used to give the fracas some kind of legitimacy; regardless, the affray was not a duel.

By the turn of the twentieth century, the term duel was used nonchalantly by the press to explain shootouts of a criminal nature, but the old excuse of the Code Duello was no longer employed. A case in point was the first page headline in the *Nashville American* of December 7, 1903: "SERVICE ENDED BY BLOODY DUEL." Just as the minister at the Grace Presbyterian church, Rev. W. B. Holmes had announced his text, Numbers xxiii., 10, "Let me die the death of the righteous," "Patrolman Benjamin F. Dowell and Thomas Cox, a man well known around town, fought a duel with pistols.... The duel was fought at close quarters ... each man claiming that the other fired first." Dowell was moribund. Earlier that afternoon, Dowell had arrested Cox's sister on charges of disorderly conduct.

> The details of the shooting were considered most sensational, both men emptying their revolvers, and after being so desperately wounded the officer ran into Grace Presbyterian Church, where the evening services were in progress. Staggering in the door just after the officiating minister had read his text, and reeling backward the officers' arms, still clutching his revolver, went up into the air. There was great excitement in the congregation, the fusillade of shots on the outside of the church having alarmed the worshippers. When the officer appeared holding up his weapon ladies in the congregation hurriedly picked up their cloaks and wraps to leave, but when it was seen that there was no danger of violence, they soon became quiet, and all did what they do. Officer Dowell was eased down to a bench and was then taken into a small room in the church. The ambulance was called from the City Hospital and promptly responded.

Patrolman Dowell shortly thereafter died of his wound.[42]

No doubt the most notorious street shootout/pseudo-duel in Tennessee history is exemplified in the killing of Edward Ward Carmack by the father and son Duncan Brown and Robin Cooper in 1908. Carmack, a Democrat, was an attorney, newspaperman, and political figure who served as a U.S. senator from Tennessee from 1901 to 1907. His career as a journalist began at the *Nashville American* in 1888. He became fast friends with the publisher and owner of the American, Duncan Cooper. He left Nashville in 1892 to become the editor of the *Memphis Commercial* in 1896. Following his single term in the U. S. Senate and his unsuccessful bid for the governorship of Tennessee in 1908, he became editor of the then one-year-old Nashville *Tennessean* newspaper and a stout foe of the liquor interests, declaring himself as a temperance advocate. He was immediately hailed as a champion of the "dry" interests in the state. The wave of support from the temperance forces caused him to enter the Democratic primary for the governorship against Malcom R. Patterson in 1908. The "wet *v.* dry" issue bitterly divided the Democratic Party. Patterson, who was endorsed by the Coopers, Carmack's old friends, won in the primary and went on to win the election. As editor of the *Tennessean*, Carmack, now the darling of the prohibitionists, wrote in a bellicose fashion, decrying all anti-prohibitionists, most especially governor Patterson and his erstwhile compatriots at the *American*, the Coopers. Resentful of his vitriolic attacks, Duncan Cooper, in a fashion reminiscent of the old Code Duello, sent a message to Carmack warning him to cease his attacks. The warning went unheeded by Carmack who continued to denigrate his one-time colleague in editorials in the *Tennessean*. Animosity between Carmack and the Coopers grew until anxieties escalated to the point that tensions exploded on November 9, 1908, when the Coopers confronted Carmack in broad daylight at the corner of Seventh Avenue and Union Street. Aware of the threat the Coopers posed, Carmack, fearing an ambush was armed, and seeing the two Coopers, opened fire, wounding young Robin Cooper. Duncan's son, Robin, although wounded, nevertheless, returned fire and Carmack fell dead.

Carmack became the martyr to the temperance forces and the state and the voters adopted statewide prohibition in 1909. Both Coopers were convicted of murder in 1909. In 1910, the Tennessee Supreme Court reversed Robin Cooper's conviction on a technicality but upheld the conviction of Duncan Cooper, who was actually innocent of having fired a shot. Literally within an hour of the high court's decision, Governor Patterson extended a pardon to his old friend and political supporter Duncan Cooper. The trial gained notoriety in newspapers throughout the nation. In the end, however, it was not the Code Duello that led to Carmack's murder, but personal and private hatred. Nevertheless, the code's nineteenth-century sway, although attenuated, had stretched its limits into the twentieth century.[43] The fact was that the trial and conviction of the Coopers proved the Code Duello was a dead letter. The widely held opinion that no gentlemen of prominence could ever be convicted of a capital offense in Tennessee was, at last, proven false. Dueling, save for a few pseudo-duels, was severely moribund, if not obsolete, in Tennessee. Instead of engaging in duels to settle scores or the adjudication of differences in the courts, differences were settled by the press reports. The recourse of gentlemen to react to archaic concepts of honor, once the justification for murder under the Code Duello had slipped into oblivion.

Further proof of that assertion can be found in what surely must have been the "last duel" in Tennessee history, in early 1921 in East Tennessee where the concluding chapter in so-called dueling, actually a shootout, was "added to the bloody record of the mountains of Polk County." On January 31, members of two prominent families, the Hicks and the Smiths, met in the street at the hamlet of Springfield and "fought a pistol duel in which Smith was probably fatally wounded." The cause for the event was a business transaction that had gone wrong months earlier. When they met, one of the Hicks young men spontaneously indicated "this would be a good time to settle our old quarrel" and drew his pistol and immediately opened fire. He was a poor shot, however, and missed Hicks, who drew his pistol and returned fire, seriously wounding Smith in the abdomen and thigh. Although Smith was taken to the hospital in Knoxville, he was not expected to survive. According to the Associated Press, it was "the fourth shooting affray in this county within the past two weeks, resulting in several deaths, one of the victims being a deputy sheriff." The incident was not a fight carried out according to the by now ancient antiquated rules of the Code Duello, but a shootout similar to the murder of Carmack in Nashville thirteen years earlier. Moreover, it was a pseudo-duel most likely resulting from a feud between the two mountain families.[44]

There was, however, one comical example of a duel attempted by sophomoric university students in Nashville. A Vanderbilt University student, infatuated with a young woman popular among the campus social fraternity circuit, took offence at what he construed as unflattering remarks concerning the object of his affection made by another student. He made a telephone call to the assumed perpetrator to determine the validity of the rumor. The upshot was a duel contrived with reference to the Code Duello. The two were to meet on the field of honor in Centennial Park, Nashville, in the early morning of January 31, 1914. Their weapons of choice were nothing more than their fists. Police were notified and were staked out to arrest the two would be duelists on charges of disorderly conduct. The students apparently got wind of the police presence and never consummated their rendezvous with destiny. While the police continued to investigate their expectations of arresting the two "Chocolate Soldier" duelists they failed to materialize. The affair was quickly forgotten, save perhaps in social fraternity lore at Vanderbilt University.[45] The use of the term Code Duello, for all intents and purposes, vanished from Tennessee lexicon and practice thereafter. Use of the word duel, however, has not expired, but is used only in reference to hotly contested elections or sports events, as in a pitchers' or quarterbacks' contest.

The Code Duello was an institution of long social standing and it was, ironically, hard to kill. Generally speaking, it did not pass out of existence till the passing of the aristocracy of the antebellum South, where it was more commonly resorted to as a deadly means to redress insult to antiquated and romantic concepts of honor, Tennessee being no exception. In the first half of the nineteenth century, there were few public men of the section but that at one time or another participated either as principal of second in an "affair of honor," and several of them more than once. If they did not participate in dueling, they approved of the Code Duello and this fostered homicide.

The same patterns were repeated in South Carolina, Kentucky, Mississippi, Arkansas, and Louisiana. General Albert Sidney Johnston, who died at the Battle of Shiloh, was wounded by General Felix Huston over who should command the Army of Texas. Thomas Hart Benton was among those who killed his opponent by the rules of the Code Duello.

By the early twentieth century, the mere suggestion of the code brought to mind a score of dueling incidents or associations intimately connected in one way or another with the imaginary and romantic "moonlight and magnolias" beliefs of many aficionados of Tennessee's place in the history of the old South. There were dueling grounds in Nashville, Memphis, the fields of East Tennessee, and just across the border in Kentucky. Weapons were generally single-shot flintlock or cap pistols. Save for the Cooper–Carmack shootout/pseudo-duel in 1908, there was never a conviction for murders brought about by the code of honor. But while the law might have looked the other way when it came to dueling, the tenets of the Code Duello permitted no such disrespect, a duel being attended with as much decorum as the crowning of a king.

As the old South died, so did the practice of dueling, although "revolver duels" as Mark Twain humorously referred to them, continued to occur among journalists and politicians sometimes referencing the antiquated code, but extemporaneously without the formality of its rules.[46] Thus, duels fought on horseback, with rifles at 50 yards, or with shotguns and revolvers in the streets of obscure towns in Tennessee, continued in a long and attenuated spiral, until the last "duel" of any statewide and national notoriety being the murder of Carmack by Cooper in Nashville in 1908.

5

Feuds and Outlaws

The Wild, Wild East: A Blood Feud in Nineteenth-Century Knoxville; the Mabry, Lusby, and O'Connor Killings, 1881–1882

In Tennessee history, the term *frontier* most often brings to mind the period just prior to statehood, when Anglo and African Americans emigrated from the eastern shore inland, settled and displaced the indigenous Indian populations. In American history and popular culture, the term often denotes the last period or the so-called "wild west" of the late nineteenth-century. Images of deadly gunfights at the dusty O.K. Corral or in the streets of Yuma, Arizona, seem somehow familiar to all. But at least one east Tennessee city, Knoxville, shared this untamed characteristic with the towns of the wild west, where violence in Tennessee continuing from the Indian wars of the late eighteenth century, the duels of Andrew Jackson, the battles of the Civil War, the coal miners' strikes of the 1890s, to the murder of Edward W. Carmack in 1908, and labor unrest in Chattanooga in 1917. The violence in nineteenth-century Knoxville expressed continuity with the state and national tradition of violence.

As in the surrounding mountains, a sense of familial honor and vengeance worked with the easy access to firearms to produce fatal conflicts. On Christmas Eve 1881, came the first of six murders revolving around the family and fortunes of General Joseph Alexander Mabry, a wealthy Knoxville landowner and speculator. (The title "general" was apparently a sobriquet inasmuch as Mabry never served in a martial capacity in the Civil War.)

The exploit, according to the *Knoxville Daily Tribune*, "has thrown a damper over the entire community, and the man who drinks his glass of whisky to produce gaiety does so with a shudder." Don C. Lusby, Constable of Knox County's second district, engaged his friend Will C. Mabry in a horse race into town on Christmas Eve. Both, "chums you might say," had earlier attended cockfights at Wade's brickyard in North

Knoxville and were flushed at the end of their galloping race at Alf Snodderly's bar at Vine and Gay Streets. Mabry apparently harbored hard feelings against Lusby, who in his official capacity had earlier barred him from Madame Maggie Day's bordello because of his rowdy conduct.

Inside, an altercation developed in which Mabry refused Constable Lusby's offer of a drink of apple brandy—hostile word were exchanged and soon he and Lusby fought a classic barroom brawl of the kind usually associated with cinematic depictions of the wild west. In the course of the row, Mabry hit Lusby on the forehead with a 1½-inch-thick coffee plate weighing a pound. Bleeding and enraged, Constable Lusby reached in his pocket and found his pistol. Mabry, realizing his predicament, straightaway ran for the door, chased closely by Lusby. Soon the antagonists were "out on the street. When Lusby shot the first time," said one witness, "I did not hear him cry. When the second shot was fired Mabry grunted. The shots were simultaneous. Mabry dropped on Vine Street about thirty feet from Gay." The second shot penetrated Mabry's left lung, cut a large blood vessel, and caused internal hemorrhaging. "Lord have mercy, he's killed me!" one witness testified as his last words. Dr. Sam Boyd testified at the preliminary hearing on Christmas Day that the first shot had lodged in Mabry's neck while the second entered his left side, striking the seventh rib. He died of internal bleeding. Some fifty witnesses, exactly twenty-five for each side, would testify, but no clear picture emerged.[1]

The *Knoxville Daily Chronicle* took the occasion to editorialize that this killing "should arouse public indignation against the unlawful practice of carrying concealed weapons. Sober men are not apt to be guilty of so foolish an act as drawing a pistol and shooting with slight provocation founded upon a trivial matter, and whisky is undoubtedly at the bottom of most infractions of the law of this kind, but if men did not carry pistols at all, they would not have them when they have lost control of themselves through the influences of strong drink."[2]

On January 11, 1882, Judge M. L. Hall determined that Lusby, while excited because of the blow to his head, "had brought his mind to the determination to kill him [Mabry] and under these circumstances he is entitled to no bail." No verdict was reached in the ensuing trial.[3]

General Mabry was a Knoxville landowner, of one of the area's oldest and most prominent families. During the Civil War, he had offered to clothe many Confederate soldiers. Prior to the war, he had been president of the Knoxville and Kentucky railroad. In that capacity and after the Civil War, he worked with General Maney, president of the Tennessee and Pacific Railway Company. Mabry likewise was a lobbyist with great influence with his personal friend, Governor De Witt Clinton Senter (1869–1871). Generals Mabry and Maney worked together to secure public funding for their mutual railroad project, but Mabry's expected payment for his influence with the state's chief executive was not forthcoming. Subsequently, Mabry took $25,000 from the T&P treasury as a loan. The subsequent lawsuit went against Mabry and he began selling land and his stables of blooded racehorses to meet his obligations. Nevertheless, the general continued to speculate in land and was still a noted businessman/developer in the city. In fact, a street in Knoxville bears his name. He was said to have a terrible temper and prone to violence, for example, "that during his career as a sporting man he killed a man whose name is not now remembered." General Mabry was also heavily in debt, and so was engaged in nearly constant litigation. All his property, it was reported, "was involved in law and was time and again sold for taxes and to satisfy judgments, but somehow he always managed to hold on to it." General Mabry was a member of the decaying *postbellum* Old South land-owning aristocracy. Certainly he was preoccupied with maintaining his social authority and political influence and bequeathing it to his sons, one of whom was now dead.[4]

By May 1882, the criminal court again began proceedings in the matter of the *State of Tennessee v. Don C. Lusby*. The Criminal Court jury acquitted him of murder in the first degree but was divided on the question of whether or not his offense could be considered manslaughter. Ultimately, he was released on bond after a mistrial was declared. One newspaper editorialized in response that when a citizen was approached by a peace officer known to carry a pistol, the smart man should "arm himself with a musket or double-barreled shot gun." A yearning for justice by vendetta was growing in some rather prominent Knoxville circles, and the feeling of bitter enmity intensified between the two families. While many contemporaries may not have thought of it this way, blood feuds were products not only of the Wild West and the Tennessee mountain clans, but occurred in more urban settings as well. Indeed, a "deadly family feud has existed between the two families" and soon the second chapter growing out of that feud would unfold.[5]

On August 26, Don C. Lusby, who was out on bond, and his father, Moses, were shot while in the presence of General Mabry and his attorney son, Joseph A. Mabry, Jr., and others inside the Recorder's Court chambers. The *Knoxville Daily Tribune* called the shootout "A Terrible Sequel to the Bloody Tragedy of Last Christmas Eve." The general was told that morning that Lusby was "hunting him and would probably kill him and to keep him out of his way." Apparently taking the information seriously, the general, although he was armed with a pistol, avoided Lusby when he saw him on the corner of Clinch and Gay Streets around 10:30 a.m. Mabry went into McCampbell's drug store to avoid a confrontation, and Lusby crossed the street positioning himself at the side door, facing Clinch Street, apparently watching for Mabry saying in no uncertain terms that he would kill the general. His father, Moses Lusby, was heard to have said "he would be damned if he (Don) did for he intended to do, it himself."[6]

It was at this juncture that Knoxville Police Chief W. Harper arrived. Lusby complained the general was following him in a threatening manner. As Chief Harper left the drugstore and stepped into the street followed by Mabry, Lusby called to the general several times, but the general paid no attention. Lusby's fervor only increased as he began shouting curses at the general saying, according to Chief Harper, "You see he will not speak to me, the damned old scoundrel!" and other bitter words. It was then Harper placed Lusby under arrest. Lusby resisted arrest for some time, but was finally subdued and taken to the Recorder's Court. His armed father joined his son in the chambers, where a warrant was taken out against Don Lusby for creating a disturbance. The general, his son—also armed with a pistol—Chief Harper, Moses Lusby, the City Recorder, and a few city policemen were in the room. The warrant was sworn and Harper then moved to disarm Lusby, to take his pistol. In the ensuing scuffle, some five shots were quickly fired. Moses was shot in the chest and because the bullet lodged near his spine, he was dead instantly, while Don was mortally wounded. It was 11:15 a.m. Don was taken towards his home borne on a cot by friends who were unable to get any further than a private house, ironically on Mabry Street, where he died.

Eyewitnesses testified that while they had seen the elder and younger Mabry with pistols immediately prior to and during the shooting, no one testified that they saw either actually shoot them at the Lusby's. Deputy Sheriff C. B. Gossett arrested the two Mabrys on charges of murder and felonious assault. Both the Mabrys posted a $2,500 bond, yet as the newspaper paraphrased Knoxville Justice Alex Allison, "he would not presume to say that a jury would find them guilty." Even though the Mabrys were indicted for the double murder, they were acquitted of the charge of murder in Criminal Court. While they were acquitted, it was widely believed they had committed the crime. In summary, they had gotten away with murder.

Suddenly, on a rain-soaked Thursday morning, October 19, 1882, just after 10 a.m. and within a period of two minutes, three leading Knoxville citizens lay prostrate on Gay Street on the west side of the block, between Church and Clinch Streets, "their life blood gushing from ghastly wounds." Shortly, only the cold, pallid, corpses of General Mabry, his son Joseph A. Mabry, Jr., and Major Thomas O' Connor remained.

The general, after his business reversals and legal troubles, had never been the same man, and had been "of late years … drinking deeply." His son, Will, had been murdered in the streets of Knoxville. His other son, Joseph, Jr., was born and raised and for the most part educated in Knoxville, and was an attorney of local merit and recognition. It was said "recontre [sic] and altercation were distasteful to him." Nevertheless, as events would demonstrate, he was at least competent with a pistol.

Major Thomas O'Conner, the third victim of this urban blood feud that day, was born in Virginia. He had come to Knoxville in the 1830s as a harness maker. His business improved, and at the time of the Civil War he enlisted as a lieutenant of Captain Howard's artillery. His unit afterwards being held a prisoner of war at Johnson's Island in Lake Erie. He made his fortune thereafter in Atlanta and returned to Knoxville and was acclaimed as one of the shrewdest politicians in the state, having been a member of the National Democratic Committee. The major had also "rapidly risen among the moneyed men of the day" and became the major owner of the corporate giant Tennessee Coal and Iron Company. He lived in Nashville, in the Maxwell House Hotel, and in his home in Knoxville. He was a noted local philanthropist, a "whole-souled man" whose latest business venture was the formation the Mechanics' National Bank on Gay Street. He was the epitome of the New South entrepreneur, whose thriving and preeminent class helped create envy and status anxiety among the remaining and rapidly displaced antebellum aristocratic class.

That the general and the major would come to share such bitter enmity can be explained. Some time before Will Mabry's death by Constable Lusby, Major O'Conner had purchased from the general two rather agreeable Knox County properties, the Cold Spring Farm and the Chevannes' place, with the condition that the major should at some later date give the farm to Will. Of course, once Will was dead, there was nothing to hold O'Conner to the deal, or so it was reported that the general reasoned. Apparently the general's mental capacities had been strained by his years of business failure, by the killing of his son, his alcohol abuse, the murder of the Lusbys, and now his anxious conviction that the major had actually plotted his son's death to maintain a claim to a piece of real estate. One paper reported that after the Lusby killings "the General has seemed to be further than ever off mental balance." A hint of this animosity occurred during the double Lusby murder trial in September, when Mabry first gave utterance to accusations that O'Conner had been responsible for his son's death. Yet there were more sour relations between the two men. Joseph, Jr. and O'Conner had been partners in an agricultural implement business which had failed. General Mabry had applied for a security loan from O'Conner's Mechanics' National Bank and had been denied the money on the grounds that he was overextended. Certainly this sustained and stoked the general's status anxieties, but the first indication of unequivocal rancor came at the Fair Grounds, south of the Tennessee River on Wednesday, October 17, 1882.

At the Wednesday afternoon races, at the Fair Grounds, an armed and incensed General Mabry, in the presence of many witnesses, confronted an unarmed and flabbergasted Major O'Conner and upbraided him, making loud threats against him, thundering that he was responsible for the murder of his son, calling him a "G_d d_d robber and murderer [*sic*]." The general declared his passion to shoot the major "then and there." The major replied calmly that the racecourse and that afternoon were neither the time nor place for gunplay. Later that evening, a frenzied General Mabry sent word to the major "that he would kill him on sight." O'Conner's supporters advised him, in light of these threats, he would be justified in carrying a weapon and shooting the general on sight. Forewarned was forearmed.[7]

At very nearly ten o'clock on the rainy morning of October 19, the general and a friend, Robert Steele, Esq., appeared walking south down the west side of Gay Street toward Church Street. Standing across the street in the doorway of his Mechanics' National Bank was Major O'Conner. Suddenly, as the general reached a point across from the Bank, O'Conner brought out a double-barreled shotgun, stepped out on the pavement, cocked the weapon, raised it to his shoulder, took deliberate aim and fired at Mabry, who was about one step in front of Steele. Mabry fell instantly on his face "and as he fell O'Conner emptied the other barrel into Mabry's body." Steele ran to the nearby People's Bank, failing to perceive that Joseph, Jr., had arrived on the site. After the younger Mabry saw his lifeless father he had reached a point on Gay Street, where he drew his pistol, took premeditated aim, and fired at the major some 50 feet away. His marksmanship was excellent, and the major was instantaneously hit with deadly effect. At the same instant, the major turned to the right and fired his shotgun at Mabry. Young Mabry sunk to the ground and before a second had lapsed Major O'Conner "sank to the pavement falling on his back, [throwing] his arm wide open and [dyeing] without tremor. Young Joe Mabry attempted to rise but only got about half way up, then fell on his back and died in a few seconds without uttering a word and no struggle was perceptible except the twitching of the muscles and the death gurgle in his throat." Four shots had been fired. One eyewitness newspaper account elegantly described the aftermath of the incident this way:

The reverberations from wall to wall of a few successive explosions, the curling up of a little sulphurous cloud upon this and that side of a narrow street and forms prone upon the wet and slippery flagging [pavement], then the hurried tramp of curious feet and pale lips are busy with eager questions. The dead are carried to houses upon either side of the street, which is made dismal by rain and the gathering throng of funeral umbrellas that block the way. The first palsy over, I hurried and fragmentary explanations are given while the curious throng gathered around the bullet hole in the wall and the horrid pool of blood on the pavement that is mingling with the descending rain.[8]

The scene was quiet after the shootout. Three of the most prominent men in Knoxville were dead on the rain- and blood-saturated street. The public's frame of mind was subdued, "everybody was cool, calm, and sorrowful.... All heads were bowed in sincerest sympathy...." *The Daily Tribune*, however, reported that its all-time record-breaking sales reached five editions before the public's thirst for news was slaked.[9]

What had been learned from this violence, which had "never been approached before in our history, and which are never likely to occur again..." There was something inherently awful in these events, and they were not held to be characteristic of Knoxville. Perhaps, philosophized an editorial in the *Daily Tribune*, it was a generational lack of respect for the old cultural canons. After all, up until the recent killings "not even the most bitter feuds—which have existed here as they do everywhere—have terminated so fearfully.... The old code of adjusting difficulties is regarded by the rising generation here as something to be shunned, and personal animosities, if entertained at all, very seldom come to the surface of society." The clash of the new and old social and entrepreneurial mores had borne bitter fruit.[10]

Funeral services for the Mabrys took place at their home on Mabry Hill, on Dandridge Pike on October 20. At about ten o'clock, two hearses conveyed the remains of General and Joseph Mabry Jr. to Old Gray Cemetery, where a double grave was prepared next to Will C. Mabry's cenotaph in the family lot. There were but six of fourteen members of the Mabry family left surviving. A Methodist service was held. Later, on the 21st, Episcopalian funeral obsequies were held for Major O'Conner at Melrose. His wife, sister, and a brother survived him. Many friends from Nashville and across the state attended his remains. He was laid to rest also in Gray Cemetery.

The feud that terminated in the streets of Knoxville claimed six lives. That such a bloody lawlessness occurred in a Tennessee city in the nineteenth century seems somehow out of character, a temporary aberration not characteristic to the civilized east. Yet the allegory of Knoxville's Mabry, Lusby, and O'Conner homicides were not affairs of honor. Instead, they indicate that in our past violence was sometimes resorted to by established, conservative men of wealth to settle with irrevocable finality certain real or imagined economic, familial, and social disputes.[11]

The Swofford–Tollett Feud Start

Never before in the history of Bledsoe County had the populace been so stirred up over a crime as it had over the murder of William L. Tollett, on July 14, 1905. Though only thirty-nine years of age, he was known to nearly every man, woman, and child in the county and was very popular. The county had a normal Republican majority of about 300, but in 1902, Mr. Tollett ran as a Democrat for County Trustee and was defeated by only twenty-two votes, and in 1904 by fifty-one. He was a hard worker from boyhood and conscientious about saving his money. He had only recently reached a point where he could afford to pay special attention to the education of his children, and the purchase of a hotel in Pikeville where he had moved were steps in realizing his ambitions.

Bledsoe County had had its share of murders before, but they had been committed in the open, where it was questionable as to who would draw the quickest; the men of this region were considered brave and high-minded, "not lurking in thickets watching for the passage of enemies and shooting them in the back when they safely passed" until July 1905.

The feud began over a century-and-a-half ago, according to a report in the Nashville *American* of July 6, 1905:

> … evil passions that destroy or blind the reason sometimes hold sway, and cause cruel murders to destroy the happiness of some of its finest homes, and encite [*sic*] the murderous instinct in all of one family connection toward all of another. Such was the Swofford–Tollett feud, originating over [150] years ago and already involving in its deadly toils four different generations. It began with the killing of John A. Tollett on April 30, 1863. Tollett was believed to have hefty sum of money on his person at the time and, it was for this reason he was murdered. The crime was charged to Aaron Swofford, but the crime against him went unproven. The Tolletts believed that Swofford was the murderer, and a deep hatred for the whole Swofford clan developed in the Tollett family, a feeling fully reciprocal by the Swoffords.

Things settled down after killing of Tollett in 1863, so much so that there were two marriages between the Tolletts and Swoffords. These two weddings eased the tensions between the families for a generation until 1892, although the families made no secret of their feelings. Marriages between the two families did not result in mutual courtesies or civilities when they passed each other on the road.

Their hatred was revealed "when one day as W. L. Tollett was coming down Walden's Ridge in his wagon … was set upon by Aaron Swofford and his son, pulled from his wagon and severely beaten with sticks." Tollett was unarmed but swore vengeance against them should they meet again. In the August 1892 election for state legislators, both voters from each family were at the polls "but so were a hundred friends of each, and all were fully armed." Tensions were palpable, but although it was expected, there was no trouble. Then came the presidential election of November 1892, between the democrat Grover Cleveland and Republican candidate Benjamin Harrison. Soon after the polls were opened, there was severe unrest. Both families were in town and armed when shooting broke out. After the air cleared, two of the

Swoffords were dead, and three others of the family were wounded. One Tollett suffered knife wounds. It "was a wonder that so few were killed." Subsequent trials found no one guilty of a crime.[12]

The next episode in the feud occurred after William. L. Tollett's father died after the incident at the polls, leaving $500 to Esau Swofford's wife, formerly a Tollett. William Tollett contested the will causing a split in his own family between him and his two brothers, Frank and Mose, and his sister, Esau Swofford's wife, and all three aligned themselves with the Swoffords in the matter of the 1892 shootout at the polls.

To add to the confusion was the fact that Esau Swofford's sons, Charley, Esau, and Sam were close with their uncle, W. L. Tollett. The youngest of the three nephews, Charley, had almost been raised by him. Charley developed a fondness for his uncle's money; on one occasion, "Charley took a satchel containing money, a deed, and a life insurance policy." Charley reluctantly confessed to the theft but remained a welcome guest at the Tollett house because of "the blood ties that bound him to the family."

In the summer of 1904, a confusing set of events involving forged checks were made on the William L. Tollett account at the Pikeville bank. All were made out to George Tollett, W. L. Tollett's brother. All were for less than $25.00. But on September 4, 1904, Charley presented a check for $220, again made payable to George Tollett. While the bank cashier was suspicious, he was familiar with the young man presenting the check, and ultimately cashed it. Like the other checks, it been signed by William L. Tollett. The payee said the check was for payment of two mules that his father, Esau Swofford, had sold to Tollett. That they were forgeries was not discovered until May 1, 1905. The cashier swore out a warrant for George Tollett, the son of Frank Tollett, a brother of W. L. Tollett. Upon seeing that George was not the person to whom the checks had been cashed, the cashier admitted a mistake had been made. But instead of the checks being simple forgeries, they were double forgeries. Charley Swofford had been passing himself off as George Tollett. Plans were made to arrest Swofford.

Tollett joined the sheriff's troop tasked with arresting his nephew. As he was on his way to rendezvous with the sheriff's party, he met Charley on the road, who was armed with a shotgun loaded with buckshot. Tollett managed to subdue his nephew, and arrest him, holding him prisoner until the posse arrived. When the sheriff arrived to take Charley, he insisted that his uncle had used unwarranted harshness when arresting him, a charge William denied.

Charley had no trouble raising the $1,000 bail and was promptly released to face trial in the Circuit Court. "Since the date of Charley's arrest there has been the bitterest feeling on the part of the entire family toward Tollett, and his three nephews. Sam, Esau, and Charley were not shy about displaying their enmity toward their uncle and making threats against him. For example, Charley Swofford was quoted by a neighbor as saying "Bill Tollett may come up to cut his hay, but he will never get back home."

On Wednesday July 5, 1905, William left Pikeville and went up to his farm for some produce for use at the hotel. He was not afraid, he said before leaving, "to meet the Swoffords face to face, but he thought they would attack him in the rear."

While Tollett seemed to have no apprehensions about being killed, his brother, Mose, did, and let him know that Esau Swafford enlisted the aid of his brother,

The Reverend J. A. Munday, itinerant anti-vice crusader in Nashville, Tennessee. While his sermons were moving, they did not result in any lasting reform of prostitution in Nashville. (*Nashville Daily American*, June 7, 1886)

CRYING FOR HELP.

Twelve Fallen Women Who Want Proper Homes.

Evangelist Munday Pushing His Work and Meeting With Success.

He Has a Word More to Say to the Kid-Gloved Christians.

ONE OF THE PENITENTS

Repentant prostitute attending one of Reverend J. A. Munday's anti-vice sermons. While initially successful, reform of prostitution, a "necessary social evil," ultimately failed. (*Nashville Daily American, June 18, 1886*)

Three "Frail Sisters," *c.* 1885. These three prostitutes posed for this novelty photograph. (Some observers question the gender of these "sisters".)

Street walker, *c.* 1870.

Left: Edward Zane Carroll
Judson ("Ned Buntline") in his
later years. A bit of a Lothario,
Buntline had compromised the
wife of a rival editor and as a
consequence fought a duel with
her incensed husband, only to be
placed on trial for murder and
nearly lynched by a mob.

Below: A brace of dueling pistols,
early nineteenth century. Such
specialized weaponry was often
used in nineteenth-century duels,
according to the Code Duello.

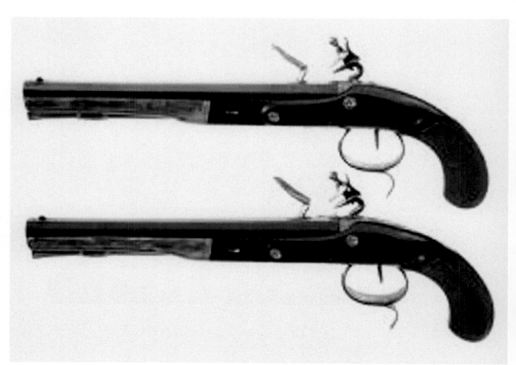

Equestrian statue of Andrew Jackson, hero of the Battle of New Orleans, victor in the Jackson-Dickinson duel, and seventh president of the United States.

Jackson-Dickinson duel, May 30, 1806. Initiated by insults resulting from a bet on a horse race, the duel was fought in Kentucky. Jackson took a bullet to the chest but prevailed and killed Dickinson, and lived to tell the tale.

Sam Houston's dueling pistol, used in his duel with William A. White, September 22, 1806. Fought near the same spot Jackson and Dickinson dueled twenty years earlier, Sam Houston, then a member of Congress, killed his rival William White over remarks made in the U.S. House of Representatives.

Revenue agents with captured still, East Tennessee, c. 1910. Such scenes were familiar during the nineteenth-century Internal Revenue Service raids on moonshine stills, when forewarned that a revenue raid was planned, moonshiners would disassemble their still and move it to another remote location only to begin illegal distillation of whisky once again. Note the shotguns.

Traditional nineteenth-century moonshine still. A variation of the sorts of stills used in the Tennessee Mountains to produce illegal whisky.

Walnut Street Bridge, Chattanooga, from which Edward Johnson was lynched, March 19, 1906. The lynching of Johnson, determined not guilty by a court of law, drew widespread national attention and condemnation, including then-President Theodore Roosevelt.

CAPTAIN B. BROWN'S CRUELTIES.

Lynching of three Unionists by Washington County (East Tennessee) Confederate Home Guard, January 23, 1863. (*Daniel Ellis, Thrilling Adventures of Daniel Ellis, (1863) p. 108*)

James, "to use his influence with the boys to prevent them from killing Tollett." Mose cautioned his brother not to go alone and to be cautious and that he would be safer if he took someone else with him.

Instead, Tollett took an alternate and longer route on the East Valley Road, in order to purchase some hams on the way. He was about a mile from the home of his three nephews when he was shot. The crack of the shotgun frightened the mules that ran with the wagon, which was halted about a mile down the road by a man who had seen the smoke from the shotgun blast.

When the team was stopped Tollett's body was hanging over the side of the wagon, his head down. His body would have fallen into the road, but his collar had caught on one the irons on the side and this held him. Examination showed that he was dead. The left side of his face and head were peppered with turkey shot, evidently fired at an angle from the rear.

His hat had fallen off and [a] reporter counted sixty holes made by the turkey shot on the left side of it. All passed through, some also passing into his head. Sixty holes made by the shot were also found on his face and head. Probably ninety shot were contained in the [shotgun] load, and as there was but one report it is possible both barrels were fired together.[13]

News of the murder was promptly reported in Pikeville and an investigation by the coroner's jury was held. Just south of the murder scene was a dense cedar thicket; on the east side of the road was a rampant growth of high weeds; the tops of the weeds had been riddled with shot. On the far side of the road, corn stalks clearly demonstrated that both barrels of a shotgun had been fired. When the scene of the murder was examined, boot prints showed plainly in the ground, leading in direction of the railroad tracks, both coming and going.

There was no eyewitness to the murder, and the coroner's inquest could only determine that Tollett "came to his death as a result of gunshot wounds inflicted by parties unknown." Tollett's friends were not satisfied with the finding and made arrangements to use bloodhounds owned by a deputy sheriff in Chattanooga. A poor railroad connection delayed the arrival of the hounds for fully three days after the shooting. There had been no rain so it was reasoned the hounds would be able to track the killer even though the scent was old. The hounds, "with noses to the ground started off on a run, the shoe-tracks leading the way.... When the party reached the house of Goly Swofford, a relative of the three boys ... they were unable to continue the scent." Although Goly was among the participants in the 1892 melee, there was no evidence to suspect him of being the murderer. Nevertheless, evidence implicating the three Swofford boys began accumulating.

Convinced that the boys were responsible the posse made its way to the farm of Esau Swofford, the boy's father, found and arrested them. In looking around for evidence, they found a pair of shoes belonging to Charley. The left shoe matched the prints left at the murder scene. It was reasoned that the three boys all waited on different roads for Tollett to pass by, intending to shoot him.

On the day of the murder, Charley Swofford was seen with a shotgun; when asked why, he replied that he had been fox hunting. Inasmuch as he was regarded as a competent hunter, he was further asked why he had not taken his hunting dogs with him his alibi seemed improbable. His reply would later be used against him during his trial. The three Swofford boys were arrested and incarcerated. "Probably a hundred men, Swoffords and Tolletts, returned to Pikesville and remained at the jail till it was seen there would be no attempt at violence, when they withdrew and returned to their homes."

The killing of Tollett was denounced by all, including the Swoffords who expressed genuine regret at the homicide. Most of them were fellow church members and wanted "the feud to be buried forever." Indeed, Swofford's burial at the family cemetery was evenly attended by both families "even though it was true that there were many revolvers buckled around the waist, but nothing passed derogatory to the dead, who were highly esteemed by all, friend and foe alike, and they joined in paying a last tribute of respect to his memory."

It was predicted that the trial of the three Swofford boys, to be held in Melvin, would "be attended by all the Swoffords and Tollett's and guns will be handy." According to a newspaper account of the affair:

> There are grave apprehensions of trouble, though there is a disposition among the cooler heads to avoid it. It cannot be denied, though, that there has cropped out some of the old feeling especially among the younger members of the two families. If trouble once starts, there is no telling where it will end.
>
> The three Swofford boys are not representative of their family ... they have been somewhat wild and have no reputation as well-behaved boys. They have been the terror of school teachers, have been charged with disturbing church services, and have aroused the fear and apprehensions of many people....
>
> An effort was made to secure an expression from the boys in jail, but they refused to talk, not even stating their ages.... They all appeared confident of being turned loose...[14]

The ultimate result of the trial is not known, although one of the Swofford boys, Sam, was released as there was no evidence to connect him to the crime.[15] Interestingly, State Senator E. G. Tollett, William's brother, contended that there was no hostility between the Swoffords and Tolletts. He stated clearly, if not incredulously:

> There is not now nor never has been a feud existing between the Swoffords and Tolletts. The Swofford family as a whole and the Tollett's have been fast friends for several generations. The lamentable encounter at the election of 1892 between certain members of one family of the Swoffords and my brothers had a perfectly harmless origin....
>
> My grandfather, John A. Tollett was murdered in 1863, at night, by a number of men in disguise ... his leaning to the cause of the Confederacy caused his murder.
>
> The Swoffords involved in the encounter of 1892 are only remotely related to those charged with the murder of my brother, and there is not the remotest probability that the bad blood of 1892 will ever be stirred again, and there is nothing to provoke a discussion of the unhappy event, save the similarity of names of the parties then and now as acted upon by the imagination of sensational journalism.

There was absolutely no attempt at violence to the prisoners ... and none but the officers accompanied them to jail, and there is no apprehension of trouble at the preliminary trial.[16]

A newspaper story from June 1915 mentions a prison break from the state penitentiary in which Charley Swofford and two other convicts participated. Charley was recaptured. Thus we know one of the Swofford's was convicted of murder. Otherwise, there is no court record to indicate any successful prosecution of Charley, or any other of the Swofford family.[17]

Tennessee Desperadoes: The Taylor Brothers

Andy Taylor, brother to John and Bob, was hanged on November 23, 1883, in Loudon. His offense was touted "one of the boldest and most atrocious ever committed in this State."[18]

He stayed indifferent to the end, even playing his banjo. Prior to his hanging, he was asked in an interview if he contemplated making a confession. His answer was revealing of a rather mercenary twist to his fate:

Yes; I have thought over it and have decided to make a full statement of my history from my boyhood. I'll do it for anyone who wants it for $150. I'll tell everything; how John got into trouble, and how the whole thing occurred, and everything about it. It'll sell. I believe 5,000 copies would be sold without much trouble.[19]

His parting words on the scaffold were profane, while his demeanor on the gallows was "wonderful and unparalleled in the annals of crime, and fully in keeping with his desperate nature and atrocious deeds." He steadfastly refused to see any minister, saying he "would die like a man." Asked if he wished to say anything to the crowd, he replied: "Not a G-d d—n word." He mounted "the gallows with a firm step, and calmly surveyed the crowd with a half-smile on his beardless, young face."[20]

While the noose was being adjusted, Sheriff Springfield, of Hamilton County, asked him if he felt angry toward him. The twenty-one-year-old Taylor unhesitatingly answered: "G-d d—n you; I'd rather drink your heart's blood than any man's I know." He asked that his body be sent to his mother. The black cap was adjusted over his head. He stood fully two minutes as the noose was adjusted, and called out impatiently, "Hurry up with your racket!"

The trap was sprung at 3:15 p.m. He was dead at the end of the ninth minute; he was cut down at the end of the twenty-seventh minute and placed in a coffin for shipment to his mother. The throng witnessing the event numbered 1,500. The gallows, screened for the execution "was the first private hanging ever had in this part of the State."[21]

Ironically, the deed that led domino-like to Andy Taylor's execution was committed by his eldest brother, John Taylor, who killed James Fletcher in Chattanooga on February 21, 1881. Taylor was the engineer on the steamboat *Tellico*. Fletcher was a boat builder, who on the fateful day was repairing the *Tellico*. A quarrel arose and John, "being of a very impetuous nature," drew a pistol. "Fletcher was an old man, Taylor a large, brawny giant in his prime." When he drew his pistol, "the old men remarked that 'none but ____ cowards carried pistols.'" Incensed, Taylor fired, killing the old man. Now a murderer, John Taylor sprang into a nearby rowboat and made his way rapidly down the Tennessee River, and was soon ensconced in the mountains. The incident created great commotion in Chattanooga, and a large posse was shortly in pursuit. But Taylor was not located until April, when he was traced to Roane County, where his mountain hideout was besieged by an armed posse. He surrendered. Even though his trial was deferred nearly a year he was finally convicted of manslaughter and sentenced for ten years in the state penitentiary; he appealed his conviction to the state Supreme Court.[22]

He was being conveyed to the Supreme Court, in Knoxville, aboard a Cincinnati & Southern railroad car on September 14, 1882. He was placed in a front car and guarded by Hamilton county Sheriff W. T. Cate and Deputy Sheriff John J. Conway. When the train reached Sweetwater, two men boarded the car from the rear and sat near to where Taylor was guarded. "They were tall, brawny, ruffian-like men and seemed intent on some deep design." The train had gone 4 miles toward Philadelphia when the pair of strangers suddenly rose; they turned out to be John's brothers, Bob and Andy Taylor. Bob walked calmly to the bench to which John was chained, placed his pistol at Deputy Sheriff Conway's head, and fired point blank, instantly blowing his brains out in an act of cold-blooded murder. Andy Taylor fired at the sheriff who came charging into the scene. John Taylor jerked the pistol from the dead deputy and, although handcuffed as he was, joined Andy and shot the sheriff, who managed to fire one shot before he died, wounding John in the wrist. Deputy Sheriff Conway's body was unceremoniously thrown from the train. The handcuffs were quickly unlocked and the three brothers promptly proceeded to the locomotive. Holding their weapons to the engineer's head, they forced him to move on, at maximum speed (40 miles an hour), through two stations to Loudon, 20 miles away. Upon reaching Loudon, they mounted waiting horses riding quickly to parts unknown. Chattanooga was in frenzy when the news reached the city. Soon a posse of 200 boarded a train and sped to Loudon. A company of African American militia from Chattanooga likewise joined the search. They scoured the country for two weeks but found no trace of the Taylor trio. Additional posses were organized in nearly every county between Chattanooga and Knoxville; at one time, no less than 2,500 men searched, but found nothing. The state offered $12,500 reward for the murderers, dead or alive, but they were not found.[22] The Taylor brothers had given the law the slip. "It was," according to the Nashville *Daily American*, "the most daring murder in the annals of crime."

When the three Taylor brothers left Loudon, they proceeded through the mountains to Kingston. They forced a physician to dress John's wound. They entered several stores, absconding with boxes of cartridges and supplies. Remounting, they continued to the densest forests and hid in the remotest recesses. They were familiar with the region and remained undetected. They were believed to be headed for the North Carolina mountains.[24]

A few days afterward, the brothers decided to split up. Bob Taylor boarded a train at Rockwood, and proceeded to Missouri where he had kin. He had been there scarcely a week when the Sheriff of Laclede County, recognized him and resolved to arrest him. Taylor was in Lebanon, Missouri purchasing supplies; as he boarded the train he was followed by the sheriff and a deputy. A few moments after he took his seat, the sheriff sidled behind him and putting a pistol to his head, ordering him to surrender. Bob Taylor was not easily daunted, and he reached for his revolver, but before he could draw, the sheriff fired and Bob Taylor fell dead. The news of his death was received with elation in Chattanooga; when his corpse arrived, 5,000 people met it at the train station. It was placed on public exhibition the next day and viewed by 15,000 persons.[25]

Andy and John Taylor, when they were left by Bob, proceeded cautiously over land in the direction of Alabama; they traveled only under cover of darkness, and made 5 or 6 miles each day. They disguised themselves as tramps, "John having his head all tied up and putting on the aspect of an idiot or crazy person, and Andy leading him." In this manner, they actually passed through Chattanooga where militia was guarding the river bridge, and some 1,000 volunteers scrutinized strangers. From Chattanooga, they trudged to Memphis and then to Missouri, intending to join their brother Bob. When they reached Missouri, they learned of Bob's death. John became very depressed; this, coupled with long exposure and neglected wound, proved too much "for his iron constitution." He fell ill at Ballenger's Mill, Missouri, and after a painful sickness of nearly a month, died of typhoid fever and "the flux" in a swamp in southeastern Missouri where Andy buried him.

The death of his two brothers left Andy despondent. He was but a boy, scarcely twenty years old, and when he realized his situation, he almost committed suicide. He left Missouri and began to work on a farm near Emporia, Kansas. Remorse seized him again and once more tried to shoot himself, but was prevented. Drinking to excess he confessed, was arrested and placed in close confinement until Tennessee lawmen were notified. The Hamilton and Loudon county sheriffs went to Kansas, and Taylor was conveyed to Nashville because the excitement was so intense in Chattanooga that it was feared he might be lynched. As a further precaution, Governor William B. Bate arranged for him to be incarcerated in Williamsburg, Kentucky.[26]

In June, Andy Taylor was transferred to Loudon to face trial. Procuring a jury proved to be difficult. Some 320 talesmen were summoned before the jury was complete. The court-appointed attorney's line of defense was that the prisoner was a minor at the time, having been persuaded into the deed by his elder brother, Bob. After a week, the case was given to the jury and in two hours they returned a verdict of guilty of murder in the first degree. His lawyers appealed to the Supreme Court. At special request, he was transported to Chattanooga to be kept in prison until the Supreme Court made its decision. When he arrived, hundreds called to see him, and all were astonished to see a beardless, dull youth instead of a demon. He remained quietly in jail in Chattanooga until September, two years after the original crime had been committed, when he was taken before the Supreme Court in Knoxville. The lower court's finding was confirmed; he received his sentence with composure and awaited his fate with indifference. Andy Taylor was sentenced to die on November 23.[27] He was transferred to Loudon to face the hangman. What *The New York Times* characterized as a "terrible tragedy" was concluded and Andy Taylor's fall was complete.[28]

The Morrow Gang, District 9, Montgomery County

In mid-June 1884, restlessness ran high in District No. 9, Montgomery County, after news of the arrest and indictment of Ransom Morrow and his two sons for murders extending back as far six years, as well as extortion, arson, and robbery since 1864. The headquarters of the Morrow gang was Bellamy Cave, near the house of their leader, Ransom Morrow.[29] In the cave was "a pit, said to be bottomless, used for disposing of their victims." The Morrows stood accused of killing "old Jim Brown," an African American farmer in the district's neighborhood of Wiley Church and Bellamy's Cave in October 1878. Also murdered was Dick Overton, also a local black farmer, in August 1884. Overton's corpse was disposed of in a "bottomless pit"—the so-called "Hell Hole"—in Bellamy's Cave.[30]

Bellamy's Cave, which played a major role in the murders, was judged to be second in size only to Mammoth Cave in Kentucky. It had a small opening and was a place of public resort, where neighbors had picnics and balls. It shared another more histrionic distinction, however, namely the "Cavern of Horrors."[31] Indeed, much of the evidence against the Morrows had been discovered in what was termed the "Hell's Hole affair." In excess of a dozen unsolved murders, innumerable house burnings, extortion, and robberies were popularly believed to be the work of the Morrow Gang. Neighbors had long suspected them but were afraid of reprisals should they speak out. In the absence of complaints, the family "carried on a regular John A. Murrell business." Around 1870, they spread rumors in ninth district that they were members of the Ku Klux Klan, keeping their neighbors in a constant state of dread. A dozen or more of the Morrow family had been tried for various crimes, including murder, horse theft, barn burning, smoke house and corn crib thievery, and setting fire to entire houses; residences were broken into and clothing and bedding were stolen. Despite being tried for such crimes, none of the family were ever convicted as they had friends who established alibis for them. The Ninth Civil District of Montgomery County, where the Morrow gang held sway, for all intents and purposes, was the family's private domain.

The county magistrates arrested Ransom and his two sons and Dr. Bellamy with no recourse to bail. They and other witnesses were questioned by the grand jury. Eyewitnesses testified about the heinous murders committed by the Morrows in Bellamy's cave, a smaller cavern in the cave now known as "Hell's Hole."

Ransom Morrow and his sons, William and Charles, were arrested and held in iron cages on the second floor of the old Clarksville jail. The sixty-six-year-old Ransom was described as "a remarkably fine looking old man, except about the eyes ... his body ... and his carriage erect. His features are clear cut, delicate and, remarkably handsome. His nose in what would be called Roman.... His ... steel gray eyes gave his face a decidedly Mephisphelean appearance." He was plainly dressed in gray clothes even though he was a man of "considerable fortune, being the owner of some 700 acres of well improved land, besides, nobody knows how much personal property."

His eldest son, William, thirty-five years old, "stood six feet in his boots," was "built like John L. Sullivan, the champion prize fighter," with heavy dull gray eyes giving him a "sullen look, that occasionally, when he gets angry, becomes diabolical."

Charles, twenty-four years old, looked very much like his father, with "delicate features, bluish eyes and rather slight frame." He wore a slight boyish yellow moustache and "would never be taken for a murderer."

In an accompanying iron cell was Dr. Pete F. Bellamy, from a locally prominent family, also implicated in the Bellamy Cave murders, largely because the entry to the cave was on his property. He had gray hair and a beard, was a well-known raconteur, and well educated. Dr. Bellamy was Ransom's son-in-law, and lived half a mile from Hell's Hole, He had been arrested "while hiding out at his brother-in-law's ... and brought in and lodged in jail without bond."[32]

It was the investigation of a robbery at a neighboring household in the ninth civil district that led to the surreptitious discovery of Dick Overton's putrefying corpse, which was found in the "Hell Hole" in Bellamy's Cave. A neighbor, Winn, procured a search warrant and with law officers, searched Dr. Bellamy's residence, but nothing incriminating was found. Acting on a hunch, the lawmen searched the cave, thinking the articles robbed from Winn would be stashed there.

They entered through the deceptively small breach to the cave using lanterns to light their way. Some 700 yards in the cave they found a smaller, deep, dark cavern that had never been known to be explored, and discovered "Hell's Hole." Dick had worked on Ransom's farm and was owed back wages, which Ransom paid in part, promising to pay the rest once he had sold some tobacco. Dick Overton was never heard of after that. The remains were thought to be too far gone to for anyone make a positive identification, but they were determined to be Overton's by four witnesses, including Overton's father, brother, and cousin. They all later swore to the Grand Jury that although the hair had fallen off the decomposing head, that the flesh was still on his face, but dropped off when the corpse was moved, they recognized the body by the features and moustache, and knew beyond doubt the hat, pants, heelless shoes, and pocket-knife were those belonging to Dick.[33]

As the *Clarksville Weekly Chronicle* put it: "Quite a sensation has been created in this county by the arrest of certain parties residing in the 9th district, charged with deeds so dark and crimes so dire as to curdle the blood of him to whom the story is told."

Upon examination by the Grand Jury, it was showed that the Morrows "had been forcing the victims, year after year, to walk over the precipice in 'Hell's Hole,' dashed them to pieces at the bottom of the chasm, at the point of shot guns, and shooting them if they refused to go." "Incongruously, "Ransom and his boys," continued a newspaper report, "were held in high esteem as pillars of the Baptist church here." Ransom Morrow was a deacon in the Baptist Church. Some of his neighbors spoke highly of him, and could not believe he could have committed the murders.[34] His son, William, however, was believed to have been the perpetrator of these two and other murders since 1869, according to "the common talk of the people of the district." Four witnesses, including William's father-in-law, testified that Morrow had confessed that he had killed Jim Brown and Dick Overton. The alleged excuse for killing Brown "was that he attempted to ravish Dr. Bellamy's wife, and for the [murder] of [Dick] Overton, that he was caught allegedly trying to ravish a little daughter of Rans [sic] Morrow's." The evidence was that Bill and Charley Morrow "carried Overton to a place near the cave where the shot him and put his body in the cave."[35] Charley would later be exonerated.

Also arrested as accomplices before and after the fact were William Outlaw and David Horn. All of their crimes extended over a period of twenty years "and during all that time they have committed many crimes, including a number of murders, and the people who could have exposed them have been afraid to do so."

In an accompanying iron cell was Dr. Pete F. Bellamy, also implicated in the Bellamy Cave murders, largely because the entry to the cave was on his property. He had gray hair and a beard, was a well-known raconteur, and well educated. Dr. Bellamy was Ransom's son-in-law.[36]

On June 10, the Grand Jury found three indictments against William "Bill" Morrow, "one for the murder of Jim Brown, colored the second for the murder of Dick Overton, colored; the third for arson, in burning Mrs. Lowry's house." Ransom was indicted as an accessory before the fact of the murder of Overton. When the sheriff read the indictments to Bill Morrow, he immediately confessed helping murder both the African Americans, "but said if he was going to hang he would deny the burning of Mrs. Lowry's house." Hell's Hole was to be explored the next day by a large party headed by the sheriff. Previously it had "been explored as far as the [Red]river which runs through the cave. By this river bones were found, showing where the victims were disposed of. A log was thrown in and soon floated entirely out of sight." [37]

Ransom, Bill and Charley Morrow, and Dr. Bellamy were refused bail and remanded to the county jail until their trial set for November 1884. Popular opinion in the ninth district held that the Morrows were guilty, that "the legal evidence, which will be admissible on a trial before a jury, is quite strong if not conclusive of the guilt of the defendants."[38]

Apparently Ransom had taken advantage of his "extraordinary and baleful influence" over his son, William, convincing him to become the scapegoat for the entire band implicated in the Bellamy cave murders. To save his own neck, he callously convinced William to turn state's evidence and "unbosom himself to the Attorney General and the grand jury." Coldly calculating that William, while in his cups, had already confessed complicity in the murders of Jim Brown and Dick Overton, Ransom reasoned it must have been plain to William that he could not escape justice unless his father could be set free to exculpate his son. The best way to get Ransom out of jail was for William to confess to the murders. William unenthusiastically agreed.[39]

William Morrow's full confession was accepted by the court in the case of *State vs. William Morrow*, on December 20, 1884. Dr. Bellamy and Ransom were to face trial at a later date and set free. William still faced trial for arson. He confessed, no doubt because of his belief in his father's promise to have him exonerated and that he would be spared once his father was set free and could set the record straight. William was sentenced to hang on January 30, 1885, for the murder of Dick Overton. Ransom Morrow received a life sentence in the state penitentiary; both he and his son-in-law, Dr. Bellamy, were remanded to jail to stand trial as accessories in the murder of Jim Brown. Bellamy and Ransom were later set free because there was not enough viable evidence to convict them.[40]

Bill Morrow was hanged on June 10, 1885. "Notwithstanding the privacy of the affair, quite a crowd of curious people gathered on the hillside in front to the jail hoping to get a glimpse of the prisoner on the gallows." At ten o'clock a.m. a special force of twelve armed deputies, marched down and surrounded the jail.

The gallows was placed between the new jail and the kitchen, a space of seven feet wide. A beam three by four inches, to which the three-fourth inch grass rope was attached, was fastened in the wall of each building, eight feet above the scaffold. All the open spaces were closed with plank, and tarpaulin was spread overhead. The scaffold was constructed of rough lumber. The trap-door swings by two hinges on one side, supported by an iron slot or trigger from the kitchen below.

A "very neat rosewood coffin" trimmed with silver, 3 by 6 feet, was brought in by the undertakers at one o'clock. Bill Morrow appeared nonchalant about "the frightful monster death so near him." At five minutes past two o'clock, deputies came for Morrow, handcuffed him, and marched down the stairway of the jail to the first floor accompanied by ministers and law officers, and was marched up the improvised steps to the scaffold, the windows and doors all being closed or darkened to prevent any outside view.

The prisoner walked with steady, active step, and appeared calm, resolute and dignified, as if about to perform some very pleasant duty, He was neatly attired in a black cloth suit, white shirt, turn-down collar and black cravat. His cheeks were shaved, showing a heavy moustache and chin whiskers.

Morrow was asked if he had anything to say in regard to the veracity of his confession, and he answered no. "'Then are you ready to die?' 'Yes, at any moment' was the prompt reply." Morrow stood erect, "as calm, as brave and dignified a specimen of humanity as was ever seen, betraying not a single emotion or sign of alarm." His hands and feet were bound and the black cap placed over his head. The sheriff asked if he was ready, to which Morrow answered in the affirmative.

The sheriff sprung the trigger and Wm. Morrow was instantly launched into eternity. The stretch of the rope gave him a seven foot drop and he was killed instantaneously, by the dislocation of the neck ... as pronounced by the attending physicians. Not a single quiver of flesh or limbs or the drawing of a muscle was perceptible.... The body was hung twenty minutes, when it was cut down and placed in the coffin and ... conveyed to his wife and children. After being viewed by friends it will be interred at Blooming Grove church, by the side of his first wife, as requested.

Before his execution, Bill was removed from the cell in which he, his father, and Dr. Bellamy were all kept prisoner. While kept in isolation, he wrote a letter to his father saying, in essence:

My father:—You said you hoped I would be hung, and tomorrow you will get your wish, for I will be hung and put out of your way. You got me into all this trouble, and promised to stand by me if it took the last cent you had. Then you got mad with me because I would not take it all on myself. Don't never get any of your children into trouble and desert them, as you have me. I ain't got no malice against you for what you have done me. I forgive you, and hope God will forgive you.[41]

The execution of Bill Morrow and prosecution his father, Ransom Morrow, and Dr. Bellamy did not result in an immediate decrease of tension among those citizens in District 9. The environs were not unfamiliar with violence. Soon after the Civil War, it took a contingent of Federal soldiers to quell the terrorist activities of the Ku Klux Klan in the district. Yet soon after quietude had been established, there followed the disappearance of an old African American by the name of Morrow, then a peddler, the killing of Jim Brown, and the killing of Dick Overton, interspersed with instances of arson, thievery, which became common gossip in the vicinity after the arrests of Dr. Bellamy, Ransom Morrow and his sons, Bill, Ben, and Charles.

After Bill's execution, public sentiment against the Morrows was expected to diminish. Ransom Morrow and his sons, Ben and Charlie, were cleared of any wrongdoing as was Dr. Bellamy. Belief that Bill's execution would prove a caution, tending to "cool the audacity and brazen impudence of these men, and that the community would in the further rest in peace," was not shared by all citizens of District 9. The acquittal of the Morrows and Bellamy led many to uneasiness among those who had testified against them. Fear of revenge gripped them. "Several prominent citizens are conscious that they are shadowed; they know not by whom, but live in constant dread of some evil consequence." One gentleman, upon being interviewed by a newspaper reporter stated "that he must hurry off to go home before night. I used to come to town and return the same day by travelling a little in the night, but there are several of us now who make it a point to stay overnight in town and go home in the morning, and *don't go out after night for any purpose.*" The reporter doggedly asked him why this was true, and "soon got the gentleman's jawbone in a quiver, and his tongue rattled freely."

> Well ... if you really want to know why, just come down there and spend a few days, and you will have no trouble learning that District No. 9 is not at all the little heaven painted by the attorneys in the Bellamy case. Oh, the devil! You needn't laugh; there is no fun in it for us fellows. About a dozen of us don't dare go out after night. We don't know when we may have to run out from a fire or take chances for life. Old Rans and Bellamy are not all of the Morrow gang ... and I don't feel at all at home when I am there. I don't sleep good. I see blazes and dream of that yawning chasm in Hell's Hole.... Oh, great God, man ... just come down to see [my] neighbors ... and hear them tell about the signs of blood, spirits without lanterns following men up at night.... Several of us met not long ago, and after telling all I knew, and hearing the experience of the other fellows, darn me if I wasn't scared so bad that I couldn't hardly summon the courage to go home, and you bet I didn't go back the same way I went, but traveled around, about five miles out of my way. That's the way it is in No. 9. The trouble with me is, the rascals all believe that I have got money, and nothing I could say or do would convince them to the contrary. If he were to kill me they wouldn't get over $2.50 for I don't keep any money at home, and I don't want to be killed for $2.50, though it is all the same to me as if the devils were to get a million ... our people are ... getting so they are afraid to talk again except just among themselves....
>
> Oh, you may talk funny about stopping up Hell's Hole. There's nothing funny about it; we don't know how many people have gone on an excursion down that

gaping gulch, trying to solve the problem of the cheapest method of stopping it, and haven't been heard from [since]....

I tell you honest citizens are growing nervous over the situation; no one feels safe; there is no confidence existing, and we are determined to have relief if we have to help ourselves; and if there is any more queer doings and sayings, you will find sign-boards hanging up all over No. 9. Since the trials and the acquittal of the gang the mysteries are all very easily cleared up; people know where missing things went, who executed this or that deviltry...[42]

It was not noted in any press report that a white man was found guilty of murdering black men. This irony is explained the result of the pervasive influence of white supremacy established in Jim Crow laws, notions, and customs. Nevertheless, this conviction was, whether noted as such at the time, an unacknowledged milestone in racial justice in Tennessee.

There were no further lawless activities attributed to the Morrow Gang of Montgomery County. In time, recollections of the Morrow Gang faded from memory, except perhaps in folklore ghost stories, shelved by the return to peaceful normality in District 9.

King of the Yeggmen

In the early twentieth century, William "Bill" Cody, known as one of Tennessee's most evasive and notorious yeggmen, jail breakers, and highway robbers, apparently disappeared sometime after his escape from the Tennessee penitentiary in 1915. He was known to have begun his life of crime after committing armed robbery in Polk County in 1903, and he perpetrated numerous felonies for the next eight years. Known as a "mocker of locksmiths," he had, despite his many arrests and convictions, never been successfully held in any jail or penitentiary. "Small in stature, almost a 'runt,' but with a keen, desperate eye, is 'Bill' Cody. The word fear is as foreign to this man's make up as is any inclination to obey the law."[43]

Cody's first arrest was made in 1911 by Special Officer W. M. Fryar, of the Nashville, Chattanooga & St. Louis railroad. He was collared for "hoboing" on a freight train near Hooker station, after a dramatic fight atop a speeding freight car. Cody was routinely brought to Chattanooga but it was not until he was incarcerated that his identity established. There it was found he was wanted for a robbery in Wauhatchie, and for a series of store robberies in East Chattanooga. Found guilty of these crimes, he was sentenced five years, and for the store robberies, he was given six years—eleven in all.

Cody made a mysterious exit from his Hamilton County jail cell early Friday morning November 26, 1911, using a wire to turn the "circle," freeing himself from the cell-block corridor. He passed quietly past the night jailer escaping pursuit. His whereabouts remained unknown until it was discovered he was incarcerated in Fort Smith, Arkansas, three years later. While awaiting trial for safecracking, he escaped by using a spoon to loosen enough bricks to create an egress. Before being jailed at Fort Smith, Cody had been captured in Texas. While manacled and escorted by

Texas Rangers to Arkansas, the spirited Cody escaped by leaping from a moving railroad car window as the train crossed a river and he floated temporarily to freedom. Then-Hamilton County Sheriff Conner was *en route* to bring the desperado to Chattanooga; but once, upon reaching Memphis, he read an Associated Press dispatch of the bandit's escape from Fort Smith, he turned back.

Offers of big rewards failed to bring about his capture until the autumn of 1914, when an officer at Fort Smith, Ark., identified him from a description furnished by Sheriff Conner. After his escape from Arkansas, reports had been received in Chattanooga that he was in Wauhatchie, where he had relatives, but he could not be apprehended.

He was finally found, however, in the late afternoon of February 25, 1915, on the Wauhatchie road near the top of Lookout Mountain. He was wearing a black suit with leather riding leggings, a long gray overcoat, and a soft black hat. Deputy Sheriff Frank Fryar saw Cody coming towards the city and called the sheriff to notify him. With two deputies, then Sheriff Nick Bush met Cody near Dr. Boyd's residence on Lookout Mountain. Their automobile was running at so high a velocity that they sped past Cody, giving him an opportunity for fight or flight. Sheriff Bush and Deputy Light turned back and met Cody face to face in the road. Day approached him from the side of the road. Sheriff Bush leveled his revolver on Cody and ordered the yeggman to stop. When within about 12 feet of Cody, he was looking down the bore of Cody's .38-caliber Colt automatic. Deputy Day, however, drew a bead on Cody and fired a shot into the fugitive's right shoulder with a jail riot gun. Crippled, Cody fell. He was arrested and taken to Erlanger hospital, spending the night under the guard of two armed deputies. His wound was not serious. His arrest was the successful result of several months of pursuit by Sheriff Bush, who inherited from Sheriff Conner the desire to take the bandit into custody.

When taken into guardianship, according to the *Chattanooga Daily Times*, Cody was heavily armed, carrying a new .38-caliber Colt automatic eight-shot pistol, loaded with steel-jacketed ammunition, a 30-30 German army Luger automatic in a holster, with an extra magazine, loaded with assorted steel-pointed and soft-nosed dumdum bullets. The Luger, it was reported, had the penetration power of a 1903 Springfield rifle, and could fire as many as 150 times a minute. Cody likewise carried a 5-inch pocket-knife, and in his left sock were found four steel hacksaw blades, capable of cutting through steel. In his leather suitcase were found more tools of his trade, namely one and a half sticks of high-grade dynamite, several yards of fuse, a box of dynamite caps, a large ratchet drill and an assortment of highly-tempered steel drills, large quantity of ammunition, brace and bits, electric searchlight and extra battery, two hacksaws and a heavy file, cake of soap, string of assorted skeleton keys, red silk mask, and a razor. Additionally, it was reported there was a pint of finely-ground black pepper, "which the officers say is used to deaden the scent of a man's trail if pursued by bloodhounds." A tin can found inside the case was said to contain nitro-glycerin.[44]

The suspect readily admitted that he was "Bill" Cody. Without complaining of the wound in his side, Cody sat quietly until confined in a ward at Erlanger hospital and chained to his bed. Two Hamilton County deputy sheriffs kept watch at Cody's bedside. Sheriff Bush was advised by Dr. B. Reisman that it was necessary to make an X-ray examination to ascertain if Cody's lungs had been penetrated by the blast from the Deputy Sheriff on Wauhatchie road. He would be sent to the hospital ward of the county jail if found healthy.

Sheriff Bush believed Cody had been the culprit in the attempt to blow the Bank of Sewanee's safe on February 16, and that he had several associates in the Chattanooga environs. Further investigation of the Sewanee job and a number of jewelry robberies in Nashville were made to see if there was circumstantial evidence implicating Cody.

Law officers congregated at the jail that night to learn details of the desperado's arrest. Deputy Sheriff Sam Henderson proved to have had the earliest acquaintance with Cody in Hamilton County. "'I went up against his gun twelve years ago in Polk County,' he said. 'He figured in two robberies up there and gave the officers considerable trouble.'"

An x-ray indicated that Cody had pneumonia and was sent to the hospital ward of the county jail. Guards remained vigilant. Cody was in serious but not critical condition. Pneumonia resulted from the load of buckshot fired into his shoulder and back by Officer Day. Thus he could not have escaped, making the heavy guard evidently superfluous, except that fears that "a gang of desperate men" would find it a "comparatively easy matter" to raid the jail and set him free. Cody's elusiveness in the past, and the presence in the city of other members of his gang who were known to be desperate, and willing to take any chances to rescue him, were responsible for his removal. Indeed, a possible henchman, about midnight on the 26th, when Cody left Erlanger hospital, at the corner of Palmetto and Fifth Street "stepped into the middle of the street and stopped his automobile." According to an account in the February 27, 1915, Chattanooga *Daily Times* the ensuing encounter and conversation went this way:

"Have you come from the hospital?" was asked of him.

When he said he had the man asked him of Cody's condition.

"Do you think he will be able to travel in a couple of days?" was asked. When he was told that it might be a week before he could be moved the man appeared to be satisfied. He returned to the sidewalk, where a companion was standing beneath a tree.

Sheriff Bush, upon learning of the incident, immediately had all the other prisoners removed from the hospital ward on the third floor of the jail. Additionally, the ward was thoroughly disinfected. Old mattresses and blankets were replaced with new and clean sheets were installed. Late in the afternoon of the 26th, Cody was taken from the hospital where he was chained to his bed, and placed in the ward at the jail, where he is under the constant care of an efficient registered nurse. Dr. Reisman held that if no complications arose his patient would be able to sit up within ten days to two weeks.

Although known to be easygoing and loquacious, Cody refused to discuss his situation with the press. He talked little since his arrest about anything, speaking only to his attorneys, J. J. Kalwick and J. W. Scott, who had defended him during his former predicaments in Chattanooga.

Cody had achieved a celebrity's status. When he reached the jail, more than 100 people waited hoping to get a glimpse of "Wild Bill." The day jailer reckoned that more than 1,000 citizens came to the jail on the 25th just to see the assortment of burglars' and safe blowers' tools taken from Cody and put on display.[45]

While at first reticent, Cody became more loquacious at the county jail. He was apparently more interested in regaining his health than an escape. He joked with his nurse: "… if you will just get me well again, I'll make you a present of the 30-30 Luger gun downstairs that everybody seems so interested in, but mind you, you've got to get me well."

It appeared his health was improving, although he was not ready to accept visitors. Sheriff Bush was allowed to question him for a few hours. Cody insisted that the blowing of the vault in the bank at Sewanee ten days earlier was not his work. His alibi was that he was in St. Louis at the time. In fact, his wife and two children and father lived there, and he made that city his headquarters. "A person of his profession" claimed the *Chattanooga Daily Times*, "seldom lives in any one place for any length of time. He says … that St. Louis has been his headquarters since his escape from the jail here in 1911."

While Cody could not receive visitors, his arsenal, save for the dynamite, continued to be the object of great curiosity. The tools were examined by hundreds of people who called at the jail, eager for a peep of the yeggman, and if not him, to see the implements of his trade. Some of the throng wanted a souvenir of the notorious thief. Cody's stock of 30-30 and .38-caliber bullets was nearly depleted by the curious souvenir seekers, causing Sheriff Bush to sequester the ammunition. Even his pocket knife was stolen. In addition to his collection of guns and explosives, a small amount of money was found on his person. When Sheriff Bush remarked about the paltry sum, Cody smiled and replied with braggadocio: "It was $8 and some cents, wasn't it? Well eight or ten dollars ought to be enough for anybody's immediate needs. If I had more I might get robbed. Had I needed more I could have gotten it."

By mid-March, Bill Cody had recovered enough so that it was judged that he could most likely be sent to the state penitentiary to serve out his sentences. A visit by his brother, employed by the Lookout Coffin and Casket Company in St. Louis, apparently brushed aside the felon's reluctance to talk to the reporters. He began talking to the press and gave an explanation for his life of crime. According to a newspaper report, Cody maintained:

> Most folks are sort of driven to being crooks, anyway. We don't want to be, but we get into it some way and it is hard to get out. I was just a youngster when I got into my first trouble, and if I had been treated half-way right at that time I don't believe I would have ended like this.
>
> I got in trouble with a man by the name of Cooke at an ice-cream supper in Benton fourteen or fifteen years ago. I had been drinking some, and when he pulled the chair out from under me I cut him.
>
> They arrested me that night, but I jumped into the river and got away and was away for several years. Several years later they arrested me down in Texas. While they were bringing me back I jumped from the train in Arkansas and got away again. A short time after that I was here in Chattanooga, and some of Sheriff Shipp's men arrested me.
>
> When they carried me back to Benton they not only locked me up, but they chained me to the cell. They wouldn't let anybody talk to me. Even when my father

came they wouldn't let him see me. I said right then that I wouldn't be arrested any more if I could help it; that the law didn't care anything about me and I wouldn't care anything about the law. They sent me up for a year then, and that's the last time I have stayed in jail until I got here.[46]

And in jail, under strong and constant guard, he did stay until he was sentenced in April. Cody was sentenced to serve only five years at Brushy Mountain prison for highway robbery. He had expected a sentence twice as long. He was elated at the smaller sentence and told a newspaper reporter: "That means that I will have five years more in which to try to make amends for the past ten or fifteen years. Some people doubtless will take the idea of an old-timer like me treading the straight and narrow way as something like a joke, but it is not. I know it is a pretty hard proposition to settle down after all this time and it may be too big a one for me, but I don't believe it is. I know how it ought to be done, and if I get the least bit of encouragement you can depend on Bill. That's me."[47] In reality, a leopard had a better chance of changing his spots to tiger's stripes.

Instead of Brushy Mountain, however, Bill Cody was to serve his sentence at the state penitentiary in Nashville.[48] On April 8, 1915, after a number of saw blades were discovered in his cell, Sheriff Bush took the "king of the yeggmen" to the state penitentiary at Nashville, to await what was believed to be a fifteen-year sentence of for breaking jail and robbery.[49] Bush warned the prison authorities that Cody was a dangerous man and strict guard should be kept over him. The warning, according to the sheriff, was not taken seriously by prison authorities, but was greeted by the blasé remark that they had "some worse than Cody."

He was ensconced at the state penitentiary on the Cumberland River in late April 1915. It appeared as though he was going to remain true to his word, but after only three months into his ten-year sentence, a headline in the *Chattanooga Daily Times* announced "'Bill' Cody Free Again," demonstrating that he either did not get the "least bit of encouragement" or that he had determined life in the penitentiary was not to his liking. In either event, he had escaped from the state pen with a fellow inmate who was serving a sentence for murder, Charles Swafford of Sequatchie County. They were hastily joined by a third convict.

The prisoners were first seen escaping by Dr. L. W. Edwards, the prison physician, as they were scaling the walls behind the prison laundry. They had made a ladder in the carpenter shop after intimidating a number of convict workmen.

The ladder was made of a single scantling, to which the escaping convicts nailed cleats that had already been provided, and had been concealed in a sack for some time by Swafford, who in some mysterious fashion also furnished the pistols with which they were armed. These, said Swafford, had been hidden for several weeks in a punching bag that he had been allowed to use in the motor room of the harness shop where he worked. How he managed to obtain the arms he refused to tell. When Dr. Edwards gave the alarm the prisoners commenced firing at him. He quickly sought cover and gave the alarm.

Guards rushed up to the ramparts and shot several times at the prisoners as they went over the wall. Several guards came out the gates and went in hot pursuit of the escapees, Cody, McKenney, and Swafford, who were by this time out of rifle range. The escapees made a beeline for the Cumberland River and jumped in. They started to swim across, but seeing citizens on the opposite, bank they came back.

McKenney was captured as he was sitting on the bank resting after his swim. Swafford's tracks were followed down the river where he was captured in a thicket. "Wild Bill," however, was nowhere to be found. He had entered the river again further downstream, and from his tracks it was assumed he either made good his escape or had drowned in the swift current of the river. No other sign was seen of him. Smooth-shaven William Cody was about thirty-two years old, weighed 137 pounds, and could be identified by multiple scars on his head. The following morning, Cody was discovered in a nearby church, but when officers arrived at the sanctuary, he was gone. Although a reward was offered for his apprehension, he remained at large.[50]

Back in Chattanooga, on September 4, 1915, Sheriff Bush received a postcard, mailed from City Point, Virginia, where it was thought Cody, an expert "soup" (nitroglycerin) man, was employed by the DuPont powder works. The post card read simply: "I have a couple of safes to blow, also a train to hold up before I leave. But, say—I shall give your city my attention soon. So lookout. Yours, BAD BILL."

The handwriting matched samples of Cody's writing in letters he had written from jail eight months earlier. Whether or not "Bad Bill" would make good his promise to return to Chattanooga was anybody's guess, but proof had been found that he visited the city soon after his escape from the state penitentiary in June. Evidence existed showing that Cody had left the Nashville environs on the Tennessee Central Railroad, came to Soddy on the Cincinnati, New Orleans & Texas Pacific Railroad, and from there he walked to Chattanooga. There he "touched" some of his former colleagues and secured a "stake" to finance his trip out of Tennessee. Cody was known as a versatile lawbreaker, taking on anything from second-story work to through express trains.[50]

Nevertheless, the trail grew cold as America entered World War I. Rumors were heard that he was robbing motorists in Marion County, but these were never substantiated and seemed not to fit his *modus operandi*. Cody may have lived an exemplary life, working incognito in a war production factory, or he may have joined the army during the war, or perished in the influenza epidemic of 1918–1919. He was rumored to be back in the Chattanooga environs in 1919, but this was never verified.[9] Whatever may have happened to this colorful Tennessee bandit, however, will never be known, but his story is just one of the more colorful pages of the Volunteer State's past.

6

Moonshining in Nineteenth-Century Tennessee

Moonshining, or the illegal production of beer and liquor, was a direct consequence of the excise tax levied on spirits by the federal government in 1791. It was unpopular and led to the "Whisky Rebellion" of 1794 in which farmers in western Pennsylvania mountainous region refused to pay. The upshot was the suppression of the insurrection by an army of 12,000 state militia, led by President George Washington. In the face of such overpowering force, the "Whisky boys" succumbed to the federal government. The tax has been maintained on and off for over 225 years, although the illegal manufacture of whisky did not cease. The scenario of Federal revenue agents ferreting out moonshiners, destroying illicit stills, and prosecuting "wildcatters" continued through the nineteenth and into the twentieth century, even as late as the present time. The still owners, generally farmers in the remote southern mountain regions, continued making "shine," engaging in a cat-and-mouse game with revenue agents. It was a dangerous business, often times involving gunfire and even death. Moonshining was familiar in Tennessee, indeed the practice has passed into folklore and cinema. Briefly, the history of illicit distilling in Tennessee, took place in two periods; from statehood in 1796 to 1817, when the excise tax was lifted, and 1862 to the late twentieth century, when it was reinstituted. Local moonshining businesses flourished along with larger established tax paying distilleries. According to Tennessee historian Michael Birdwell: "Distilling was among the first industries established in Tennessee, and by 1860 it was the state's biggest industry." After the Civil War, illegal distilling became common place and competed with legitimate distillers in Tennessee. Therein lay the rub.

Before and especially after the Civil War, small amounts of distilled spirits were commonly produced mostly by mountaineers for "personal consumption, medicine and to supplement their meager incomes." Wildcatters, or moonshiners, continued defying the law and persisted in making moonshine throughout the nineteenth century. The enforcement of the tax on unlicensed liquor led to violent confrontations between Internal Revenue Collectors and moonshiners mostly, but not exclusively, in the mountainous regions of the Cumberland Plateau and Eastern Tennessee. Shutting down these remote distilleries became a costly task for the Federal government's Internal Revenue Service agents.

Opposition to paying the tax rested on a number of factors:

> With corn the primary crop, particularly among semi-subsistence farmers in the mountainous Appalachian backcountry, it was only natural for the production of distilled liquor to become the occupation or avocation of many farmers. Demand was high enough to stimulate production. Coupled with poor or corrupt local law enforcement and inhospitality to federal "revenuers," a tradition was formed of resistance to Federal authority that would last to the present.

Resistance was robust enough to cause the Federal government to find an alternative to its strong-arm "search and destroy" policy. To reduce the cost in dollars and in life, the Federal government needed an alternative course of action. Consequently, the Internal Revenue Service, the agency responsible for collecting the tax, changed its approach and initiated a system based upon a blanket amnesty for moonshiners in 1878. Many accepted the offer, yet many also surreptitiously continued to ply their vocation.[1]

The term "moonshine" apparently came into popular use in Tennessee in 1871. Newspapers in Morristown and Memphis that year, representing the eastern and western regions of the state, printed a short notice that read: "Illicit distilling in East Tennessee is called moonshine business. The whisky is also called moonshine." "Wildcat distilleries," as they were called, were not the object of suppression, claimed the Bureau of Internal Revenue, "because of any desire to oppress or harass moonshiners as a class, but to protect legitimate tax-paying distillers and the interests of the federal government." Illegitimate producers could sell their whisky for about one-half the price demanded by legal distilleries. If illicit distillers were allowed to operate unmolested, competition would be so high that all tax stamped liquors would be undersold and result in the closing of all legitimate distilleries. More importantly, moonshine sales would deprive the Federal government of substantial revenues on spirits. In this manner, enforcement of the excise tax on whisky was an effort on the part of the government to interfere with the "invisible hand" of the market and enforce competition by protecting legal tax-paying distillers.

To suppress moonshining and prosecute offenders was easier said than done. Many almost insurmountable difficulties were encountered by the revenue collectors, commonly given the sobriquet "revenuers." One problem was that revenue cases were tried in state courts with locally sympathetic juries. The *Tennessee v. Davis* Supreme Court decision of 1879 established federal supremacy in moonshine prosecution cases, eliminating local jurisdiction. The Internal Revenue Service divided Tennessee into eight collection districts. They were: First, Johnson City; Second, Knoxville; Third, Chattanooga; Fourth, Murfreesboro; Fifth, Nashville; Sixth, Clarksville; Seventh, Huntingdon; and Eighth, Memphis. Most of the illicit distilleries were in the First, Second, Fourth, Fifth, and Sixth Districts. Fewer were found in the Seventh and Eighth districts.

Illegal stills were most often located in deep, almost impenetrable ravines, in sequestered recesses, in dark and twisted thickets, at the head of small streams, and other extremely inaccessible places, "reached only by obscure hog paths." A story in the Nashville *Republican Banner,* October 18, 1871 described a typical still this way:

> In most instances the very small sour mash distilleries, consisting of an old copper still, well patched, and much worn from long use.... The apparatus is usually covered by a rough shed of a temporary nature.... The still and its equipment's are arranged in such a manner as to admit to their being moved on very short notice to a place of safety after a warning has been received of the approach of revenue officers and soldiers, whose object, they well enough know, is capture and destruction.

The techniques of moonshining were passed down, like the stills themselves, from generation to generation. Moonshine stills generally had an output of 10–20 gallons, although some sophisticated outfits could sometimes produce an entire barrel of whisky. Making the whisky was chiefly a male-dominated communal event. The liquor was usually made, or "run out," on Saturday nights. The men of the locality congregated at the still to test the first "run," or "singlings," and discuss topics of mountain community gossip. The following Monday morning, the whisky was generally drunk up, or sold to some crossroads grocery. It was these kinds of moonshine stills that were generally the object of revenuers' raids.

A raid followed a generic pattern. First of all the wildcatters had a well-established system to warn them that a raid was eminent. When approaching danger became known the system was initiated throughout the rugged terrain, allowing moonshiners to cease distilling and to abscond with their liquor and still into the wild. Usually a runner traveled 5 or 6 miles ahead of the revenue agents and soldiers, circulating the news that raiders were approaching. The runner, having accomplished this task returned to the still's location and made an additional report. Because they were familiar with local topography, the runners took shortcuts and were able to deliver the news hours before collectors and the soldiers could reach the stills. Unless the revenuers made a forced march, it was nearly impossible to arrest the moonshiners. Although with the help of a capable guide, they sometimes succeeded in destroying a still. Yet the more they infiltrated the mountains the more challenging their task became.

The wildcatters' code of honor held those who would inform on them or acted as guides were traitors; retribution followed. For example, in one instance in 1878, a wildcatter who had been working as an informer in Clay County was awakened one night by an angry set of men who carried out the "vengeance of the entire moonshine fraternity." He was told in no uncertain terms to leave the county and vacate immediately. To demonstrate their point further, the wildcatters burned his home and all its contents, leaving his family destitute and homeless.[2]

When confronted by revenue agents, friends and family members invariably professed to know nothing about it, and sent revenue agents on a wild goose chase in search of a supposed distillery in an opposite direction, many miles away. This allowed the guilty party to escape, but also provided an opportunity to remove their distilling equipment should the ruse prove ineffective.

Often it was the case that wildcat distilleries were owned by the local gentry. They hired an indigent neighbor who was familiar with producing whisky; if caught, it was considered *noblesse oblige* to pay his bail and all expenses resulting from his arrest and trial. The people in the "wildcat" districts distrusted all strangers suspiciously regarding them as revenue officers until the contrary was proven. In the words of an experienced raider: "They can almost smell a revenue man and know his position by ... intuition." It was believed that the only way in which distilleries could be successfully destroyed and the owners arrested would be by eschewing the assistance of soldiers and employ a posse of plainclothes deputies.[3]

Moonshiners resorted to trickery to hide their stills. One mountaineer went so far as to place his still under his house. The smoke that came out of the chimney appeared to emanate from a normal hearth fire. In another case, a still was located at the bottom of a steep bluff; all the ingredients for whisky and the still itself had to be let down by ropes from a narrow and steep pathway leading to it "barely permitting the passage of a man or dog."

In the districts where moonshine whisky was produced, no dealer in legitimate taxed spirits could sell it for more than half the price he paid for it. Some grocery keepers in these regions purchased a used, stamped barrel of whisky, out of which they might sell shine for years, the barrel constantly replenished from the wildcat concerns.

In East Tennessee, the counties where the revenue officers had most trouble with the illicit distillers were Campbell, Claiborne, Union, Anderson, Hancock, Grainger, Greene, Cocke, Hawkins, Carter, Johnson, Bradley, and Polk. Comparatively little illicit distilling was carried out in West Tennessee, the nature of the country's topography not being favorable for moonshine production. Resistance to revenue agents was stiff in all eight collection districts.[4]

In 1873, a raid on wildcat distilleries in East Tennessee resulted in the destruction of twenty stills, 20,000 gallons of beer, 250 gallons of singlings and 100 barrels of unbonded whisky. In the two months preceding in the Second Revenue Collection District, a total of twenty-four distilleries and four stills had been destroyed according the *Knoxville Tribune*. The Third Revenue District of Tennessee underwent a three-week raid in Overton, Fentress, and Putnam counties in which revenuers destroyed twenty-five stills, 18 gallons of whisky, 300 gallons of singlings, large quantities of corn and mash, and jugs. They even eight hogs were captured. The value of all the moonshine and paraphernalia involved in the raids was determined to be nearly $60,000. Additionally, several thousand dollars of other unrelated property was destroyed.[5]

The Federal government followed a strong-arm policy to prosecute illicit distillers and destroy their stills. A report in July 1878 to the Office of Internal Revenue in Washington demonstrated that save for the Fifth District the policy was working. A reign of terror existed in Tennessee. A deputy collector had killed a moonshiner in self-defense and had been indicted for murder. The local population was enraged. Nevertheless, the occurrence "had the effect to render the arrest of persons more hazardous and has encouraged the violators of law to open resistance, as they are given to understand that the state courts will protect them." The Eighth District of Tennessee manifested a slightly lower degree of armed resistance to paying the excise tax. Chief Internal Revenue Collector W. M. Woodcock was determined to rid Putnam and Overton counties of illicit distillers.[6]

Commissioner of the Internal Revenue Service in Washington, D.C., Green B. Raum had ordered collectors to reinforce the beleaguered revenue agents in Overton and Putnam Counties by an additional force of forty additional men each, "to make it so hot for the moonshiners to compel them to surrender." Large bodies of deputy collectors were required to force compliance with the law. That expectation was bolstered by a statement from a group of Putnam County "leading citizens" who wrote to Chief Collector Woodcock expressing confidence that most of the moonshiners would cease distillation efforts, surrender to authorities, in return for the payment of a reasonable fine *in lieu* of incarceration. The compromise, it was believed, would most likely be accepted. Commissioner Raum was confident that by following a zero tolerance policy "all illicit whisky distilling will cease in Tennessee before thirty days expire."[7] His confidence was unwarranted, however, as events in Overton County would shortly demonstrate.

Moonshining on the Cumberland Plateau was most prevalent in Overton and Putnam Counties. While hunting for moonshine stills in Overton County on August 23, 1878, tax collectors were attacked by the "Campbell Morgan's band [and were] under heavy fire for forty-five minutes." Finding themselves outmaneuvered and nearly out of ammunition, the revenuers retreated to adjacent Putnam County. The first action of what would be dubbed the "Second Battle of Waterloo" had been fought.

Revenue agents regrouped and returned to Overton County the next day where some 200 moonshiners had surrounded revenue collectors at the James Peek residence at Waterloo Falls, 9 miles north of Cookeville on the Roaring River. The agents ended up holed up in Peek's two-story log house. It was "one of the most determined, bloody and fierce attacks ... ever known in the history of the internal revenue matters of this State, or, perhaps, in the United States." Firing was kept up all day on both sides from August 24–25. According to the official report by the leader of the revenue raiders, Collector S. D. Mather:

> About sundown [August 24] it seemed as though there were a thousand men around us, from the sound of the bugles, shouting and firing, many of the balls penetrating the house, and we prepared ourselves to resist a charge. The whole night was pandemonium itself, and Sunday morning dawned, with men in sight in every direction ... the roads had been barricaded by high fences with large poles on top, and the blockade was complete. Firing was kept up regular [*sic*] about every ten minutes...

As the fight continued, according to the moonshiners' leader, Campbell Morgan, "citizens in the neighborhood brought us plenty of wildcat whisky, and bacon, and eggs and biscuits" in a show of support for the moonshiner's siege. It was not so much that the collectors were enforcing the law that enraged the mountaineers, but more the "abuse of innocent men" by the revenue agents. Finally a delegation of citizens from nearby Livingston and Cookeville arrived and arranged a truce. Morgan suggested that the siege would be lifted "if we could petition the President and Federal Court to pardon all their offenses up to date [and] they would let us out." These terms were rejected, and Morgan was told by the beleaguered collection agents that they "had plenty of ammunition and help was coming." Campbell was certain that one of the revenue agents, James Davis, had a personal vendetta against him, but that if his safety could be guaranteed he would surrender, give bond, and the battle could end. This was acceptable: Morgan "and his men, some sixty or seventy, soon came out of their stations and filed past, and went their way. They looked like determined men, and we know to our sorrow that they can fight.... The second battle of Waterloo was over."

The lesson Woodcock learned was that granting amnesty to moonshiners would be a much better way to end illicit distilling. For all his confidence about a policy of amnesty after the fight at Waterloo Falls, however, Woodcock admitted in October 1878 that "Jackson County is apparently invincible. My raiders can march through the county and receive fire of the enemy from every hilltop, and return fire, but the nature of the ground is such that no arrests can be made." There was still resistance to Federal authority, even though I.R.S. Commissioner Raum boasted the amnesty program in Tennessee had "forgiven some three thousand moonshiners who pled guilty to illicit distilling and received amnesty." Those who did not seek an official pardon would be hunted "to the earth" and arrested and their stills destroyed. By 1881 Raum stated that the general result of this carrot-and-stick approach was "most gratifying."[8]

Part of the problem stemmed from the forbidden nature of moonshining. Few cared to engage in it when distilling was legal. By the 1880s, the romance of the business as well as the opportunity to profit enticed many to take up illicit distilling. Additionally, a standard argument in its favor was the notion that moonshining was an activity directed against a tyrannical government's censure of a legitimate use of personal resources. Such ideas gave rise to the increase of moonshining. Conversely, no one doubted the right of the government to raise revenue by imposing an excise tax on beer and spirits. Legitimate tax-paying distilleries were an accepted fact as was the knowledge that moonshining undercut the profit margins of legitimate distilleries.

The amnesty program was the best remedy to stop moonshining. As one editorial concluded, it "will in the future array society on the side of those who will defy the law upon the others."

One report explained that the "moonshiners ... of the Tennessee mountains are a rough set of people, but not so bad as they are represented to be, particularly in northern newspapers. True, they are constantly breaking the internal revenue laws, but not always with the spirit of outlaw. They don't make whisky because the United States Government says they shall not. They make it because they want it to drink." Moreover, "they produce their own corn, peaches and apples and all the District Judges, Attorney-Generals [sic] Grand Juries, Commissioners, and Deputy Marshals in the country can never convince them by argument, [or] imprisonment ... that they have no right to turn their fruit or corn into brandy or whisky if they see fit to do so..."[9]

In a novel, *Sons of Vengeance: A Tale of the Cumberland Highlands*, (1901) this notion is reinforced in a soliloquy following the unprecedented and illusory rescue of a revenue agent from an impromptu firing squad by the elder-most member of a remote Cumberland mountain community, Uncle Havre. His answer to the revenuer's inquiry as to why he would not quit making moonshine is a superb epitome of the moonshiners' motivation for distilling illegal whisky:

I don't think it's wrong ... we plants the corn an' ploughs it, and' when we pulls it we puts in in our cribs, it's 'ourn, and no gover'ment nor anythin' nor anybody else hez a right tuh one grain of it.

We kin grin' it fer bred ur feed it to pork, ur gin it fer feed fer our horses an' cattle, an' no gover'men hez anythin' tuh say ur do about it, but if we makes a mash o' it, an' runs it throough a crooked pipe and geets the spirits out o' it and then drinks a drap our o' it ur gives some on it tu a frien, ur even hev it in our house, 'ithout usin' on it, y'u comes down on us an' burns an' breaks up our thin's en' drags us off from home in chains, and puts us in jail, sometimes for years.

We haint don' nothin' mean, we just doin' whut we heve a right to, an' it's nobody's concern but 'ourn. Let the gover'ment we fought and shed our blood fer let us 'lone, and we'll tend tuh our own business.[10]

Moonshine stills were kept in secret and remote areas of the wilderness of the mountains. It was a necessity to hide their stills in select locations in the most inaccessible mountainous environs. A newspaper report, Nashville *Daily American*, March 6, 1879, held that stills were generally located in:

A deep ravine far from any human habitation or public road is generally selected. A small hut is built, which is deftly covered with brush. The moonshiner carries his grain, fruit and wood on his back. His work is done at night, and in the day time he sleeps and watches by turns. He keeps a rifle and a brace of revolvers in the house, and ... his wife or daughter can use them with as much skill as he can. If a stranger appears in the neighborhood he is closely watched and even more closely questioned.... Nine chances out of ten the poor stranger finds it impossible to find a night's lodging or a meal within five miles of the distillery. If he is so fortunate as to find a place to lay his head he will be entertained by the female portion of the household. The men folks are always scarce about that time, and ... the hospitality of the mountaineer is something wonderful to behold. In the days before revenue officers and Deputy Marshals, a stranger traveling in the mountains was received with open arms and it was considered a great breach of duty to charge a man for a night's lodging. But the relentless and continued war on the mountaineers has made them distrustful and caused them to seal their humble cottages against the intruder whatever his business may be. The watch for the Deputy Marshal [is] like the chicken for the hawk.

The wildcatter was more an illiterate character and less an outlaw. He was an ordinary individual, uneducated but "naturally shrewd and intelligent." The U.S. District Court for East Tennessee met in Knoxville in January and July. Sometimes there were as many as 300 to 500 moonshine cases on the docket, with an average of three witnesses per case. The defendants came from all parts of East Tennessee and are required to answer all kinds of charges from "chuckin'" up a fire under moonshine still to selling a barrel of illicit whisky. Some of the charges were of an insignificant nature and were made as a result of malice of insistence of a deputy marshal in order to increase their fees. Often court was held in the dead of winter and many of the witnesses were compelled to travel on foot in thinly clad shoes 60 or 75 miles over frozen terrain. Many witnesses were women or half-grown boys, who, when they arrived at the court's venue were forced to seek shelter in the streets or lounge in the halls of the government buildings until they received their *per diem* fees, while some were unable to obtain these for a week or ten days. As an index of the success of the amnesty program, by early April 1879, it was reported that some 188 moonshiners had accepted amnesty agreeing to quit illicit distilling at the U.S. Circuit Court in Nashville, while hundreds of others waited in and out of the courthouse to seek a pardon.[11]

In April, 1886, a mass trial of over 100 moonshiners was held in Nashville. Many popular myths about the habits and character of illicit distillers were aired, and sensational misrepresentations were corrected during the proceedings. Additionally, moonshiners were shown not to be the bloodthirsty barbarians as newspaper reports characterized them. Many traveled a hundred miles on foot to redeem their pledge to cease moonshining once they accepted amnesty. Only a few were given small fines, while many penalties were suspended; only a few were actually sentenced to jail. They made no more than 30 gallons of whisky a year. According to one report: "There is no class of men on top of the earth who are more slandered than what are termed 'moonshiners.'" The Nashville *Daily American*, of February 15, 1878, claimed:

> [The average moonshiner may have been] poor and ignorant of the ways of the world.... But he is not bloodthirsty. It is easy ... to account for the formation of this erroneous idea. In the last twenty years many revenue officers have been killed in this State by moonshiners, but the danger to officers is rapidly on the decrease. Directly after the minions of the Government went into the midst of the moonshiners and severely oppressed them [this was shown to be true]. Outrages were perpetrated by these "carpet baggers" ... which incensed the inhabitants to bloodshed. Many of the residents of the localities visited were ex-Confederate soldiers, and the wrongs done them under ... enforcement of the revenue law excited them to fight the officers. With the improvement of services in later years conflicts ... have become fewer and fewer, and it is seldom ... that any serious difficulty occurs.

In addition wildcatters were beginning to understand the law better, and so were more willing to obey it. When found in violation of it they quietly agreed to the penalty. "The proportion of moonshiners who resist the officers of the law to those who do not ... is one to twenty, but unfortunately for the remaining nineteen the deeds of the one are considered the deeds of all." According to the Nashville *Daily American* of March 6, 1879, one deputy collector put it this way:

> The trouble is this: The moonshiners believe that they have the right to make whisky and, liking it, they make it. The say that they raise the corn and, therefore, [they question] why might they not convert it into whisky ... or pay a license to do so ... they are coming to know the law better, to realize their obligations to

the Federal Government, and not only is less "wildcat" ... whisky being made, but antagonisms to the officers is rapidly decreasing. The moonshiner is a hardy son of toil, industrious, economical by nature and necessity and brave and generous. They think they have the right to be moonshiners.... They are true to each other, for they are a world to themselves. There is a code of honor among them, too.... The officers realize full well that when a moonshiner makes a promise, he keeps it. Such is the general character of the moonshiner.

Most of the accused that in Nashville that April day were, according to the sheriff of Jackson County (erstwhile leader of the insurgents during the Battle at Waterloo Falls in 1878), were mostly "men brought here not thinking about the law when he bought a pint of illegal liquor.... There's more schools and Sunday schools in the country, and education is doing as much as the law. Wildcat distilling is about playin' out anyway."[11]

Moonshining activity have been diminished, but it was not completely eradicated. There were many who would defy the revenue law. Reports of excellent corn harvests in the mountainous regions of Districts One and Two predicted an uptick in moonshining at summer's end 1879. Still, moonshiners were not accepting amnesty *en masse*. A sweep of moonshine stills from November 9, 1877 to June 29, 1878, through Putnam, Hickman, White, Sumner, Grundy, Macon, De Kalb, Lawrence, Wayne, Van Buren, Hardin, Jackson, Rutherford, and Overton Counties resulted in the destruction of ninety-two distilleries, with an estimated worth of $22,832. The last raid in Putnam County resulted in the seizure of 100 gallons of moonshine whisky. Continued raids were made in Putnam, Fentress, White, Overton, Clay, and Macon Counties from February to March 1879, White and Van Buren Counties in April 1879. While many erstwhile moonshiners had accepted amnesty, it was estimated that fully 20 percent of pardoned moonshiners were once again distilling illegal whisky in the wildcat sections. The legal stills established by Chief Collector W. M. Woodcock were doing well, although a "whisky team" from Cincinnati had been discovered in Chattanooga selling unstamped whisky on the Cincinnati-Southern Railway near Rhea Springs. This, however, was a relatively minor matter considering the overall negative effect amnesty had produced in the reduction of illegal distilling in Hamilton County and indeed to a wide extent in East Tennessee.[12]

Further hostilities toward revenue collectors were made evident in reports of a local Polk County law enforcement officer who had been shot and killed as he attempted to arrest moonshiners in early August 1878. An account from Grainger County, told of a deputy U.S. marshal being fired upon during a raid by wildcat distillers; even though some forty shots had been fired, no one was hurt.[13] But the death of an agent during a raid in Blount County on August 9 indicated that the practice was both a continuing phenomenon and one with deadly consequences for revenue collectors.[14] The perpetrator was Hutsel ("Hut") Amarine, an infamous wildcat distiller and outlaw of Blount County. In a rare interview with a reporter from the *Chicago Times,* as cited in the Nashville *Daily American* of August 31, 1878, Hut, was presented "as 'mild-mannered' a 'man as ever cut a throat or scuttled a ship,' and a stranger would be prepossessed in his favor by his appearance." Hut expressed his opinion that the revenue officers were often out of bounds when doing their duty, treating the families of moonshiners roughly and conducted the their raids "more with the object of making money than for the suppression of violations of law—that they were in many instances men guilty not only of making illicit whisky, but of far worse crimes."[15] The Chicago *Tribune* account continued:

> He did not object of an officer doing his duty, but [not when] his wife and children's lives had been threatened and pistols put to their heads to induce them to tell where he was.... Other families had been insulted in a similar manner on diverse occasions. Some of these fellows who had probably made a raid frequently quartered themselves on the unwilling hospitality of the people of the mountain section without paying for anything. In fact, he knew of but one officer who had paid his bills—was a good officer, and always had conducted himself as a gentleman should. But the Blount county revenue officials were ... very bad men.

According to the *Times* reporter: "Most of the illicit distillers are stanch Republicans and having served in the Federal army ... think that having saved the government it has no right to interfere with them while robbing it." Hut had in the past kept a "supply of the dew at his house, a fact which the revenue officers were aware of, and [when they] made a raid and captured a small keg, which they emptied in the yard, reserving a bucketful for their own use; but while one of them had the vessel up to his lips, Mrs. Amarine tipped it up, spilling the fiery contents in the still-smasher's face, completely drenching him, and depriving them of a free treat." Hut Amarine was constantly on the run and could not be captured by Federal agents. According to the Chicago *Tribune* reporter:

> Wildly exaggerated stories of his prowess, hair-breadth escapes, and proverbial daring, were recounted with enthusiasm by those who know him, and they were widely believed. He was a popular folk-hero in Blount County legerdemain. He was said to be weighted down with weapons and surrounded by desperadoes when he disappeared from home, and that his house was a small fortress, with the walls crenellated for musketry.... These stories inspire a wholesome dread in the minds of many, and it would require a very brave officer to tackle the veteran distiller.

The constant harassment led Hut to leave his Blount County home for Texas, but he returned shortly thereafter.[15] Still, Hut continued his distilling and was persistently tracked by determined revenuers. He was apprehended in early February, 1879.[16] His capture was accomplished after a serious gunfight in which he killed a collector, James Cooper. He was tried and convicted of the murder and sentenced to twenty-two years in the penitentiary.[17] But Hut escaped from his holding cell in Knoxville on November 10, 1879, and made his way to Texas where he was recaptured and sequestered in the penitentiary. He escaped from the penitentiary also and was captured and returned to the penitentiary where served his sentence.[18]

While moonshining was largely a vocation dominated by men, there were two notable examples of women engaging in the practice, Mollie Miller of Polk County and Mahala Mullins who lived on Walden's Ridge in Hancock County. Each was notorious in her own right.

Mollie Miller, "the woman moonshiner of Polk County," died in June 1894 in her home in the mountains. Her operations were at one time very extensive, and she ran a gang that was involved in "more bloody fights with revenue officers than any other organized in the south." She first became known in the mountains of Sevier County, where her moonshining father taught her how to distill alcohol in the 1870s. Her first encounter with revenue agents was in Sevier County when collectors raided her father's operation, its location having been made known by an informer. In an almost inaccessible gorge the officers encountered the moonshiners. A bloody fight followed, and three of the federal agents were killed while the remaining force retreated. The officers noted that there was a young girl in the moonshiner's band, and it was believed she was responsible for the killing of one of the three. In another raid, her father was killed and all his associates captured. Soon thereafter, revenue officers received a rude wooden coffin containing the remains of the man who had informed upon the Miller gang. "There was nothing to indicate from whom it came, and the box must have been carried by wagon and left at the marshal's house. It was soon established that Mollie was behind the grisly delivery, but she was not to be found."

In a few months, Polk County, which had a reputation for furnishing illicit whisky, became the headquarters of the moonshiners "throughout east Tennessee, and raid followed raid until there was scarcely a cave on the Hiawassee River that had not been the scene of some bloody fight between the moonshiners and the revenue men." It was soon discovered Mollie was the leader of the gang; she had been arrested once but not convicted. After the Knoxville Southern railroad was constructed the isolated areas of Polk County became easier to access, and the gang was broken up. Mollie retired to a little farm, where she remained undisturbed. It was commonly believed she had personally killed three revenue agents and five informers, while her gang was responsible for the death of several others, but it was never proven. She died without ever having been prosecuted for murder or moonshining.[19]

Described as one of the mysterious race of Melungeons in the highlands of East Tennessee, Mahala Mullins was distinctive in that she was said to have weighed 400 to 600 pounds, and did her distilling at her cabin on Walden Ridge in Hancock County. She supplied moonshine to anyone who could climb up the rocky path to her cabin. Her specialty was apple and peach brandy. She made no attempt to hide her moonshining operation, virtually gaining immunity from arrest because of her tremendous girth. One revenue agent declared that she "was catchable but not fetchable." She could not walk, stand, or lie down, but "sits on her bed day and night…. Beside her is a cask of whiskey on which stand tin cups and measures. The faucet is at her hand that she may conveniently dispense liquor to all who want it."[20] When asked why she distilled illegal whisky she replied matter-of-factly "It's the only way I can make a livin'." She could see no evil of it. The sentiment of the mountaineers made it "innocent, the notoriety makes it pleasant, and the money makes it profitable…"[21]

One unique example of brazen lawlessness by moonshiners took place in Celina, in October 1895. Sam Smith, from just above the Kentucky–Tennessee state line, had been arrested for wildcatting in Tennessee. He was released after making bond and was to go on trial in Celina, Clay County, Tennessee, in late October. Smith lived "over in the edge of the State of Kentucky, among ... wildcatters and has rambled, drank whisky and associated with them all his life." Known as a domineering man, he was "always threatening the revenue officers with a hundred different deaths." It was rumored a mob of his Kentucky moonshining associates would ride to Celina on the day of his trial "and sweep not only the revenue officers, but all who might assist them, off the face of the earth."

Smith appeared on the appointed day, escorted by twenty of "the most notorious wildcatters ... heavily armed with Colt's pistols, [who] came pouring into the town of Celina." The horde demanded that Smith be set free without having a trial, an ultimatum that was refused by law enforcement. The deputy marshal was then surrounded by the mob, while Smith drew "a long bladed dirk knife ... and with wild curses, threatened to stab [the Marshal]...to death instantly, the whole mob drawing their heavy pistols. It looked as though death was knocking at [the Deputy's] door." Into the breach jumped the Clay County deputy sheriff "a brave man ... and demanded the peace." Smith then sprang forward and fired his pistol, shooting the sheriff in the hip, fatally wounding him.

Soon the Clay County sheriff arrived with a number of deputies, but "the mob at once whirled upon them, with pistols drawn" and held the sheriff and deputies at bay until Smith could get to his horse, "and the whole mob ... went sailing out of town on swift horses, with pistols in hand, and made their way back to Kentucky."[22]

The most legendary revenue collector in nineteenth-century Tennessee was Captain James M. Davis. A Confederate scout during the Civil War, Davis was noted for his remarkable ability in tracking lawbreakers. According to one source, "he could follow a trail like an Indian..." He was involved in two deadly altercations with moonshiners. In each, he killed a wildcat distiller. In one instance, according to the *Nashville American*, December 22, 1895, he killed a moonshiner named Hampton, near Estelle Springs:

> This fight occurred partly in Hampton's house, and was continued out of the house and around a chimney. Here they fired almost simultaneously, Davis shooting Hampton in the breast, and Hampton filling Davis' gum coat which was folded and tied over his shoulder, with buckshot. Hampton attempted to club Davis with his gun, which was caught by Davis. Seeing that he had mortally wounded Hampton, Davis eased him to the ground, and, with the help of another man, carried him into the house. One of the [buck] shot from Hampton's gun struck Davis in the cheek, tearing up the skin.

In the second affair, Davis shot and killed a prisoner near Tracy City in Grundy County, while taking him to jail on charges of illicit distilling. After a lengthy and sensational trial, he was exonerated, the death having been determined to have taken place in the course of duty.

Davis was in the thick of the Waterloo Falls battle, and was later wounded by rifle fire and nearly beaten to death during a raid in 1880 during a raid in Putnam County. It was in Warren County that Davis met his own Waterloo on March 13, 1882. He was shot and killed in an ambush by eight to ten malcontents in the McMinnville environs of Warren County. "His assailants had concealed themselves behind an entrenchment ten feet from the road and about thirty feet long, make of logs and cordwood and covered with fresh-cut cedar and were armed with shot guns and pistols.... All of Davis' brains were shot out, and there were over thirty bullet holes in his body." Another account told how the wounded Davis attempted to return fire when "one of the assassins stepped up ... and shot the whole top of his head off with a shot gun. He was interred in the family cemetery in Fayetteville the next day." Those responsible for the act were never discovered. In his career he had arrested nearly 3,000 wildcatters and destroyed over 500 stills, a tally that most certainly made for deadly enemies.[23]

Wildcat distilling was also a problem in Western Tennessee. A report on a raid in 1881 indicated a successful undertaking in Lawrence, Giles, Wayne, Hardin, Perry, and Decatur Counties, including the destruction of 4,500 gallons of beer, numerous stills, and the arrest of multiple moonshiners principally in Hardin County.[24]

While Hardin County was preeminent in the history of moonshining in late nineteenth-century West Tennessee, it was not the only venue for wildcat distilling and violence. For example, a report in *The New York Times* told how a man had "mysteriously disappeared" after unthinkingly stating he was a detective while in the presence of moonshiners. Henderson County wildcatters were suspected. The deputy collector for the I.R.S. Region urged "the taking of immediate steps to put a stop to the illicit distilling business, as the present force is inadequate to cope with the men who ... murder officials who are sent in search of them." The report ended with the statement that "Tennessee has been the scene of many battles between revenue men and moonshiners, and a repetition of the war is regarded as certain."[25]

The example of Hardin County wildcat distilling was unique not just because it took place in West Tennessee, but also because of the violence it characterized. Revenue collection there took on a murderous aspect in which one wildcatter, Ed Thomas, was killed after opening fire on officers who had captured his still. It was more than a story of the death of one moonshiner, and one that included jealousy and deceit, treachery and murder, revenge and outlawry all combined. Hardin County is one of the southern border counties, touching Mississippi, and is divided by the Tennessee River. The county's Ninth Civil District, known as the Red Sulphur Springs neighborhood, lay on the west side of the Tennessee River. Chambers Creek forms the western and northern boundaries, while Yellow Creek was the southern boundary. The country between these creeks is rugged and then covered with a growth of small pines. There are high hills, "deep ravines and shady glens, where sparkling streams gush forth and by tortuous course find their way to the Tennessee River." The district was an ideal one for moonshiners, and for nearly thirty years after the Civil War it was their favorite location. Revenue raids were checked until the 1880s because the wildcatters were so well organized that revenue agents were unable to find a trustworthy guide into the Red Sulphur Springs territory. Moreover, it had become too dangerous for traveling business men who knew to stay out of the district as the moonshiners always regarded strangers with skepticism.

In the spring of 1885, for example, State Senator Simms, while going through the country on business, was captured by a party of wildcatters who suspected him of being a revenue officer and intended to lynch him. He paid one of them $10 to find a witness in the nearest town to identify him. He was released, with a warning to never return or face death.

The making of moonshine whisky in the Ninth District had been a leading occupation since the end of the Civil War. Two cousins, Gus and Ed Thomas, were moonshiners, following in their ancestors' footsteps. Gus's and Ed's fathers were notorious Confederate bushwhackers during the war. Directly after the hostilities ended, Ed's father killed a man in his own still-house for an insult to his wife. This crime necessitated his departure from Tennessee, and he moved to the Indian Territory (i.e. Oklahoma), taking Ed with him. Gus Thomas' father was later killed in a quarrel, and Ed's father later was murdered in a fight. The Thomas boys were legitimate products of the backwoods. "They tread the ground like a cat and never go without a rifle, and intuitively throw it to their shoulders upon the slightest noise."

George Davis, then serving a four-year sentence at Columbus, Ohio, for illicit distilling was called the "king of the Hardin County moonshiners," the leader of the notorious "Davis Gang." He was described as a bright, fearless man, of sharp native intelligence, "easy in manners and fairly well educated." He made moonshine, but refused to sell whisky on Sunday or to a minor, and ironically, he was a nephalist. Davis was feared and respected. He exercised great influence over the Thomas boys, who became Davis Gang members, and they all stuck together to prevent successful revenuer raids into their section of the country. A deputy U.S. marshal was sent into the district with warrants for the arrest of moonshiners. His task was interrupted by men armed with shotguns, who convinced him turn around and swear never to return. He remained true to his promise.

In November 1891, a moonshine raid was made into the Red Sulphur Springs District and captured a still. Capt. A. A. Anderson, recently assistant doorkeeper of the National House of Representatives, was along on this raid. After the still was discovered the officers hid and waited for the wildcatters to arrive. The first moonshiner appeared and was immediately arrested. Anderson requested the privilege of capturing the next man by himself, and he entered the still-house and waited, concealed in the meal box, wrapping himself in empty grain sacks. A newspaper account from the Nashville *American* of December 22, 1895 had it that:

> [He soon] became very comfortable and fell asleep. Soon a moonshiner came down the ravine with a two-bushel sack of malt on his shoulder. Entering the still-house with a great grunt of relief, he tossed the sack into the meal box. It struck Anderson on the head he raised an outcry. The moonshiner, thinking it was his partner, removed the sack, but when Anderson arose with a six-shooter in his hand he fled precipitately, and it as necessary for one of the men outside to chase him over a hundred yards before finally capturing him.

However, the first significant raid made into Hardin County was in June 1893, when U.S. Marshal Brown, of Memphis, led a party into the Red Sulphur Springs District. They first went to Gus Thomas' house, and, finding him asleep, arrested him. He was then wanted only for selling moonshine. While Gus was dressing he "whispered to his wife to send his teen-aged brother Jesse, then about 13 years old, to warn George Davis." When the posse reached Davis' home, they were greeted by four men standing on the porch with rifles in their hands. When ordered to surrender they retreated into the house and immediately opened fire. Deputy Marshal Garner was killed and Marshal Brown was wounded, the posse being compelled to beat a retreat. Later, in June 1894, Revenue Agent Clark and General Deputy Collector Rutledge led another raid into the country and captured Gus Thomas and his brothers, Bob and Dick, but were unable to locate the stills, so no arrests were made.

George Davis was in the meantime leading a duplicitous life. He continued his illicit distilling operation, convincing revenue officers he was not engaged in the business. His aim was to clear himself of suspicion that he had murdered Deputy Marshal Garner. Gus Thomas, in the meantime, was perceptive enough to dodge all serious charges, and had decided never to surrender. Ed Thomas returned from the Indian Territory in October 1894, to escape prosecution for several murders there.

On New Year's Day 1895, Gus and Ed Thomas attended a party at the Red Sulphur Springs Hotel. A Kentucky lumberman stopped there overnight, and was eyed with suspicion by the Thomas boys, who picked a fight with him and shot him through the leg. Fearful that he would be killed, the lumberman stumbled to the stable, hitched his horse to his buggy when Gus arrived with a shotgun "and blew the whole top of his head off." They then led the horse nearly a mile across the Mississippi line and hitched him. The body was robbed and left, being found by a mail rider the next morning. A reward of $1,000 was offered for the arrest and conviction of the murderers.

This egregious crime attracted considerable attention. George Davis saw an opportunity of removing Gus whom he could no longer control and simultaneously succeed in distracting attention from himself in connection with the killing of Deputy Marshal Garner. He eventually agreed with the Hardin County sheriff to betray Gus and assist in his capture. The Thomas cousins suspected Davis' intentions, and they split up and went into hiding.

In the meantime, the revenue men were endeavoring to locate the Thomas boys' stills. The sheriff hired a guide to go into the Red Sulphur Springs district and find them. This guide made a trip in company with Deputy Marshal Hawkins, who posed as a lumberman. Gus and Ed happened to meet them and actually arrested them. Hawkins negotiated his release. The Thomas boys decided to try the guide on a charge of stealing hogs. After a lengthy trial, conducted before a sympathetic district Magistrate; the guide was found guilty and bound over to jail in Savannah. He stayed incarcerated for two months until revenue officers succeeded in securing his release.

Another foray was made into the moonshining Ninth District in February 1895. Led by General Deputy Collector Rutledge, Deputy Collector Trice, and Commissioner Stump the party had a 40-mile ride through a snowstorm and reached Gus and Ed Thomas' house about three o'clock in the morning, almost frozen. They surrounded the house demanding admission, but were rebuffed. When they forced the door open, they found that the two men had escaped through a trap door in the floor and fled, firing back as they ran. The revenue party did capture a still belonging to the neighboring "Poindexter Boys," also members of the Davis Gang. The buggy in which the party traveled broke down about 10 miles from Selmer, and it was destroyed.

There was another raid in September 1895. Some weeks before the raid Gus Thomas, who learned of George Davis' betrayal, wrote to the revenue officers that

Davis, while posing as a changed man, was making wildcat whisky all the time. Gus proposed to lead the way to Davis' still house if he would be granted amnesty. The officers agreed. Thomas said to the officers: "I hate like h—l [sic] to do this. He has always been a good friend, but he turned traitor on me, and I'll cut down him if I can." He led them to Davis' still and immediately vamoosed. Davis was successfully captured and his still destroyed. He suspected Gus was the turncoat. In November, Davis was tried at Jackson and did not contest the moonshining charges, receiving a four-year sentence for illicit distilling. There are no witnesses against him in connection with the killing of Deputy Marshal Garner. Jesse Thomas, the boy who acted as messenger, was the only witness who could testify against Davis, but he was accidently killed in a suspicious hunting accident in Arkansas, where he was visiting one of Davis' kin.

In an act of revenge, Davis' brother-in-law, John Kennedy, directed the revenue officers to the Thomas boys' stills. Both were destroyed. Ed Thomas was killed by the officers just as he was attempting to shoot them. Gus Thomas would probably have met the same fate had he not been warned by the shot while eating his breakfast. He quickly took to the woods evading capture. Gus promptly killed John Kennedy the next morning as the old man was working at his wood-pile.

Gus was still at large in the Red Sulphur Springs District. One witness some days after the Kennedy murder quoted him as saying that he expected to live but a short time anyhow, and he would remain at home and kill as many of his enemies as possible before he died. The affair now amounted to a feud between Davis' friends on one side and Thomas' kin on the other. Perhaps the feud eventually "would lead to break up the moonshine district and eliminate the vilest men on each side."[26]

Gus Thomas, "the most desperate and murderous moonshiner in Tennessee" was captured on January 30, 1896 and imprisoned in Savannah. Three of his "pals" were likewise taken prisoner, including his brother, Dick. "The great effect will be the breaking up of the most desperate [gang of] outlaws in the State and making the lives of officers more safe in that mountainous [sic] district."[27] Gus was incarcerated in the state penitentiary, and save for an abortive escape attempt, served a life sentence for murder of a federal agent.[28] George Davis was convicted of conspiracy and was sentenced to fifteen years at the state penitentiary in Nashville in June 1901. Moonshining in the Red Sulphur Springs District had reached its end.[29]

Moonshining did not cease with the turning of the twentieth century. For all intents and purposes, the nineteenth-century history of the practice was but a precedent for the continuation of illicit distilling in the twentieth century, when it was fueled by the prohibition resulting from the 19th Amendment and the Volstead Act. Wildcatting was also an expression of cultural continuity in the moonshine districts in Tennessee. A raid in 1901 in Lawrence County resulted in the destruction of large still, while a shootout with revenue agents took place in Fentress and Putnam counties in the same year. It was announced by the Internal Revenue Department in 1904 that despite its popular reputation for its production, Tennessee was no longer the leader in the production of moonshine. However, wildcatting continued, for example in Sevier County in 1910.

A trial of twenty-eight moonshiners was held in Jackson in 1916 and by 1921 an increase in the number of revenue agents was inaugurated in the Volunteer State to continue the suppression of increased illicit distilling in Tennessee. An indication of the persistence of moonshining in the state was demonstrated in the story of Reverend Joseph R. Smith in Sewanee. He plead guilty to charges of making illegal whisky in the Federal Court in 1912. For several months, Smith had been the pastor at three small churches. In the smokehouse a few yards from the parsonage, revenue agents found a still. They destroyed it along with nearly 100 gallons of illicit alcohol. Smith declared that he did not know it was against the law to make moonshine, yet he professed he knew it was wrong to drink it. He had never sold any, but did give some to a few of his parishioners "for medicinal purposes." In 1931, the trial of a hoary "gray bearded mountaineer" took place in Anderson County. After he was found not guilty of running a moonshine still, "the spirit of celebration came over him and in front of the jury of his peers he took a swig of liquor from a pint bottle." Ever alert, the chief court officer snatched the bottle from his hands and placed him in custody. The court held him under a $2,000 bond for illegal possession of alcohol.[30] Today, an explosion of legal whisky is sold under various names, which include the word "moonshine" or "white lightning" in their brand, conjuring up nostalgic romanticism for a bygone era in Tennessee history.[31] The growth and sale of marijuana is on the increase and is rapidly replacing moonshine in twenty-first-century Tennessee as the illegal drug of choice.

7

Lynching in Tennessee's Past

To best gain an understanding of lynching, it is necessary to define it. It is the extra-legal and premeditated killing of one or more individuals by a group of assailants. It is most often used to characterize executions by a mob in order to punish an alleged transgressor or to intimidate a group. In Tennessee, and in the totality of American history, the intimidated group and victims have in the main rightfully been characterized as African American. While this is not comprehensively true in the case of Tennessee, minor variances do not absolve the crime of murder overwhelmingly committed against black men by white men. Lynching was often based in Jim Crow notions of racial superiority, ersatz concepts about black sexuality and a variety of other purported provocations. In popular understanding lynching is generally associated exclusively with the illegal hanging of black men; however, there were white victims as well. Whatever the causes of the lynchings, they must be categorized as alleged crimes, as the cases were neither proven in a court of law, nor was death sentencing a result of a jury trial. Lynching itself was the crime.

According to the Equal Justice Initiative: "Lynching created a fearful environment where racial subordination and segregation was maintained ... for decades. Most critically, lynching reinforced a legacy of racial inequality..."[1] In Tennessee, as elsewhere in the old South, the history of terrorism and subordination of African Americans followed the Civil War and was radically enforced by a nearly ritualistic practice of lynching.

Some characterizations sequester lynching into a variety known as "terror lynchings," defined as murders, carried out with impunity, sometimes in broad daylight, often "on the courthouse lawn." These lynchings were not "frontier justice," because they generally took place in communities where there was a functioning criminal justice system that was deemed "too good" for African Americans. Terror lynchings were horrific acts of violence whose perpetrators were never held accountable. Some lynchings may be termed public spectacle lynching as they were attended by the entire white community and conducted as celebratory acts of racial control and domination.[2] It is not going too far, however, to say that all lynchings were terror lynchings, especially from the point of view of the victim and the black community they successfully intimidated. To call them terror lynchings is to belabor the atrocity they represented; in a macabre sense, to gild the lily.

Lynching reinforced existing racist attitudes, made fiat by the Tennessee General Assembly.[3] From 1866 to 1901, thirteen laws and one amendment to the Tennessee State Constitution made segregation an ironclad policy prohibiting integration in public schools, the criminalization of intermarriage between "white persons and Negroes, or descendants of Negro ancestors to the third generation" (a state constitutional amendment); while a statue reinforced the amendment making miscegenation a felony punishable by imprisonment from one to five years. In addition, hotel keepers, carriers of passengers, and keepers of places of amusement had the right, if not duty, to control access and exclude African Americans, while railroads were required to provide separate cars for black passengers, and later separate but equal facilities for all persons paying first-class rates; and while "all well-behaved persons" were to be admitted to theaters, parks, shows, or other public amusements, with the stipulation that that proprietors had the right to create separate accommodations for whites and blacks.[4] The idea and fact of segregation of the races could not be more officially explicit, as was the unofficial and murderous enforcement of these decrees made manifest by lynching.

The history of lynching must have begun sometime during the antebellum period. Enslaved African Americans may have been lynched by slave patrols, but given that these were not recorded and the fact that slaves were valuable property, it was likely few victims were black in the decades before the Civil War. Additionally, blacks were not then citizens with civil rights. Lynching of whites, appears to offer a countervailing narrative and for all intents and purposes, begins at or before 1821. The date is approximate, but it is documented in the records of the McMinnville County Archives (Warren County) as having occurred "many years ago." The victim's name, race, gender, and alleged crime are unspecified. The next lynching verified by a publication took place in Franklin, Tennessee, in 1821. The white victim, Adkinson (or Adkins), was lynched for murdering his wife.[5] These two events might best be characterized as the result of "frontier justice" as both victims were white. As the Civil War began, Committees of Vigilance groups formed in many cities and counties in Tennessee. These self-appointed vigilante organizations took it upon themselves to root out all so-called disloyal Northerners and northern influences to insure the supremacy of the Confederacy. In early May 1861, two hapless white men, "Morton and Sampson Kennedy," were abducted in Shelby County and summarily lynched by one such group because they were returning to their homes in the North; they were thought to be spies.[6]

During the Civil War, two documented lynchings involving a Confederate soldier and another entangling five East Tennessee Unionists occurred in 1861 and 1863. One in Fayetteville, Lincoln County, of Joseph C. Taylor, a Confederate soldier, who was taken from the jail by a mob and lynched for an unknown offense on October 20, 1861.[7] On January 23, 1863, the lynching by the Confederate Home Guard of Washington County of five unionists who were caught trying to cross into Kentucky to join the Federal Army took place. All victims were white, and the gruesome sight was witnessed by a unionist guide who saw the entire proceeding.[8]

Directly after the defeat of the Confederacy, just before the institution of reconstruction policies in Tennessee, one Rolly Davidson was lynched for an unknown reason in Franklin County in 1865; one Baker, "late of the rebel army," killed the Knox County Circuit Court Clerk in an altercation and was taken from his jail cell by an angry mob and lynched immediately from a tree in the street on September 6, 1865.[9] The fact that these victims of lynching were all whites is explained by the fact that African Americans were considered property, and to lynch a slave would be to deprive the white owner of his chattels. After freedom at the end of the war, this caveat was no longer applicable, but racist attitudes had not changed.

Without a doubt, the first lynchings of formerly enslaved African Americans in Tennessee occurred in Memphis on May 1-3, 1866, in what is known as the Memphis Race Riot. During the Civil War, thousands of slaves left plantations on their own volition and settled in refugee camps in Memphis. Their presence annoyed many whites, particularly the Irish-American community. According to the text of a National Association for the Advancement of Colored People/National Park Service historic marker placed at Army-Navy Park in Memphis:

> On May 1, 2 and 3, 1866, mobs of white men led by law enforcement attacked black people in the areas near South St. (aka Calhoun & G. E. Patterson). By the end of the attack, the mobs had killed an estimated 46 black people; raped several black women; and committed numerous robberies, assaults and arsons. A congressional investigative committee reported that four churches, twelve schools and 91 other dwellings were burned. Although no one was ever prosecuted for this massacre, it became a rallying cry in the battle over the nation's reconstruction following the Civil War. Ultimately, the outrage that followed the massacre helped to ensure the adoption of the 14th Amendment to the United States Constitution.[10]

Some may argue that the number of forty-six killed were not lynched, but indeed they were, keeping in mind the definition of lynching as defined above as "the extra-legal and premeditated killing of one or more individuals by a group of assailants." That the African Americans were killed in a riot is of less importance than the fact that the estimated forty-six were lynched during the racially motivated rampage.

Usually the brutality was limited to one victim, but that was not always the case. In this chapter, the total number of victims per lynching are counted, not just the fact that a lynching occurred at a given date and location. Sometimes, as in the Memphis Race Riot, a lynching took the lives of more than one victim. The multiple murders of sixteen unidentified African Americans in Gibson County, in West Tennessee, in 1874, along with the lynchings associated with the Memphis Race Riot eight years earlier, are examples of such white-on-black brutality. Racial tensions were already high due to the Congressional attempt to pass the so-called "Force Bill" that would protect black voting rights. On August 24, 1874, a large group of African Americans had allegedly shot at two white men near the town of Picketsville, Gibson County. The shots were fired either over a quarrel over a 50-cent debt a white owed to a black after eating some barbeque, or as retaliation for white depredations committed against blacks. The two white men galloped to Picketsville, warning the white inhabitants of a possible attack. A posse was quickly formed and sixteen blacks were arrested and placed in the county jail at Humboldt.

Around 2 a.m. on August 26, some 100 masked horsemen broke into the jail, forcibly removing the sixteen African Americans. Half a mile out of town on Huntingdon Road, the nightriders shot six of their captives. Farther up the Forked Deer River, 10 miles off Picketsville Road, they hanged the remaining ten blacks from tree branches. Governor John C. Brown offered a $500 reward for the arrest of the terrorists. He also ordered the sheriff to form a posse and apprehend the lynchers. Despite the outrage in black (and some white) circles, no one was ever found culpable in the crime, which was a *de rigueur* outcome in the vast majority of lynching cases. Rumors abounded in the white communities that an armed force of 500 blacks was forming to retaliate. This indicates the paranoia of the white community, since the existence of such a formidable force of blacks was wholly unsubstantiated. Though there was an initial investigation by the U.S. Attorney's Office, a trial was never held. This remains the most infamous, save for the Memphis Race Riot, unsolved and unprosecuted terrorist-mass-murder in Tennessee history.[11]

Springfield, Robertson County, was the scene of a number of lynchings, in 1878, 1880, and 1881, which all shared the characteristic of the murder of multiple victims. In 1878, two African Americans, Pearson and Sadler, accused of the murder of a white man, according to *The New York Times*: "... were taken from [the] Springfield jail at 1 o'clock this morning [June 20] by about 100 armed but unmasked men. The jailor, not apprehending such a visit, was unprepared, and ... delivered up the keys. The accused were taken five miles from the town and hanged. A doubt existed as to the guilt of the men, and both protested their innocence to the last."[12]

Another multiple lynching of greater magnitude took place on September 1880 near Springfield. An eccentric, senior white man, LaPrade, was allegedly murdered by a group of seven black men who were searching for money it was rumored he had inherited. He denied having the money and he was tortured and brutally killed by his attackers on the night of September 6. They dismembered his body and dumped it in a sink hole not too far from LaPrade's log cabin residence.

Suspicion fell upon some seven African Americans who were arrested; all but two were released on the basis of their alibis. The five set free left post-haste for Kentucky, indicating their desire to escape a possible lynching. Their egress was stopped by a posse near Sadlersville, where they were jailed. The two remaining in Springfield, Bell and Jamison, were joined by another black man known only as Ramsey. The latter had allegedly shot and fatally wounded a white woman who had refused his amorous approaches. On the night of the 16th, an equestrian mob rode into Springfield with the intention of lynching all three suspects. According to a story in the Nashville *Daily American* of September 16, 1880:

> A quieter, more orderly or better regulated mob there never was. They were sixty in number, and drilled with the precision of a cavalry company. Entering the town two abreast from the Port Royal road, they rode directly to the jail, placing their horses directly in front of the building and in charge of eight men. Pickets were also placed a different parts of the city. Their coming had been anticipated, and

many persons were up and eager to see the proceedings. When they approached too near the jail the lynchers would warn them off. Some of the spectators were only a few feet from the horses, and talked pleasantly with the mobbers, although not able to recognize them. All of the lynchers were disguised—some of their hats drawn down, and nearly all their faces covers with handkerchiefs.

In what was almost a ritual in such events, the mob's leaders demanded the sheriff give them the keys to the jail, which he refused. They then took possession of the jail, and with tools taken from three local blacksmiths managed to break down the iron door between the cells and the sheriff's office. Bell and Jamison were taken from their cells, but it was not so easy to extricate Ramsey, who, anticipating a mob, had declared "he would sell his life dearly." His cell was atop that of the cell that held Bell and Jamison, and it was necessary to use a ladder to reach him. Ramsey had torn off a stout leg from a chair in the cell and used it as a club to keep the lynchers at bay. The intruders managed to break the lock of his cell, but found Ramsey to be less than cooperative. Ramsey, as the Nashville *Daily American* story continued, defied them:

> ... and with a heavy hickory club, taken from a chair, showered blows on his assailants; only two of them could come within reach.... Fiercely the battle raged for one hour. Coal Oil was poured and lighted paper was thrown, but without success. By the light they could see to aim, and shot after shot was poured in, so that ... the cell wall looked as if peppered. Whenever Ramsey was hit he would exclaim "You hit me _____ you." At the third shot he said "you have hit me three times" "You're a liar," shouted a lyncher. "Stop a minute and I'll show you." The fight stopped while Ramsey exhibited his right hand, the forefinger and thumb of which had been ploughed by the bullets. The fight was resumed. From his place behind the wall, Ramsey could have kept a thousand foes at bay. But the loss of blood was telling on him. A perfect stream was running down his right leg, and he stood in a large pools of his own gore. At last he sunk. A bystander seized the opportunity and fired from the top of the ladder, the ball piercing Ramsey's breast. There were other shots fired, and finally seizing on the lifeless body, they eased down the ladder and dropped it to the floor. Bell and Jamison, quiet, but trembling witnessed this singular struggle of one man against half a hundred. The prisoners say the combat was a fierce one. Ramsey would declare his intention to die game, and so would send some of the lynchers to hell, while the mob captain urged his men to be careful and not get any marks that would lead to future detection. The cell door and Ramsey's improvised club were spattered with blood. It was not known that any of the lynchers were hurt. Ramsey's body lay extended across the floor until the coroner's jury had decided he came to his death by an unknown mob.

Bell and Jamison were tied to horses and taken 6 miles out of town to where the railroad crossed the Port Royal road. The struggle at the jail lasted from about 12:20 to 3 a.m. The mob's original plan had been to invade Sadlersville (Robertson County) and take the remaining five suspects in the LaPrade murder and lynch all seven of them. However, as day was about to break, and knowing that in daylight they might be recognized, they reconsidered. It was too late to rush to capture the other five suspects and so it was decided to lynch Bell and Jamison at once. Before being murdered the two gave up the names of their accomplices in the Sadlersville jail. The newspaper account continued:

> [Then] [t]wo large pieces of black crepe were ... placed on the negroes' face and hands. Jamison was then strung up to a sapling, with a most convenient branch. Bell was carried sixty yards further up the road and hanged to a dogwood tree. The cord used was very small but strong, and cut into his flesh, strangulation caused his death. Both were only six or eight inches from the ground.

The lynchers left the bodies hanging, which were discovered about 7 a.m., and the sheriff notified. Passengers on the southbound train had seen the victims about 5 a.m. The suspects in the Sadlersville jail, in the meantime, had been sent to the jail in Springfield. Recognizing the danger that another lynching could occur, the prisoners were moved to Nashville and imprisoned there by order of Governor Albert Smith Marks (1879–1881).

The remaining suspects were transferred to Springfield to face trial on February 19, 1881. In order to avoid a lynching, the judge held their trial that evening. All went well until the judge charged the jury and the sheriff was about to take the prisoners to jail. Two of the suspects had turned state's evidence and were released. Abruptly, a mob of 200 men rushed in and seized the captives in the courthouse; startled spectators jumped out of courtroom windows. All lights in the court were extinguished to obscure the identities of the lynchers. The prisoners were taken upstairs to the second-story balcony bound and hanged. All died quickly, without a struggle, but one, who "had to be thrown down, tied and then raised." Hundreds of shots were fired, but, oddly, none at the victims, whose bodies were "all suspended from the small veranda, close together" were hit. The lynchers made it clear that anyone who would cut the bodies down "did so at their own peril." The details provided in the newspaper report indicate the reporter may have accompanied the mob. The two alleged suspects who had turned state's evidence were similarly murdered after having been hunted down by an equestrian lynch mob.

The members of the mob were never publicly identified and the crime was never prosecuted. Lawless mob violence enforced the statutory segregation. Despite the fact that such vicious mob murders were condemned by many, including governors, the terrorist lynchings were tolerated. The many episodes of lynching then enabled and gave power to the historically brutal reality of segregation and racial oppression of African Americans in Jim Crow Tennessee.[13]

According to the assessment of *The New York Times*:

> [Ten men, counting LaPrade,] have been hustled into eternity as a result of this atrocious crime and not one of them has met his death at the hands of the law. Judge Lynch has reigned supreme in Tennessee, so far as this case is concerned, and he chose his executioners with such good judgment that not one of them is known to the officers of justice whose duty is to apprehend them; or if they are known the officers are so thoroughly in sympathy with them that they wink at the

crime, and profess their ignorance of their identity. It is a sad commentary on the civilization of Tennessee that nine men can be hurried to death without warrant of law, and the lynchers remain unknown and undisturbed, but the fact remains to the eternal discredit of the State.[14]

The State Senate unanimously adopted a resolution condemning the action of the mob at Springfield and pronounced that such actions must be suppressed even if it required the whole power of the state. The resolution called upon the governor to use all means and measures to lead to the arrest and punishment of the perpetrators, promising the support of the legislature in such efforts. In the end, no one was arrested or held responsible for the deed. This was not atypical, and even when perpetrators were arrested, indicted, and tried they were never convicted.[15]

In the South, the purity of white women was held nearly sacred. Many lynchings were justified on the basis of alleged attempted and actual black-on-white rape. Seldom were such cases given the summary courtesy of a legal trial, and mob dictates prevailed. Not only was the ideal of white female purity and chastity assumed, but it was the duty of white men to protect it and punish those who violated the ideal. This was true even of whites who merely insulted white women, as an incident in Knoxville in May 1882 demonstrates. A young man had "spoken defamatory words" about the sister of another man, "at whose hand he met his death."

> [The killing was justified because] a brother is not worthy of the name brother if not ready to protect the fair name of a sister. The low creature who will speak in derogatory terms of a woman, who will spread stories prejudicial to her character inflicts an irreparable injury.... No man ... who speaks disrespectfully of a lady ... or of any female ... is no man.... Barlow knives might even be put to worse uses than eradicating the foul tongues of those ... who make a business of libeling females.[16]

As a means to insure the belief in white female purity from the imaginary primal sexual prowess of African American male lust, the state legislature on June 29, 1870, passed a law to enforce the state constitutional provision against the "Intermarriage of White persons with Negroes, Mulattoes and persons of mixed blood ... descended from a negro from the third generation inclusive." It was a felonious offense, punishable by "not more than one nor less than five years imprisonment."[17]

Yet separation for the purposes of banning sexual relations between blacks and whites was not always so well observed or punished when cases of white men cohabiting with black women. For example, in Memphis in 1889, it was announced that the grand jury would meet and "devote the entire day to investigating charges of illegal cohabitation against twenty white men and seventy-five Negresses," brought by an organization of African Americans known as the "Black Caps." They meant to gain enforcement of the miscegenation laws. "A meeting of white men was held at the corner of South and Main streets ... and an organization calling themselves 'White Caps,' decided upon. The exact purpose of the 'White Caps' is unknown, but a number expressed their intention to sit down on sassy negroes."[18] The outcome of any grand jury probe is not known.

One of the earliest lynchings having to do with violation of the miscegenation law and racist mores occurred in 1872 in the Rutherford County hamlet of Christiana. A black man and a white woman had been cohabitating and a child was a result of their illegal union. He left Christiana to avoid the "indignation against him." He returned a few years later and rented a room at a local boarding house and lived peacefully there for a few weeks. One morning, seven masked men appeared in the boarding house looking for the assumed guilty party, who, becoming aware of their presence and purpose, jumped out the window and began running. As he approached the wooden fence, the hooded figures fired and killed him. The murderers were known to witnesses and while a notice was sent to Murfreesboro to apprehend them, they were never arrested.[19] The message was clear to any African American male. Many cases of miscegenation are noted giving rise to the inference that regardless of the law, the practice was more common than previously imagined.[20]

Research indicates that thirty-three lynchings in Tennessee were committed on the basis of alleged rape committed by the murdered victim. There were no judicial proceedings to prove or disprove such allegations, only assumptions based upon hearsay. That represents 1.5 percent of the total number of the 213 lynching events. In no case did murder for alleged rape involve more than one victim, and all but one event involved African American men. This number is surprising as it indicates rape was either not a matter of great concern to whites, or the fear of mob-controlled execution was so great that few blacks ventured to carry out such "outrages." Yet lynchings carried out on the assumption of guilt of the rape of white women by African American men were horrific events. One little-known example occurred in an extremely rural setting near the community of Braden, at the Clinton Summit crossroads, in Fayette County, in October 1895.

After eluding gangs of enraged, armed white men in Mississippi and in West Tennessee for a week, Jefferson Ellis, black, thought to be the perpetrator of a rape in Fayette County, was apprehended and early in the morning of the 16th lynched by a mob of several hundred. The Memphis *Commercial Appeal* indicated in a report with the egregiously gruesome headline "TORTURED AND HANGED," that Fayette County Constable Farrow was taking Ellis to the Somerville jail in his buggy. The prisoner, secured to the seat with his elbows tide behind him with rope nearly managed to free himself and make an escape, but was deterred and securely handcuffed to the buggy seat. The constable stopped at the home of the alleged rape victim in order to positively identify Ellis as the perpetrator. He could not help but notice the 200 men following him "with shotguns in their hands or pistols in their pockets [who] galloped after the buggy, while another fifty men followed in buggies." He was powerless to stop them.

Arriving at the alleged victim's house, he found that another 100 men had already assembled, waiting for Ellis. A masked and armed squad followed Farrow into the house but did not try to take Ellis. The victim identified Ellis as the accused and the masked men immediately took control of the prisoner. He was taken to the nearby woods and interrogated, and according to a lengthy account found in the *Memphis Commercial Appeal* of October 16, 1895:

"... while the rest of the crowd arrayed themselves around the two big fires that had been built in the yard." Constable Farrow was kept in the house, guarded by armed men. Then, according to the newspaper report: At about 1:10 the mob started with Ellis for the pike where the public road crosses the Louisville & Nashville Railroad. Here there is also a telegraph pole. A big fire had been built at the place and around it the mob gathered in a circle. The handcuffed negro was on his knees before the fire. The leaders of the mob told Ellis to pray, but he only looked at them in a stupid manner. Being told he was about to die, he raised his voice in a negro "hymn." By the time he finished the mob was looking ugly. The fiercer element were in complete control. Cries of "burn him!" were heard on all sides. This fearful fate would probably have been fortunate for the negro as subsequent events proved. Amid shouts of the mob, a man jumped to the negro's side with a drawn knife in his hand.

"Cut off his ears," they cried.

"Give me a finger," shouted one man.

"Give me a thumb," cried another.

Being urged by the fierce ones in the mob, the man with his knife cut off the negro's right ear and held up the bleeding trophy in full view of the crowd.

The better element [*sic*] in the mob drew off at this time, and said they were not in favor of doing anything but hanging the negro. Their protests were not noticed. The negro screamed from his torture but his other ear was cut off a few moments later. The men became madder at the sight of this work, and those who were mutilating the negro, found ample encouragement. They next cut off his fingers and carried away part of his clothes. They mutilated him in a horrible manner. The negro was covered with blood, and it looked like his head had been scalped. The mob was not even then willing to end the negro's agonies. They made him stand up so all the crowd could see him. Finally, fully thirty-five minutes after the torture began, the rope [was thrown over the telegraph] pole ... seventy-five feet away. The rope was a very long one. The free end was taken by a man, who quietly climbed the telegraph pole and threw it over the cross-arm. The crowd jerked the negro to the foot of the pole, and while the mob shouted the bleeding and mutilated form of the negro was swung to the cross-arm.

Then the negro was lowered to the ground, and his head was cut from his body with pocket knives. The noose was then put over the negro's feet, and the headless body was again swung up.... A placard was put on the negro's headless body with the words: "Death to the man who cuts him down before 4:40 this evening."

"No doubt," the report concluded, "the injunction of the mob will be obeyed to the letter, and the passengers on the Louisville & Nashville Railroad today can see the horrible sight."

The mob quickly dispersed after the ghoulish lynching was concluded.[21] All lynchings in Jim Crow Tennessee were illegal and brutal, yet this example was particularly cruel and bizarre.

Another lynching for alleged rape occurred in Dyersburg, Dyer County, on November 7, 1913. John Talley, an "18-year-old mulatto negro ... attempted rape and ... was threaded up to a locust tree..." It did not matter that he had no trial, he was assumed to be guilty by the woman he allegedly tried to rape, it was said. He protested his innocence and was even glad to be locked in jail to protect him from an anticipated lynching. It did him little good, however. An angry mob of some 200 white men rushed the jail but were unable to find the keys to the cell. Blacksmith's tools were procured and the frightened teenager was extricated and carried to the courthouse a few blocks away. Although the district attorney and sheriff pleaded with the mob to wait for a proper trial, "the mob procured a new one inch rope [which] was placed around [Talley's] neck and the men, slowly and with deliberation threw the rope over a limb of a locust tree." According to a story under the heading "DYER MOB AVENGES CRIME," in the *Nashville Tennessean and Nashville American* dated November 8, 1913:

> The negro was again asked if he was guilty, and he still protested his innocence, and even as he was pulled up to the limb he was let quickly down to give him another opportunity to confess, but he was then too weak to speak. One long pull was given the rope, which was immediately attached to the trunk of another tree, leaving the negro hanging in midair some twenty feet from the ground with the Dyer County Courthouse as a background and the beautiful Confederate monument to his left. The mob immediately dispersed.... The mob was composed of well-known white men, and no effort was made to conceal their identity.... There was a rush by souvenir fiends for pieces of the rope. During the hour the negro's body was dangling in midair, none of the colored population of the city went near the scene.... There was so little excitement attending the affair that some businessmen on the square did not know of the incident ... until the mob dispersed.

A press report concluded that Talley was a "bad negro" and was known for "attempting familiarity with white women."[22] The reports of such lynchings dehumanized the victims as "the negro" instead of "the victim" or "the man."

At the root of such brutal lynchings was the concept of the purity of white Southern womanhood. A lynching in the small Montgomery County community of Guthrie elicited the following in the *Clarksville Tobacco Leaf Chronicle* as an explanation and excuse for such murders. According to an editorial on the subject, the lynching of the "negro Barnes" on December 19, 1892 was a deplorable affair, yet the alleged crime was enough to arouse the indignation of the white people of that community.

> There is no use to denounce mob-law so long as negro men will persist in crossing the color line and committing such a crime as the negro Barnes attempted. So long as this is kept up so long will the people take the law into their own hands and mete out swift and sure justice to the guilty party ... there was no undue haste in lynching the negro on Thursday night, and the lynching took place on Monday evening. From the time the crime was attempted until the lynching sober men were working on the case getting all the evidence pro and con [on] the negro, willing to give him a fair and impartial hearing. If he were found guilty they were in favor of hanging him; if innocent, he would have been released. The evidence was all against him ... his body was riddled with bullets and his neck had been broken by a rope. *The people have again said by their actions that the women of the South shall and will be protected from the lust of brutes masquerading in citizen's clothing. Let this be a warning to all such in the future.*[23] [Emphasis added.]

White men were not excluded from mob murder either. In one case, in Dyer County, five white horse thieves were rounded up and incarcerated in 1869. In what would become a familiar *modus operandi*, they were taken into the custody of a lynch mob who summarily executed them, in this case shooting them to death. This particular lynching was nether racially, nor economically, based. It was more a matter of "frontier justice." It was likewise, in an era of intense political division, nonpartisan. According to a newspaper account: "The citizens engaged in this act were of all shades of politics and were among the best men in the county. The leading man, indeed, in the whole affair, was a former Radical [Republican] member of the Legislature. They were not disguised in the slightest and seemed to justify their conduct and glory in it ... [and] think that the death of these desperadoes is a benefit to the country." This and a previous lynching of two similar horse thieves were expected to stop horse thievery in Dyer County and can be placed in the category of "frontier justice."[24]

In Knoxville in early September 1885, Lee Sellers, white, was abducted from the Knox County jail by a mob estimated at some 100 masked men who battered down the jail yard fence. He was accused of murder. As usual, the sheriff pleaded that the mob wait for a court of law to decide Sellers' fate, and as usual, the mob refused and broke down the cell door and took him away. Sellers, however, had a knife and defended himself as best he could, cutting two of the mob in the process. He was soon subdued and taken for hanging at the "high bridge which spans the [Tennessee] river here." Upon arriving at the bridge, it was discovered that the rope was not long enough to be secured to the bridge girder. Nevertheless, Sellers was released and swung out to hang, but miraculously freed himself from his bonds and climbed to the relative safety of the bridge's supporting iron work. As he ran up fifty shots were fired at him. Though wounded and choking he reached the girder above, slipped his head from the noose and made his way to one of the broad stringers which runs from end to end of the bridge, about a third of a mile long. His intention seemed to make his way to the south side of the river. According to a story in the Nashville *Daily American* of September 5, 1885, the crowd began firing at him and exhausted their ammunition, when:

> Sellers, wounded, bleeding and exhausted from his struggle lay upon the stingers and for a time it was thought he would make his escape. A ladder had arrived ... and a party went above to look for Sellers, it happened that the ladder had been set directly under him and the man first reaching the top first grappled with Sellers. Sellers made a violent effort to break loose, and did so, falling over the bridge the frightful distance of a hundred and fifty feet, on a pile of stone on the base of the pier, the fall crushing him to death. The body was found to be perforated by over a dozen bullets. No resistance seemed to have been made by the police authorities or the sheriff and his deputies. When it became known that the number of men actively engaged in the lynching was not greater than the number of police the good citizens [*sic*] were indignant that a better show [*sic*] had not prevailed.[25]

"Oh, God, have mercy on my soul!" were his last words the morning of June 27, 1892, in Bedford County. when an "alleged wife murderer ... entered into eternity this morning.... The delays of human justice dissatisfied the people who thirsted for vengeance, and the case against Will Bates, [white] charged with wife murder was appealed to a higher tribunal, before whose awful bar he now appears." After Mrs. Bate's funeral that evening a crowd gathered before the house of the local magistrate where a preliminary hearing in the murder charge was to be held. Bates was delivered to the hands of the county sheriff, who took him to the jail in Shelbyville "before the indignant citizens could prevent it." While a mob was expected at any moment, none appeared, according to the report under the headline "BATES SWUNG UP," in the Nashville *Daily American* of June 8, 1892:

> ... people began to wonder what manner of men the citizens of that local were, who would not even make a demonstration on behalf of outraged womanhood. But the people of that end of old Bedford have shown their ability to organize and conduct a mob to the latest improved methods. They only waited until mature deliberation had thoroughly convinced them of the accused's guilt, when they arose as one man and meted out justice swift and stern. [That] morning, almost at day break, the pioneers reached town and quietly hitching their horses, began waiting. No weapons were displayed, no boasting was heard, but it was evident to all who looked upon the determined faces that Bate's days on earth were numbered.
>
> All interest centered on the incoming train at ten o'clock. The train was late. Excitement increased. Suddenly as Depot Street awaited in silence, the cry arose "Here they come!" Down the street from the depot, with heads erect, with set and stern features, came the avengers. Men from Haley, from Wartrace, from Tullahoma and from all the county around had gathered themselves together with one common aim and purpose. They marched four abreast and looked neither to the right nor to the left.

Scaling the fence to the jail and overpowering the sheriff and his deputies, the mob found Will Bates, and in another cell his father, Scott, incarcerated on horse stealing charges. A noose was placed around Scott's neck and it appeared he too might be lynched when Will was found and dragged out of the jail. He protested his innocence to the last. The report ended:

> The crowd went in the jail about 10:30. They forced the door at 10:35. They found their man at 10:45 and brought him to the ... courthouse at 10:50. [In the courthouse yard there stood] a lonely tree of the species commonly known as the "heaven tree." Here the crowd decided to hang him.

*   *   *   *

> A relative of the deceased woman then climbed the tree, rope was thrown over the limb, and as the great town clock struck eleven, the body of Will B. Bates, alleged wife murderer, swung into the air. There was no ... struggle.

The crowd then decided to make a clean sweep of it and lynch Will's father, Scott. After considerable argument the mob was dissuaded by the sheriff, and Scott was taken to Murfreesboro where he was kept in safety in jail there. The rope by which Will was lynched was cut into pieces as souvenirs while an "enterprising photographer took [a picture] of the body as it was swung up and these pictures will be in great demand."[26]

A newspaper report of May 28, 1891 reported on the lynching of a black man, Green Wells, in a story with the appallingly crass headline: "JERKED MEAT." According to the article, the day before, after mistakenly taking a black man, Alan Head, as their victim, at the Polk Station railroad depot in Columbia, a mob realized its error and stormed the Columbia jail, looking for the alleged murderer. Initially successful attempts were made by the sheriff to thwart the onslaught by appeals to allow the law to take its course. Wells was believed to have killed a white man, John Fry. The next day, however, the crowd, "under the leadership of one ... impetuous spirit, who led the way with a Winchester rifle in one hand and a rope in the other" stormed the jail. Using crowbars and sledgehammers, they took Wells from his cell and "quickly reached the bridge which spans the Duck River about 400 yards from the jail. A large crowd of the morbidly curious followed upon the steep bluffs below the bridge and upon the tops of adjacent fences, piles of lumber and housetops." After securing the rope, Wells was brusquely thrown off the bridge, but the rope was too short and his hands were not bound. Consequently, Wells managed to climb back up the bridge, only to be greeted by the blood thirsty mob. "The second time the mob made no mistake," and tied his hands behind his back and used a longer strand of rope. Horrifyingly, Wells was "again lifted above the railing and in another instant his body shot swiftly downward, a distance of eighteen or twenty feet." He "quivered for a moment and then hung motionless except when the river breezes swayed it to and fro or turned it slowly about as if to exhibit to all the morbid spectators the brutal face, distorted with its hideous, ghastly grin, it staring eyeballs starting from their sockets." As his body fell a "wild, weird wail went up from among the crowd of negroes upon the bank. It came from the lips of the murderer's mother, who followed him to his doom." Another African-American man, George Warner, was lynched at the same bridge on May 26, 1890.[27]

Some lynchings in the Volunteer State were of sufficient magnitude to attract statewide and even national attention, and even drew widespread condemnation in the first decade of the twentieth century. Already mentioned was the Gibson County massacre-lynching of 1874. Two others garnered attention in August 1894, at the crossroads community of Kerrville in Shelby County, and in Chattanooga in March 1906, with the murder of Ed Johnson.

Shortly prior to midnight on August 31, 1894, a heavy wagon drawn by a horse and mule team, traveled slowly over an antiquated wooden-plank road two miles north of Lucy, near the Kerrville community, Shelby County, on its way to Memphis. It had reached a stretch of road that was heavily timbered on both sides, limiting visibility. Shelby County Deputy Sherriff and Detective W. S. Richardson walked ahead of the team as a guide to test the stability of the road while the wagon followed after. The wagon, handled by A. T. Atkinson, carried six black prisoners, handcuffed and chained together. The prisoners were in transit to Memphis for placement in the Shelby County jail. They were suspected of committing arson, having burned some thirty-two barns.

The wagon approached Big Creek, which intersected with the road in three different places. Bridges erected at each of these junctions were said to be very likely impassable. As the wagon reached the first bridge, the deputy sheriff tested its strength. He lit a match to better ascertain the condition of the bridge. Suddenly a voice from out of the darkness called out: "You better not cross that bridge." When he asked why the voice called out "Because it's in bad condition" was the response. After inspecting the bridge, it was determined it was strong enough carry the prisoner-wagon over the creek. When the second bridge was reached another voice warned the guide not to cross it because it was out of repair. His response was to ask why and again to be told the "bridge is broken, be careful."

Richardson feared an ambush had been set, but he went ahead to find the mysterious voice had this time spoken the truth, the bridge was out. It was impossible to ford the stream so the wagon was stopped. He found a detour that would allow the wagon to ford the creek. "At the moment the wagon made it across the creek they found themselves confronted by fifty armed men and was told to raise his hands." The detective hesitated. "What does this mean," he asked. "Never you mind. It means business, shove up your hands!" Suddenly he was surrounded. "The muzzles of shotguns, rifles and revolvers were poked up to his face, pressed against his chest and tickled his back. Up went his hands." A volley of shots fired at the prisoner wagon broke the stillness. According to an account in the Memphis *Commercial Appeal*:

> When the mob surrounded the wagon the negroes seemed to know instinctively what was about to be done. They were sitting on boxes that had been thrown about on the floor of the wagon. One sat on the seat beside the driver, Atkinson. One negro in the body of the wagon rose up on his feet and threw up his shackled hands.... That motion was his last, for a shower of bullets was poured into his body. He fell over and out of the wanton into the road dead.
>
> The negro sitting beside the driver threw his arms about Atkinson with a gesture and exclamation of supplication. The muzzle of a shotgun was shoved against his stomach and the charge was sent through his body.
>
> Atkinson was seized by the mob, hustled up to the side of Richardson and there held until the murders had taken place.
>
> Volley after volley was poured into the bodies of the shackled and manacled negroes in the wagon until all of them must have been dead.
>
> Then the mob yanked the bodies out of the wagon, threw them on the road and continued to fire volley after volley into them.

Atkinson and Deputy Sheriff Richardson later testified that there were fifty people in the mob, most of them wore a disguise but "had their heads incased in a sort of hood of black cloth," but it was too dark to identify any one of them. After the murders were committed a voice commanded: "'Forward boys,' guns were shouldered and the unknown men walked back into the woods that lined the road. Soon the officers heard sounds which led to the belief the lynchers had tethered their horses nearby and that they had mounted and ridden away."

Three of the six lynched prisoners had been arrested on charges of arson. They were said to belong to an organized band of barn burners that had in five years destroyed thirty-two barns, as many residences and other property of great value in the vicinity of Kerrville, Lucy, Millington, and Bolton's College, all in Shelby County. Atkinson left to find a magistrate while Richardson stayed behind with the six lynched men. "In the morning it was found when the rising sun threw light on the scene, that the negroes had been perforated again and again with bullets and small shot. They had been fired into repeatedly, apparently out of pure malice or deviltry. Especially did it appear that [one of the deceased] ... had been mutilated purposely, for his head was shot into jelly, and the same is true to a less degree of the other bodies." The coroner's jury, which included two black men, had no evidence except that given by Richardson and Atkinson, and a verdict held that the black prisoners came to their death from "gunshot wounds fired by unknown parties."

Racial tensions in the community were exacerbated as a result of conflicting land claims. Before the war most of the property in the area was owned by the Kerr family, from which the village got its name. When the direct line of the Kerr family died the property was divided among more distant heirs "and later was cut into smaller tracts and passed into the hands of aliens."

A dynamic had developed that created tensions between the black and white communities, further complicated by a rift in the white community. Blacks, who had been on the land since antebellum days, firmly believed they had rights on the property, but there was much difficulty convincing them that their rights as squatters were not permanent. In addition to this was the differences in the kinds of crops black and white farmers grew. Essentially, the black community depended upon raising cotton, while white farmers raised grain and livestock. They formed a white Farmers' Association. Whether or not the association was dedicated to progressive farming and agricultural fairs, the black community viewed it askance. It promoted economic competition with cotton cultivation, and so pitted white against black, already at odds in the Jim Crow era.

The blacks, it was alleged, conceived the idea of improving their own condition and retaliating upon the whites by burning down the barns of such persons who followed diversified agriculture. Barn burning became common, and the black farmers allegedly extended their operation by burning residences and stores. White farmers who showed the greatest tendency toward improvement of conditions were most likely to be visited by the incendiaries. "A couple of dozen fires have been this caused in the last year, and within the past fortnight there have been several fires of importance in that vicinity."

Economic competition and the rule of Jim Crow were the root causes for the troubles. This social and economic dynamic may well have resulted in barn burning, but there is little but circumstantial conjecture that blacks had formed an arson ring. Economic segregation and oppression of the Jim Crow era lent themselves to a rise of racial conflict manifesting itself as barn burning. The murders at Kerrville, carried out with such excess, suggest the lynching was as much a personal matter as one stimulated by local economic pressures and racist Jim Crow fiat.

Prominent citizens of Memphis met on September 7 and presented resolutions and denounced the lynching, "The spirit ... was indicative of a general determination that the murderers should be brought to justice and the good name of the county preserved." Judge Cooper was serious about getting to the bottom of the matter. He was not persuaded Deputy Sheriff Richardson's report was truthful and knew that the deputy sheriff had a bad reputation, having been tried for extortion while with the Memphis police force. Evidence of a conspiracy between the lynchers and Richardson mounted. Aside from extending the grand jury's investigation, Cooper visited Governor Peter Turney who on the judge's recommendation, offered a $5,000 reward for information. In the end, Richardson and H. N. Smith, indicted as co-conspirators in the lynching, were found not guilty despite overwhelming evidence to the contrary.[28] Visceral white racism had prevailed over factual evidence of white guilt in the murder of six African Americans and justice was denied. Jim Crow ruled supreme.

After receiving a stay of execution from the U.S. Supreme Court, Ed Johnson, an African American, was lynched by an angry mob of some 300 livid whites. He was wrongfully convicted of the rape of a Chattanooga woman and in a rare instance the U.S. Supreme Court reversed the conviction. An incensed racist mob, using sledgehammers stormed the jail and with the involuntary acquiescence of jail officials, Johnson was removed him from his cell. The mob took him to the Walnut Street bridge and made ready to hang him. Bravely remaining calm in the face of the mob's terroristic action, Johnson said: "I am not guilty ... I know I am going to die and I have no fear to die. God bless you all." Shots were fired into his body as it was hoisted up and hung.

Racial tensions increased as the black community learned of the illegal act. There was fear that a race riot would occur. To prevent the likelihood of a riot, some 400 heavily armed special police officers patrolled the streets "to keep down a race war.... The negroes congregated in large crowds, threatening to shoot white people and burn houses." Two white men, one a deputy sheriff, were wounded by shots fired by African Americans. An attempt was made to set fire to the commission house on West Ninth Street, dousing it with gasoline.

The next day, nearly 1,000 blacks stopped work in several of the larger industrial plants and stood in groups discussing what action to take to avenge his death. "The woman servants," according to one newspaper account, "in many cases left their employment, and are more sullen and angry than the men."

> Law and order won a signal victory in Chattanooga tonight when a squad of less than 100 policemen, backed up by four companies of militia, held a huge crowd of negroes, variously estimated at from 2,000 to 4,000 in number, in check preserved peace and prevented a riot which might have resulted in a great loss of life.
>
> There are in this city three companies of infantry, a troop of cavalry, and a section of artillery belonging to the National State Guard. They expect to be called out for duty, there is a feeling of unrest, and excitement that may end in a race riot. Fearing such a contingency the police board had ordered all saloons closed for the day and night.

Governor John I. Cox and other state and national politicians, including President Theodore Roosevelt, condemned the lynching and "mob law." Since Johnson's case had already been accepted by the U.S. Supreme Court, the justices directed federal officers to investigate the lynching, in particular whether or not Sheriff Joseph Shipp and his deputies were involved. The court ruled that Shipp, his deputy, and three others were guilty of contempt of court in Johnson's death after an investigation and hearing were held. Shipp was sentenced to nine months in a federal prison, and when released, he received a hero's welcome by unrepentant whites in Chattanooga.[29]

At least three women were the victims of lynching violence in Tennessee history, all of them African American. Julia Hayden, a slave before the war, a young, attractive mulatto school teacher, was murdered on August 22, 1874. She was visiting her aunt and uncle, Hembry Lowe, "a worthy colored man," in Maury County where she had recently accepted a position in the county's segregated public school system. Two horsemen rode up to the house that night and repeatedly asked for Julia Hayden shouting to her uncle: "We do not want to hurt you uncle Hem, we want that teacher!" Their demand having been denied they fired indiscriminately into house "in their fury of disappointment..." One shot passed through the door, "the ball striking her just below the collar bone, passing through her neck and possibly breaking her spinal column" killing the young woman instantly. It was rumored it was the act of Ku Klux Klan terrorists, but it was later revealed the perpetrators were two inebriated young men bent upon some sort of violent sexual liaison with Ms. Hayden. According to a newspaper report:

> The two men had been drinking and having conceived the idea of outraging the girl's person, they had gone to house expecting little difficulty in getting possession of her, but discovering they could not gain admittance, even by force, grew exasperated and commenced firing into the house, with the fatal result already mentioned.

There is no record to indicate if the two young men were tried and/or convicted of their lynching of Julia Hayden.[30] She had done nothing to deserve her fate but was the victim of the drunken sexual desire of her two would-be white assailants.

In Sumner County, two African-American brothers, Chick and Will Martin, were acquitted on charges of barn burning in the Hendersonville environs. Afterwards they returned to visit with their mother at her cabin. On the night of February 2, 1892, a mob of mounted horsemen surrounded the cabin and demanded that the brothers come out to face them. Knowing the horde intended to lynch them, they refused and the mob began firing indiscriminately into the cabin windows. One of the shots hit and instantly killed Mrs. Martin, after which the mob "took their departure." While the incident was widely denounced, there is no record of anyone being tried for this murder.[31]

Eliza Wood, an African-American domestic cook, was lynched at the Madison County Courthouse on August 18, 1886. She was killed on suspicion of having killed her former employer, a Mrs. Wooten, with "Rough on Rats" a common brand rodent toxin laced heavily with arsenic. The evening of the 18th, a mob estimated at 1,000 gathered to attack the Madison County Jail. When the courthouse bell was tapped, the signal had been given to assault the jail. Voices from the mob were heard yelling "Every man who has a wife come forward!" Eliza was dragged from the jail and at first there was no consensus as to whether Eliza should be hanged or burned. The latter option was chosen. The Nashville *Daily American* reported the event in its August 19, 1886 number:

Finally she was borne, amid the horrible yelling of the mob to Court Square, every rag of clothing being torn from her body. After being drawn up once she admitted having purchased some poison but said it was some time ago, and was for a sore mouth. Finally, amid great shouting she was drawn up and the crowd was told to get away and five shots were fired into her body as it swung. A notable feature was the large number of negroes present, including a number of women. All of them endorsed the action of the mob. All of them feared her. It is believed firmly that she not only poisoned Mrs. Wooten but also poisoned her little babe over a year ago. It is claimed she had a regular mania for poisoning people, and has during her life of 57 years murdered more than a dozen people. A negro woman walked seven miles from the country ... to see her hung ... who said she had poisoned eleven children in her neighborhood. Leading citizens watched the hanging. Nobody is found to defend her. Few of the mob were masked at first. Everybody thinks the city is free of a she devil.

Her mangled body was left hanging until the next morning. According to a newspaper report: "A sheet had been wrapped around her body, and the bloated features presented a horrible spectacle ... an inquest was held. A verdict of death by hanging at the hands of unknown men was returned." One eyewitness, Madison Count farmer Robert R. Cartmel, remarked curtly in his diary: "She will poison no more."[32]

On March 9, 1892, in Memphis, according to the Nashville *Daily American* of March 10, 1892:

The dawn of a bright spring morning as it cast its light across Tennessee's second city disclosed the dead bodies of three negroes riddled with bullets and partially covered with brush, lying in an open lot about one and a half miles from the heart of city.

The bodies as they lay outstretched with faces heavenward were mute reminders of the terrible work of seventy-five masked men in this city at 3 o'clock this morning. The names of the negroes whose bodies were literally shot to pieces are:

CALVIN McDOWELL,

WILLIAM STUART,

THEODORE MOSS.

The alleged crime of these three African-American men was their alleged ambush of four deputy sheriffs "in a bad negro locality" known as "The Curve," as they searched for a suspect for whose arrest they had a warrant. In retaliation later that night, some seventy-five masked men appeared near the Shelby County jail on Front Street. Three masked men, by means of subterfuge, overpowered the turnkey and after a search of the segregated black portion of the jail, extracted McDowell, Stuart, and Moss. They were among twenty-seven blacks arrested for complicity in the ambush of the four sheriff's deputies, and were at first difficult to locate. The three were found and were securely bound and gagged and hauled into the street. Their destination was an open field by the tracks of the Chesapeake & Ohio Railroad near Wolf River. Their gags were removed. Moss reportedly said to his captors: "If you're going to kill us, turn our faces to the West!" A single shot rang out hitting Moss in the cheek, after which "a terrible volley was poured in upon the shivering negroes who instantly fell dead on the tracks." Shelby County Sheriff McLendon half-heartedly expressed his willingness to do what he could to find the killers. An inquest was held that rendered the verdict: "We find that the deceased were taken from the Shelby County jail by a masked mob of men, the men overpowered [the guards] and ... [took] all to an old field and [were] shot to death by parties unknown to the jury."

The roots of this lynching lay in a combination of racism and economic competition between two grocery stores in "The Curve," one owned by whites, the other, "The People's Grocery," by blacks. Friction caused by the combination of these two factors led to difficulties that resulted in Shelby County deputy sheriff's being dispatched to the Curve to arrest the owners of the People's Grocery. Mistaking the deputies as the vanguard of a lynch mob, shots were fired wounding some law men. The racist anger and resentment that followed led to the lynching.

The text of Tennessee Historical Commission Historical Marker "People's Grocery" in Memphis explains:

> Thomas Moss, Calvin McDowell, and Will Stewart, all African-Americans and co-owners of People's Grocery (located at this site), were arrested in connection with a disturbance near their store. Rather than being brought to trial, they were lynched on March 9, 1892. Moss' dying words were, "Tell my people to go west—there is no justice for them here." This lynching prompted Ida B. Wells, editor of *Memphis Free Speech*, to begin her anti-lynching campaign in this country and abroad.[33]

The headline of the December 16, 1924 Nashville *Tennessean* read: "Mob Lynches Negro Boy Who Shot Grocer." Samuel Smith, a fifteen-year-old African American boy, accused of shooting Ike Eastwood, white, "a popular Nolensville grocer," on Friday the 14th, and was wounded from returned fire by Eastwood. Smith's uncle apparently had had some car trouble and was trying to purloin parts from Eastwood's parked car. Samuel was left with his uncle's car. Eastwood was aroused by the noise and fired and wounded Samuel. Samuel returned fire, wounding Eastwood, who was taken to St. Thomas' Hospital. Samuel Smith was found in the next morning in a clump of weeds, badly wounded, and almost unconscious and was taken to Nashville General Hospital where he was later abducted from his bed by "a masked and armed mob at midnight, Monday night." All telephone lines were severed. In less than an hour, his naked, bullet-ridden body was found, "hung from a tree by the side of the road 100 yards from where he shot Eastwood, and the exact spot where he was captured last Saturday morning. Some thirty automobiles filled with vigilantes arrived in the night."

Finding Smith they demanded at gunpoint that he get up—he was already wounded from the previous night's incident. "The scared negro in trembling tones answered that he was wounded and unable to rise." The men then drew their shotguns and said, "We'll kill you here then." Smith reluctantly stood up and was marched, unrobed, outside. Because the telephone lines had been cut, hospital staff were unable to summon the police, and the automobile armada sped into the night. After reaching their destination on the Nolensville Road, Smith was tied to a tree on the Nolensville Road. Soon "shotguns boomed" from the cars, which thereafter disappeared, leaving no trace of their identity. An anonymous telephone call informed the sheriff's office and the newspaper soon after the lynching occurred. There had been incidents with "gun-carrying negroes" that summer but this was the first time a lynching had occurred in Nashville in thirty-two years.

Smith's corpse was found tied to the tree with a plow rope "with the manacles and part of the severed chains still clamped to the ankles, the feet hanging about two feet from the ground." The scene of the lynching was approximately 200 yards from the Williamson County line, near Nolensville. Smith's uncle was charged with accessory to attempted murder and incarcerated. Although the usual lip service denounced the lynching, and while the Mayor and virtually all civic clubs decried the lynchings—the Nashville Chamber of Commerce even offered a staggering $5,000 reward for information—none of the lynchers, branded as "a gang of fugitive slayers" were apprehended and the case was never solved.[34]

The body of Cordie Cheek, a twenty-year-old black man, was found suspended from a limb of a cedar tree near Columbia on December 15, 1933. The Maury County Grand Jury had recently refused to indict him on charges of an attack on an eleven-year-old girl, a decision that in itself was nearly unprecedented. He had been transferred to Nashville for protection from a threatened lynching in Columbia. Maury County authorities informed Nashville agencies of the grand jury's verdict, along with instructions to set Cheek free. In less than an hour, he was kidnapped from the residence of a relative in Nashville by an unidentified group of white men from Maury County. The murder of this innocent man was handled, according to Maury County Sheriff Godwin "in a very quiet manner ... no one knew anything about it." An editorial in the Nashville *Tennessean* expressed outrage. A mass meeting by leading citizens and civic clubs was held to encourage a proper investigation of Cheek's murder. Yet their outrage was more about the violation of the dominion of Davidson County as much as the lynching itself. According to an editorial in the Nashville *Tennessean*:

> Clearly a crime was committed when the negro was kidnapped from his relative's home here. The sovereignty of this county was ignored by a gang from Maury County in the abduction of this negro. There is a crime for the Davidson County Grand Jury to investigate, and the new Central Committee has asked that especial care be taken in selecting men of the highest calbre to form the jury which will be entrusted with this investigation....

*   *   *   *

> Cordie Creek was not killed as the result of a sudden inflaming of a hasty mob action. Weeks lapsed between the time of his alleged crime and abduction. The abduction was carefully planned to follow upon his release here, and it was carried out in a cold, skillful manner. His abduction in Davidson County and his killing in this or in Maury County were the result of carefully considered plans. It was a gang killing rather than a mob lynching.[35]

The nuance between a "mob lynching" and a "gang killing" no doubt was not appreciated by the Nashville African American community. It is interesting that the word "negro" was still being used in the accounting of a racist murder, a convention that only served to dehumanize the victim and maintain white control of the black community by means of terrorism inspired by segregation long ordained by Jim Crow laws and accepted social notions of race.

A political lynching, a type previously unknown in the history of lynching in Tennessee, occurred in Brownsville on June 22, 1940. Elbert Williams was born in Haywood County, Tennessee, in 1908 to sharecropper parents. Williams received his education in the African American church that served as the segregated school for black children in the Haywood County.

In 1939, he joined the Brownsville chapter of the National Association for the Advancement of Colored People (NAACP) as a founding member. Given the racial climate of the day, and the fact that lynchings were not unknown in the county, his action spoke well of his brave commitment to the struggle for equal political and civil rights. Haywood County was not without distinction in regard to its history of African American involvement in politics. Samuel Allen McElwee, an African American from Haywood County, was elected to the Tennessee House of Representatives in 1886, where he served until the rigged election of 1888 cast him out of his leadership role. Nevertheless, McElwee worked with other black legislators fighting for equal education opportunities for formerly enslaved people of Tennessee, and was heavily involved in working to defeat Jim Crow and contract labor laws. He was a man ahead of his time, yet was forced out of Haywood County by white supremacists who threatened him with violence. The county was a hotbed for the Ku Klux Klan, yet simultaneously, African Americans were involved in county politics in the 1880s and throughout the rest of the nineteenth century.

Williams' activism in joining the NAACP was of some concern to local vigilantes, who abducted him from his home late in the night on June 22, 1940. His captors beat him brutally, questioning him about the activities of the NAACP, and whether or not he was planning a meeting to recruit new members for the local chapter and carry out a voter registration drive. Williams never returned from the interrogation.

A few days later, his bruised, bloated, and beaten corpse was found 6 miles from Brownsville, floating in the Hatchie River. There were two bullet holes in his chest. A hastily convened all-white coroner's jury produced a hackneyed verdict that he had died "of foul means by parties unknown." The coroner swiftly ordered that his body be quickly and clandestinely interred in an unmarked grave.

A special county grand jury was convened in August to rule on his death. Future Associate Justice of the U.S. Supreme Court assisted in the investigation. Despite his best efforts, the U.S. Department of Justice did not follow through with its own investigation, and the case went cold. Elbert Williams was one of many scarcely celebrated heroes of the civil rights movement, whose lives were taken in efforts to fulfill the exercise of America's most fundamental right, the freedom to vote.

On June 20, 2015, the Tennessee Historical Commission honored Williams with the placement of a historical marker, in a public ceremony in Brownsville. The text reads:

ELBERT WILLIAMS 1908-1940 Elbert Williams, an African American Haywood County native, was one of the early members of the National Association for the Advancement of Colored People (NAACP) killed in the United States for his civil rights work. He and his wife Annie became charter members of the NAACP Brownsville Branch in 1939. On May 6, 1940, five African Americans tried to register to vote. A white terror campaign followed and destroyed the NAACP Branch. More than 20 African American families fled the area. Williams disappeared on the night of June 20, 1940, after police took him from his home and questioned him about planning an NAACP meeting. After three days, Williams' mutilated body was found in the Hatchie River. His death was ruled a homicide by unknown parties, and he was buried in Taylor Cemetery. Annie Williams quickly moved to New York. After interviewing witnesses in Brownsville, Thurgood Marshall, NAACP Special Counsel, criticized the U.S. Department of Justice's investigation and failure to prosecute. The NAACP Brownsville Branch reorganized in 1961.[36]

Events in late February 1946 led to the killing of two African-American men in Columbia under circumstances of intense racial disturbance. The difficulties sprang from an incident on the 25th when a white radio repairman was thrown through plate glass window of his shop by a young black man. Shortly thereafter, shots were heard in the "Mink Slide District," the center of the town's African American business and residential community. Columbia policemen were sent to patrol the neighborhood. Either blacks were the first to draw fire or first to fire, but in either case four policemen were wounded. As the news spread crowds of infuriated whites gathered at the Maury County Courthouse. Blacks overheard threats that there was to be a lynching. Believing in the real possibility of such a killing, the black community prepared itself for an onslaught of white mob violence. White businessmen were so convinced there would be trouble that they "barricaded themselves in a two block part of their business section." That night, white gangs on the periphery of Mink Slide fired pistol shots into the community, while blacks shot back. A race riot seemed to be in the offing. There were no fatalities, although ten blacks were said to be wounded. There was no lynching.

The next day the police, bolstered by 400 state highway patrolmen and state guard troops, carried out a sweep, without search warrants, of Mink Slide. They confiscated weapons. There was no corresponding sweep of white neighborhoods. The sweep garnered a collection of rifles and resulted in the arrest of 100 suspects. Among them were James "Digger" Johnson and William F. Goodwin.

During their interrogation, held in a storeroom storing the confiscated weapons, Johnson and Goodwin, most likely believing a lynching was a distinct possibility, grabbed two of the stockpiled weapons. Goodwin fired and wounded a sheriff's deputy. Hearing the noise, state troopers entered the room with revolvers blazing and mortally wounded Johnson and Goodwin. Because the Columbia hospital was segregated, the two were rushed to a black facility in Spring Hill, some twelve away. They died in transit.

The killing of Johnson and Goodwin did not fit the characteristics of historical lynchings, although it did bear some resemblance. It is not difficult to understand the likely motives of the two men, inasmuch as Columbia had experienced racial murders in its past, one as recent as 1933. It is most probable the men were keenly aware of that history and were convinced their fate would end in a lynching. Rather than submit meekly and perhaps hoping to escape custody, they grabbed the rifles in an attempt at saving themselves from mob murder. In that regard, it can be seen that this was a lynching, but one occurring under unique circumstances contaminated with a history of violence toward African Americans in Columbia and the state of Tennessee.

Black and white local clergy attempted to address what they saw as the real root of the Mink Slide incident, namely inadequate housing, schools, and hospitals. Their talks, however well-meaning, did not result in any policies addressing those issues. Litigation resulted in the acquittal of all but two on charges of attempted murder and helped stimulate the formation of the President's Committee on Civil Rights by Harry S. Truman.

The Tennessee Historical Commission erected a historical marker to the Mink Slide troubles. The text reads:

> 1946 Columbia Race Riot—In February 1946 a struggle between an African American World War II veteran, James Stevenson, and a white shopkeeper over a radio repair order sparked a riot, fueled by law enforcement officers who raided the African American business district without search warrants and confiscated weapons. Police arrested over 100 African American men, charging them with attempted murder. With legal defense headed by Z. Alexander Looby, Thurgood Marshal, Leon Ransom and Maurice Weaver an all-white jury acquitted 23 of the 25 men. Because of this incident and others in the South, President Harry Truman established the President's Committee on Civil Rights.[37]

There have been no lynchings in the Volunteer State for over seventy years, notwithstanding the 1968 assassination of Dr. Martin Luther King in Memphis. Indeed, most of the lynchings occurred well over 100 years ago. The number of lynchings declined with the advent of the twentieth century. This in itself is testament to the successful Civil Rights struggle of the twentieth century and a concomitant change in racial bias. While racism still exists in a systemic fashion, great strides have been made with the elimination of lynching in the Volunteer State, and the South in general. The following list of 213 lynchings is presented to give a picture of the totality of lynching murders, in Tennessee's history from 1821 to 1946.

Research indicates a total of 213 documented lynchings in the Volunteer State's history. Of the 213 documented lynchings, thirty-two involved whites, or 14 percent, while 187, or 86 percent, involved African Americans. Using the figure of 213 lynchings as the total the following subtotals and percentages are shown: lynched whites, thirty-three or 1.5 percent; 182 blacks, or 89 percent; nineteen for alleged rape, or 8 percent; five white, alleged rape, or 3 percent; multiple victims per lynching, 117 or 54 percent. The remaining categories are unknown as they relate to causes. Some 180 took place in the nineteenth century, or 82 percent, while thirty-nine, or 18 percent occurred in the twentieth century.

Chronological List of 213 Lynchings in Tennessee, 1821–1946[38]

McMinn County (w) "many years ago," unknown person, unknown date.

Adkins or Adkinson, (w), murder, in Franklin 1821.

Morton and Sampson Kennedy (w), in Shelby County by "Confederate Authorities" (Vigilance Committee) for being Northerners, early May, 1861.

Joseph C. Taylor (w) CSA soldier, by a mob in Fayetteville, Lincoln County, October 20, 1861.

James Taylor, Samuel Tatum, Alfred Kite, Alexander Dugger, and David Shuffield, (w) East Tennessee Unionists, by Confederate Home Guard, Washington County, January 23, 1863.

Rolly Doleson, (w) Franklin County, 1865.

Ex-CSA soldier, (w) Baker, Knoxville, by mob September 4, 1865.

Forty-six unidentified African Americans lynched in the Memphis race riot, April 30 to May 2, 1866.

Simon Peters, alleged rape, Pulaski, June 30, 1868.

William Burk, Cornersville, July 4 1868.

Three unidentified blacks murdered Maury County, July 15 1868.

William Gustine (Guthrie?), Williamson County, July 17, 1868.

Samuel Bierfield (Jew), Franklin environs, August 25, 1868.

Unidentified man Pulaski, December 18, 1868.

Detective Seymour Barmore (w) murdered Columbia, January 11, 1869.

Five horse thieves (w) Dyersburg, January 29–30, 1869.

Unknown man near Dresden, alleged rape, *c.* August 25, 1869.

Col Coleman murdered (w) Carroll County, January 22, 1870.

Matt Brown and George Ballou, (possibly three more) in Huntingdon, Carroll County January 22, 1870.

Lynching, Cuba on or about August 20, 1870.

Three lynched from bridge, Franklin County 1871.

John Starkey, Manchester, alleged rape, September 2, 1871.

Henry Clinton, Christiana, miscegenation, September 5, 1872.

Sandy Peebles, Rutherford County, August 5, 1874.

Robert Banks, Kingston Springs, August 15, 1874.

Julia Hayden, Maury County, August 22, 1874.

Sixteen unidentified men, Trenton, Gibson County, August 26, 1874.

B. H. Nelson, Pulaski August (?) 1874.

Joe Reed, Nashville, April 30, 1875.

Jesse Woodson, murder, Murfreesboro, August 13, 1875.

Porter Williamson, Lebanon, February 27, 1876.

William Mockbee, Dover, April 20, 1877.

Frank McGhee, (alias George Roper), Columbia, November 27, 1877.

Henry "Boot" Alexander, murder, Murfreesboro, November 15, 1877.

Winston Anderson, near Clarksville, March 3, 1878.

Pearson and Sadler, murder, Springfield, June 20. 1878.

Pinkney Bell (w), Murfreesboro, September 1, 1878.

Unidentified, Murfreesboro, September 26, 1878.

Dennis Beeler (w), near Shelbyville, August 22, 1878.

James Russell, Murfreesboro, October 27, 1878.

George Washington, Dover, July 22, 1880.

Jack Bell, Arch Jamison & Ramsey, Springfield, September 14, (16?) 1880.

Daniel Smith, Nashville, December 2, 1880.

Fish and John Poe, Winchester February 16, 1881.

Five men, at Springfield Courthouse, February 19, 1881.

Houston Taylor, Murfreesboro, alleged rape, July 18, 1881.

Mike Walls, Dyer County, August 1, 1881.

Wilson Wade, Obion County, September 5, 1882.

Henry Huddleston, alleged rape, Franklin County, 1883.

Mormon missionaries, William S. Berry, John H. Gibbs, lynched, Lewis County, August 10, 1884.

Taylor, first name unknown, (w), McKenzie, November 1, 1884.

Three men, Frank Freeman, Charles Latham, Alinus Young, Union City, TN March 11, 1885.

Freeman Ward and Bud Farris (w), Union City, April 14, 1885.

Unidentified "young negro man," near Brownsville, July 15, 1885.

Lee Sellers, (w), murdered on bridge Knoxville, September 4, 1885.

Charles Williams, Chattanooga, September 7, 1885.

John C. Thompson (w) Roane County, *c.* October 30, 1885.

Samuel Fowlkes, (place unknown) December 9, 1885.

John Gillesspie, (w) murder, Loudon 19 March 1886

Eliza Wood, Jackson, Madison County, August 18, 1886.

Matthew Washington, Dyer County, October 14, 1886.

Joseph Thomas, (place unknown) April 13, 1887.

Unidentified, lynching, Hunter's Bluff, *c.* January 27, 1888.

Amos Miller, alleged rape of white woman, Franklin, August 10, 1888.

John Wolfinbarger (w), 1889 Grainger County, April 3, 1889.

Dan Bealer (w), murder Grainger County April 5, 1889.

Alf Grizzard Tiptonville, June 20, 1889.

John Hanner, Pairs, alleged murder, August 13, 1889.

"Doc" Jones, Chester, Henderson County, December 18, 1889.

Frank Simpson alleged rape, Henderson County (Lexington) January 8, 1890.

Jacob Staples, Heiskell's Station, February 19, 1890.

Henry Williams, Gadsden, assault, Crockett County, March 16 1890.

Unknown (w), Grainger County, alleged murder April 5, 1890.

Steve Jacobs, Fayetteville, alleged barn burner April 21, 1890.

George Warner, attempted rape, Columbia May 26, 1890.

Henderson Fox, alleged rape, Trenton, August 16, 1890.

Thomas Woodward (?), Humboldt, August 18, 1890.

Edward Stearns (or Stevens), Savannah, Hardin County, November 17, 1890.

Bradford Scott, Pinson, March 10, 1891.

Henry Sanders, Lavernia (LaVergne?), March 13, 1891.

Thomas Huntley (or Tom Hurley), alleged murder Cumberland Gap, March 26, 1891.

Martin Mayberry, Bryant Station, April 2, 1891.

William (or Jim) Taylor, Franklin County, April [26?] 30, 1891.
Green Wells, murder, Columbia, May 26, 1891.
Thompson, Gibson County, June 5, 1891.
Robert Clark, Bristol, June 13, 1891.
Ben Walling alleged rape, Decatur County, June 19, 1891 (July 19?).
Thompson, Dyer, July 5, 1891.
Jim Taylor, Williamson County, July 17, 1891.
John Brown, Dyer, July 26, 1891.
Fox Henderson, Trenton, August 21, 1891.
William Lewis, Tullahoma, August 25, 1891.
Joseph Mitchell, McConnell, November 13, 1891.
Frinch Haynie, Hendersonville, February 16, 1891.
Martin, female, Sumner County, February 3, 1892.
Unidentified, Waynesboro, March 4, 1892.
Charles White (w), Blount County, March 5, 1892.
Calvin McDonnell, Thomas Moss, William Stuart, murder, "the Curve," Memphis, March 8, 1892.
Henry Grizzard, rape Goodlettsville, April 28, 1892.
Ephraim Grizzard, rape Nashville, April 30, 1892.
Charles Everett, Manchester, May 19, 1892.
Heck Willis, Lebanon, May 31, 1892.
Will Bates, (w) alleged murder, Bedford County June 2, 1892.
Thomas Lillard, Woodbury, July 1, 1892.
H. H. Wynne (w), murder, Dickson County, July 25, 1892.
Andy Beshears (w), John Willis (w) alleged rape, Campbell County July 29, 1892.
Loeb Landers, Dresden, August 1, 1892.
Dennis Blackwell, Alamo, August 27, 1892.
Alex Bell, Mount Pelia, October 5, 1892.
Two unidentified, Jellico, (Campbell County), December 7, 1892.
Unidentified, Nashville, December 15, 1892.
Irwin Roberts, alleged murder "Shady Valley" near Mountain City, Johnson County, December 17, 1892.
Barnes, alleged rape, (South) Guthrie (Montgomery County), December 19, 1892.
One unidentified, Forest Hill, February 11, 1893.
Alfred (Andy?) Blount, Chattanooga, alleged rape, February 21, 1893.
Jessie Jones, Jellico, March 19, 1893.
L. C. Dumas, Gleason, June 8, 1893.
One unidentified, Memphis, July 18, 1893.
Lee Walker, Memphis, July 22, 1893.
Edgar Bell, alleged murder, Dresden July 27, 1893.
Charles Tait, Memphis, August 21, 1893.
John Williams, Jackson, September 14, 1893.
John Gamble, Pikeville, October 22, 1893.
Henry McGreeg, Pioneer, February 11, 1894.
Lampson Gregory, Bells Depot, March 6, 1894.
Henry Montgomery, Lewisburg, April 18, 1894.

Frank Ballard, Jackson, June 1, 1894.

James Perry, Knoxville, June 10, 1894.

James Ball, Charlotte, July 7, 1894.

William Bell, alleged murder, Dixon County, July 14, 1894.

William Nershbred, Rossville, August 12 1894.

Six men, Warren Williams, John Hays, Ed Hall, Robert Hays, Graham White and Dan Hawking, alleged barn burners, at Kerrville, (Shelby County), August 31, 1894.

Needham (Neely?) Smith, Tipton Co, November 10, 1894.

Jim Allen, Brownsville, alleged barn burner, December 20, 1894.

Harriet Talley, Petersburg, March 20, 1895.

Unidentified man, Parsons, April 25, 1895.

Jerry Johnson, Farmington, September 3, 1895.

"Doc" King, Fayetteville, September 6, 1895.

Eugene Vancy, Manchester, October 15, 1895.

Jefferson Ellis near Braden, Fayette County, October 16, 1895.

Charles Hurd, Wartburg, November 21, 1895.

Cad Smith, (w) for rape in James County, *circa* November 27, 1895.

Joseph Robinson, Fayetteville, November 29, 1895.

Ozias McGahey, Joe Robinson, attempted, rape, Fayetteville, November 29, 1895.

Frank Simpson, Lexington, January 8, 1896.

Harrison Fuller, Lexington, January 8, 1896.

York Douglas, McMinnville, April 17, 1896.

William and Victor Hillis, (w) McMinnville, murder April 26, 1896.

G. H. Givens, (w) Mountain City, April 27, 1896.

Samuel Clay, Martin, June 12, 1896.

Unidentified man, Trenton, June 30, 1896.

Nimrod Cross, Sardis, July 6, 1896.

Dave Powell, William Loving, Will Dixon alleged murder, McKenzie, November 15, 1896.

Samuel McDonald, for making threats against white man, November 19, 1896.

Two unidentified men, Webb City, February 17, 1897.

Charles Brown, Rathburn, Hamilton County, February 24 (25?), 1897.

One unidentified man, Newcastle, June 23, 1897.

Tony Williamson, West Point, July 15, 1897.

Richard Thurman, Ripley, August 9, 1897.

John Collar, Godson, March 21, 1898.

Joseph Mitchell, Rives, May 27, 1898.

Charles Washington, Mine Lick, June 23, 1898.

Richard Thurmond, Ripley, August 8, 1898.

John Williams, Mountain City, September 26, 1898.

John Smart, Chapelton, November 19, 1898.

George Call, John Shaw, Lynchburg, January 17, 1899.

A. M. Larme (w) murder, Chester County, April 18, 1899.

William Chambers, Bell Buckle, August 11, 1899.

Henry (Frank) and Rueben Giveney, Ripley, TN January 9, 1900.

Anderson Gauge, (place unknown), January 15, 1900.

Louis Rice, (place unknown), March 22, 1900.

Hugh Jones, (place unknown), July 14, 1900.

Logan Beams, Duplex, September 10, 1900.

Unidentified man, South Pittsburg, September 26, 1900.

Williams, Tiptonville, October 3, 1900.

Fred King, Dyersburg, February 18, 1901.

Charles Davis, (w) alleged rape, Smithville, August 2, 1901.

Henry Knoles, tortured burned, murder, Winchester, August 25, 1901.

Garfield Burley and Curtis Brown (Broom?), Newbern, Dyer County, October 8, 1902.

John Davis, Lewisburg, *c.* November 12–13, 1902.

Casey Jones, Elk Valley, June 24, 1903.

Allen Small, Lynchburg, September 25, 1903.

Joseph Brake, Ripley, December 19, 1903.

Thomas Searcy, Brownsville, alleged rape, April 29, 1904.

Ronce Gwyn theft, Coffee County, March 8, 1905.

Ed Johnson, Chattanooga, (national protest results), March 19, 1906.

Bob Williams, (place unknown), May 30, 1906.

[Blacks flogged, Dresden, attempted rape, April 9, 1908]

George Johnson, attempted rape Murfreesboro, August 28, 1908.

Marshall, Edward, Jim Stinbeck (brothers), Tiptonville, November 24, 1908.

Albert Lawson, murder, Paris, Henry County, July 19, 1909.

Leo Sloan, and "Daddy" Baker and one unidentified, Hale's Bar, February 8, 1910.

Walter Greer, David Neal, Green Bauman murder, Shelbyville February 19, 1912.

William Carden, (w) rape, Bradley County, December 12, 1912.

John Talley, Dyer County, alleged rape, November 7, 1913.

Thomas Brooks, alleged murder, April 28, 1915.

Eli Parsons, alleged rape, Memphis, May 22, 1917.

Lation Scott (place unknown) December 2, 1917.

G. W. Lynch, (a.k.a. Nych or Wych), Prairie Springs February 10, 1918.

Jim McIlheron, Franklin County, February 12, 1918.

Berry Noyes, Lexington April 25, 1918.

Henry Booth, attempted rape, Gibson County, October 26, 1919.

Edmund Hartley, (w) George Haley (w) murder Benton County, October 20, 1922.

Samuel Smith, fifteen years old, taken from deathbed, Nashville, December 15, 1924.

Near Dover, unknown, October 8 (3?), 1926.

Joe Baxley, Alamo, May 29, 1929.

George Smith, Union City, April 18, 1931.

Cordie Cheek, Maury County, December 15, 1933.

(Attempted lynching of E. K. Harris, Shelbyville, courthouse razed, December 19, 1934)

Richard "Dick" Wilkerson, Manchester, Tennessee, June 24, 1934.

Unidentified, near Dresden, August 5, 1934.

Baxter Bell, White Bluff, November 3, 1935.

Albert Gooden, (place unknown), August 13, 1937.

Elbert Williams, NAACP officer in Brownsville, June 22, 1940.

James Thomas Scales, Pikeville, November 23, 1944.

James "Digger" Johnson and William F. Goodwin, Columbia, ("Mink Slide") February 28, 1946.

Endnotes

Chapter 1

1 Isaac, P. C., *Prohibition and Politics: Turbulent Decades in Tennessee* (Knoxville, Tenn.: University of Tennessee Press, 1965), and Corlew, R. E., *Tennessee: A Short History*, 2nd ed., (Knoxville, Tenn.: University of Tennessee Press, 1981), 378-381, 416-419, 428-429.

2 Gunn, J. C., *Gunn's Domestic Medicine: A Facsimile of the First Edition, Tennessean Editions,* intro. by Charles E. Rosenberg (Knoxville, Tennessee: The University of Tennessee Press, 1986), v-xxi, 312, 318-321, 401-404.

3 *Ibid.*, 401.

4 *Ibid.*, 21, 52, 134, 139, 142, 145, 150, 174, 183, 192, 193, 195, 200, 202, 203, 204, 206, 216, 243, 249, 284, 312, 315, 317, 332, 347, 352, 355.

5 *Ibid.*, 402.

6 Terry, Charles E. and Pellens, Mildred, "The Extent of Chronic Opium Use in the United States Prior to 1921," in Ball John C., and Chambers, Carl D., eds., *The Epidemiology of Opiate Addiction in the United States* Springfield 1989.

7 Chestnut, Mary Boykin, *A Diary from Dixie,* ed. Ben Ames Williams, (Boston, 1949), pp. 84, 504-506.

8 Gunn, *op. cit.*, p. 402.

9 *Ibid.*, 491.

10 *Ibid.*, 404.

11 War Department, U.S., Office of the Surgeon General, *Military and Surgical History of the War of the Rebellion* (Washington, DC: GPO), Part 1, II, 646, Part 2, II, 207, Part 3, I, 547, 966.

12 War Department, U.S., *Official Records of the War of Rebellion*, Series 1, vol. 30, pt. 3, 246.

13 *Official Records of the War of Rebellion*, Series 1, vol. 30, pt. 3, p. 246.

14   Courtwright David T., "Opiate Addiction as a Consequence of the Civil War," *Civil War History,* XXXIV, II, (June 1978), 107. Terry and Pellens, *op. cit.*, p. 39

15   Williamson, J. C., ed., "The Civil War Diary of John Coffee Williamson," *Tennessee Historical Quarterly,* vol. XV, no. 1 (March, 1956). p. 65; "A Diary Kept through 1863 and into 1864 by Mary L. Pearre" (Williamson County) (Tennessee State Library and Archives, Nashville: TSLA) [emphasis added]; War Journal of Lucy Smith French June 15, 1863, typed transcription, Tennessee State Library and Archives (TSLA).

16   Courtwright, David T., "Opiate Addiction as a Consequence of the Civil War," *Civil War History,* XXXIV, II, (June 1978), 107. It casually has been suggested that Confederate General John Bell Hood was addicted to pain killers of the type described above. He may have acquired an addiction as a result of the serious wounds he suffered at Gettysburg and later at Chickamauga. It may be likely that Hood became addicted to some kind of opiate pain killer. One wonders if narcotic dependency may have impaired his martial judgment, for example, at the Battle of Franklin. There he ordered Confederate soldiers to undertake a frontal attack on a fortified Federal position sitting on the high ground. Federal General John M. Schofield had already obeyed the first dictum of military science namely "take the high ground." The second precept is to go around the high ground if it cannot be taken. Hood may have been better served to go around the hill and attack Nashville than to waste so many lives. Why would he behave so? Thomas L. Connelly in his *Civil War Tennessee: Battles and Leaders,* (Knoxville:1990), 87-98, makes allusions to Hood having "fumbled" a chance to destroy Schofield's army, that Hood "whether from exhaustion or other reasons" did not strike when he had an opportunity, that erstwhile Kentuckian was "totally unreasonable" or that he was "too emotionally distraught to continue in command." Could drug addiction, perhaps one of the "other reasons" have caused Hood to make such unbefitting actions? At the same time, however, there appears to be no direct primary evidence that Hood was addicted to opiates.

17   Williamson, J. C., *op. cit.* p. 65. War Journal of Lucy Smith French June 15, 1863, typed transcription, Tennessee State Library and Archives (TSLA).

18   Musto, David F., M.D., *The American Disease: Origins of Narcotic Control* (London: Yale University Press), 2.

19   *Chattanooga Daily Times,* October 24, 1889, and August 3, 1911.

20   Memphis *Daily Avalanche,* May 27, 1879.

21   Memphis *Daily Avalanche,* Memphis *Public Ledger,* June 27, 1879, *Memphis Daily Appeal,* June 28, 1879.

22   Memphis *Daily Avalanche,* June 27, 1879. (See also Memphis *Public Ledger,* June 27 1879.)

23   *Memphis Daily Appeal,* June 28, 1879.

24   *Ibid.*

25   Memphis *Public Ledger,* June 27, 1879.

26   *Ibid.,* June 28, 1879.

27   *Memphis Daily Appeal,* June 29, 1879.

28   *Ibid.*

29   Memphis *Public Ledger,* July 2, 1879

30   *Memphis Daily Appeal,* July 12, 1879.

31 *Daily Memphis Avalanche,* August 23, 1885.

32 Nashville *Daily American,* March 30, 1888.

33 Thomas, Miss Jane, *Old Days in Nashville: 1800 to 1899,* (Nashville, Tenn.: Publishing House of the Methodist Episcopal Church, Barbee & Smith, Agents, 1899), 80. Her use of the phrase "they had just started inhaling morphine here" seems ambiguous and could mean the drug was then widely popular in Nashville or perhaps the drug was just then being inhaled at the soiree.

34 *Nashville American,* March 23, 1895.

35 *Chattanooga Daily Times,* August 13, 1911.

36 *Knoxville Journal and Tribune,* July 8, 1900. [Emphasis added.]

37 See for example: Nashville *Daily American,* February 20, 1876, October 5, 1878, August 26, 1884, October 8, 1884, July 14, 1888, December 28, 1888, December 12, 1890, April 8, 1983, June 27, 1886, October 10, 1894, March 23, 1901, October 28, 1904; Nashville *Tennessean,* June 27, 1896, September 9, 1887, October 4, 1895, August 18, 1902, April 22, 1908, April 26, 1908, July 3, 1909, February 26, 1910, January 13, 1912, February 10, 1914, February 26, 1918, February 23, 1922; *Nashville Tennessean and Nashville American,* April 22, 1908, June 13, 1912, July 22, 1912, February 10, 1914; Nashville *Republican Banner,* May 31, 1854, April 10, 1869, August 14, 1869, January 25, 1870.

38 *Chattanooga Daily Times,* October 24, 1889, and August 3, 1911.

39 *Memphis Daily Avalanche,* June 3, 1874, June 19, 1885.

40 Nashville *Republican Banner,* August 4 1867; Nashville *Union and Dispatch,* August 4, 1867; Nashville *Daily Press and Times,* August 5, 1867; Nashville *Republican Banner,* August 22, 1874.

41 Nashville *Daily American,* December 7, 1878.

42 *Ibid.,* April 13, 1889.

43 Memphis *Public Ledger,* July, 28, 1874; Memphis *Commercial Appeal,* August 23, 1885, May 5, 1901, July 27, 1903 September 25, 1905, August 15, 1917; *Memphis Daily Avalanche,* September 4, 1885 *Knoxville Journal and Tribune,* February 25, 1900, and "Knoxville City Council Minute Books," Meeting of the January 6, 1905, 162, 167; *Chattanooga Daily Times, May 7, 1911, and;* John C. Ball, Carl D. Chambers, comp. & ed., pref. by Griffith Edwards, M.D., *The Epidemiology of Opiate Addiction in the United States,* (Springfield, Ill.: Charles C. Thomas, 1970), 37-78.

44 Musto, *op. cit.,* p 3; 61st U.S. Congress, 2d session, *op. cit.,* pp.32-33

45 U.S. Congress, *House Report No. 140: Report of the Committee on Military Affairs, to Which Were Referred the Correspondence and Documents from the War Department, in Relation to the Proceedings of a Court Martial, Ordered for the Trial of Certain Tennessee Militiamen, February 11, 1822,* 32, 36; Hudson, Charles, *The Southeastern Indians,* (Knoxville, TN: University of Tennessee Press, 1987) 226-229, 348.

46 *Memphis Daily Avalanche,* December 6, 1885, and Morgan H,. Wayne, *Drugs in America: A Social History, 1800-1980,* (Syracuse, NY: Syracuse University Press, 1981), 91, and *Memphis Commercial, Appeal,* July 27, 1903.

47 Memphis *Commercial Appeal,* July 27, 1903. Musto, *op. cit.,* p. 3. See also: 61st U.S. Congress, 2d session, *op. cit.,* 32-33.

48 *Memphis Daily Avalanche,* December 6, 1885.

49   "The Decline of Cocaine," *Medical and Surgical Reporter,* 54 (April 3, 1886), 446, and *op. cit.* Morgan, 16. Memphis *Commercial Appeal,* July 27, 1903.

50   Musto, *op. cit.,* p. 7.

51   *1897 Sears Roebuck Catalog,* p. 36.

52   61st U.S. Congress, 2d session, *op. cit.,* p. 48.

53   *Knoxville Journal and Tribune,* February 25, 1900.

54   Musto, *op. cit.,* p. 7; *Chattanooga Daily Times,* February 24, 1914.

55   61st U.S. Congress, 2d session, *op. cit.,* p.49.

56   *Nashville American,* October 24, 1899.

57   *Chattanooga Daily Times,* May 1, 1900.

58   *Ibid.,* June 7, 1900.

59   *Ibid.,* June 8, 1900.

60   Musto, *op. cit.,* p. 7.

61   *1897 Sears Roebuck Catalog,* p. 36.

62   61st U.S. Congress, 2d session, *op. cit.,* p. 48.

63   *Knoxville Journal and Tribune,* February 25, 1900.

64   *Ibid.,* June 8, 12, 1900.

65   Jones, Jr., James B. "Municipal Vice: The Management of Prostitution in Tennessee's Urban Experience. Part II: The Examples of Chattanooga and Knoxville, 1838-1917," *Tennessee Historical Quarterly,* L, 2 (1991), 115-117.

66   *Knoxville Journal and Tribune,* March 4, 1900.

67   *Chattanooga Daily Times,* June 8, 1900.

68   *Knoxville Journal and Tribune,* July 21, 1900.

69   Knoxville City Minute Books, Book N, Meeting of December 2, 1904, 139, and Meeting of January 6, 1905, 162, 167. Nashville either had no problem with drug addiction, or if it did the city authorities apparently did not consider it a problem worthy of their attention.

70   Memphis *Commercial Appeal,* July 27, 1903. [Emphasis added.] According to the account, one of the lullabies sung at these coke parties went like this: "I's don been drun on absenthe/Way down in New Orleans/I been drinkin' steamboat likker/Since I was in my teens/I been drinkin' corjal, wine an' rum/I been drinkin' corjal, wine an' rum/Bud de quickes' action, and de mos' satisfaction/Is a little sniff ob coke/It mak me feel lak ridin' on a cloud/An' floatin' thru de air on wings/An' I hears sweet voices a singin' loud/An' dis am de song dey sings:/Refrain: Honey take a sniff on me/No mo' trubble we'll see/Baby, take a sniff on me/An' we'll sail thru de jasper sea/Take a sniff on me! [*sic*]."

71   *Op. cit.,*Morgan, 93, as cited from Ways and Means Committee, *Importation and Use of Opium,* 12-13.

72   *Ibid.,* September 26, 1905.

73   *Chattanooga Daily Times,* July 5, 1911.

74   *Ibid.,* July 13, 1911.

75   *Nashville American,* October 23, 1899.

76   *Ibid.,* June 29, 1903.

77   *Public Acts of the State of Tennessee by the Fifty-Eighth General Assembly, 1913,* (Nashville, Tenn.: McQuiddy Co., 1913), 403-407. See also: Wolfe, Margaret Ripley, *Lucius Polk Brown and Progressive Food and Drug Control: Tennessee and New*

York City, 1908-1920, (Lawrence, Kansas: Regents Press of Kansas, 1978), 69-70.

78 Brown, Lucius P., "Enforcement of the Tennessee Anti-Narcotics Law," *American Journal of Public Health,* 5 (April 5, 1915), 323-324.

79 Terry and Pellens, *op. cit.,* p.66.

80 Brown, *op. cit.,* pp. 326-327. See also: Terry and Pellens, *op. cit.,* pp. 52-55.

81 *Public Acts of the State of Tennessee by the Fifty-Eighth General Assembly, op. cit.,* pp.403-407. See also: Wolfe, *op. cit.,* 69-70.

82 Brown, *op. cit.,* pp. 326-327. See also: Terry and Pellens, *op. cit.,* pp.52-55.

83 Brown, *op. cit.* p. 332.

84 *Ibid.,* 333.

85 *Ibid.*

86 Memphis *Commercial Appeal,* October 10, 1915.

87 Brown, *op. cit.,* 333.

88 *Ibid.*

89 *Chattanooga Daily Times,* June 27, 1917.

90 Brown, *op. cit.,* p. 333.

91 *Ibid.*

92 Memphis *Commercial Appeal,* August 15, 1917.

93 Brown, *op. cit.,* p.333. See also, Jones, Jr. James, B., *Drug Abuse and Prostitution in Tennessee History* (Self-Published: 2014) pp. 27-32.

Chapter 2

1 *Minutes of the Nashville Board of Aldermen,* Meeting of November 9, 1854. See also: Nashville *Republican Banner,* November 9, 1854.

2 Nashville *Union,* November 28, 1854

3 Yet, according to the Nashville *Republican Banner* February 11, 1851, there existed a "house of industry" that housed girls under 18 teaching them domestic and occupational skills. Whether these girls were former prostitutes or orphans is not known.

4 Minutes of the Nashville Board of Aldermen, Meeting of January 11, 1855.

5 Minutes of the Nashville Board of Aldermen, op. cit., Meeting of April 10, 1856; according to Anita Shafer Goodstein, the expulsion of the prostitutes became a local political issue; see Goodstein, Anita Shafer *Nashville, 1780-1860: From Frontier to City,* (Gainesville, Fla., 1989), 249.

6 Nashville *Republican Banner,* March 30, 1860. The article cited came from the *Memphis Appeal* which had quoted it from the *Nashville Methodist Banner.* The claim that there were 1,500 prostitutes in Nashville is probably an exaggeration.

7 Kaser, David, "Nashville's Women of Pleasure in 1860," *Tennessee Historical Quarterly,* 23 (1964):382.

8 United States Surgeon General's Office, *The Medical and Surgical History of the War of the Rebellion,* Vol. 1, Pt. 3, ed. Charles Smartt (Washington, D.C.: GPO, 1888), 891 For an account of the "floating whore house" as given by Captain John M. Newcomb of the *Idahoe,* see: Record Group 29, Records of the State Historian, Box 23, folder 19 at the Tennessee State Library and Archives in Nashville.

9   United States Surgeon General's Office, *ibid.*, p. 895; *Memphis Daily Bulletin*, January 19, April 2 and 22, May 7, June 3 and 14, 1864; and Jones, *op. cit.*, 275-76.

10 *Nashville Daily Press*, February 15, 1864; Chambers, William M., *Sanitary Report of the Condition of the Prostitutes of Nashville*, January 31, 1865, William P. Palmer Collection, Western Reserve Historical Society, Cleveland, 3-4, and Jones, *op. cit.*, 273-75. On September 10, 1864, the *Nashville Daily Press* reported the citizens of Cherry Street between Broad and Cedar were "treated to a sight ... that ... should be allowed no mention. A fleshy ... *fille de joie*, whose sense of modesty seemed wholly to have merged in the large development of her physical charms, entirely nude from the waist heavenward, in an open hack, drove rapidly up Cherry Street.... As she passed the Maxwell Barracks, the hundreds of soldiers ... set up lusty and continuous shouts of admiration ... an enthusiasm so wild and hearty that it can ... better be imagined than described." Because the army was administering the first legalized system of prostitution in American history, there can be little doubt as to the profession of this half-naked woman. She may have done it on a bet, or maybe she was just advertising.

11 Memphis City Council Meeting Minutes, Meeting of August 6, 1861 and Meeting for October 15, 1861

12 *Memphis Daily Bulletin*, April 30, May 1, 1863.

13 United States Surgeon General's Office, *op. cit.*, p 895; *Memphis Daily Bulletin*, January 19, April 2 and 22, May 7; *Ibid.*, June 3 and 14, 1864.

14 Napheys, George H., *The Transmission of Life; Counsels on the Nature and Hygiene of the Masculine Function*, fourteenth edition, (Atlanta, Ga., 1873), 111-12.

15 Nashville *Daily American*, June 11, 1886

16 *Ibid.*, June 16, 1886

17 *Ibid.*

18 *Ibid.*, June 18, 1886

19 Nashville *Republican Banner*, September 13, 1874; October 24, 29, 30, 1874; March 25, 1875; April 9, 1875; September 22, 1875; November 12, 1875: Nashville *Daily American*, March 25, 1875; February 17, 1876; August 9, 1876; February 14, 1878; December 8, 1878; March 27, 1879; May 1, 22, 1879; September 11, 1879; February 26, 1880; March 7, 1880; April 13, 1880; May 9, 1880; December 15, 1881; March 9, 1882; November 15 1883; May 8, 1883; August, 1883; November 15, 1883; May 15, 1884; May 29, 1887; February 6, 26, 1888; May 30, 1888; September 13, 1888; January 11, 1893; March 18, 1894; May 9, 1895; August 30, 1895; May 23, 1899. October 25, 1901; Nashville *Tennessean*, January 1, 1896; February 17, 1910; April 10, 17, 19, 1910. *Nashville Tennessean and Nashville American*, December 29, 1918.

20 Nashville *Daily American*, June 18, 1886

21 Doyle, Don, *Nashville in the New South: 1880-1930*, (Knoxville, 1985), pp. 71, 80, 82, and; Thomason, Philip, "The Men's Quarter in Downtown Nashville," *Tennessee Historical Quarterly*, 41, No. 1 (Spring 1982), pp. 48-66. See also: Nashville *Daily American*, August 8, 9, 11, 1885. [Extant physical evidence at one club in the Men's Quarter ironically named the "Climax Hotel," contradicts Thomason's claim that prostitution was not a part of the Men's Quarter. The Climax featured false walls on the third floor which housed prostitutes. Hidden panels in the small bedrooms opened into a closet running the length of the building. Here

prostitutes and their customers could safely evade any police search. See: Whitt, Wayne, "Climax is Gone: Memories Linger," *The Tennessean Magazine*, July 8, 1973, pp. 10-12, esp. p. 11.]

22 *Nashville Banner*, November 11, 1915.

23 *Ibid.*, November 12, 1915. See also: *Nashville Tennessean and Nashville American*, November 12, 13, 1915; and *Nashville Union*, November 28, 1854. [The so-called "Nuisance Act" provided for the prohibition of brothels, gaming dens, and saloons by injunction. See: State of Tennessee, *Fifth-Eighth General Assembly*, 1913 (Nashville 1913), 665-666.], and; Rosen, Ruth, *The Lost Sisterhood: Prostitution in America*, 1900-1918, (Baltimore, 1982), pp. 90-97.

24 *Nashville Banner*, November 11, 1915 and *Nashville Tennessean and the Nashville American*, November 25, 27, 1915.

25 Boyer, Paul, *Urban Masses and Moral Order in America, 1820-1920.*, (Cambridge, 1978), 191.

26 Hofstadter, Richard, *The Age of Reform: From Bryan to FDR*, (New York: Vintage Books, 1960), p. 289; Boyer John C. "The Progressive Era Revolution in America Attitudes toward Sex," *Journal of American History*, Vol. 59, (March 1973), pp. 885-908; Lubove, Roy, "The Progressives and the Prostitute," *Historian*, 24 (May 1962), pp. 308-313; LeHever, Harry G. "Prostitution, Politics and Religion; The Crusade Against Vice in Atlanta in 1912," *Atlanta Historical Journal*, 24, (September 1980), 7-29; Petrik, Paula, "Capitalists with Rooms: Prostitution in Helena Montana, 1865-1900," *Montana*, 31 (April 1981), 28-41; Degler, Carl N., "What Ought To Be and What Was: Women's Sexuality in the Nineteenth Century," *American Historical Review*, 79 (December 1974), pp. 1467-90; Rose, Al, *Storyville, New Orleans: Being an Illustrated Account of the Notorious Red Light District*, (University of Alabama; Tuscaloosa, 1978); McGovern, James R. "Prostitution in Progressive Era Pensacola," *Florida Historical Quarterly*, 54 (October 1975), pp. 131-54; Rosen, *op. cit.*, pp. 112-137, and; *Chattanooga Daily Times*, August 1, 1911.

27 Rosen, *op. cit.*, pp. 7, 44-49, and; Connelly, Mark Thomas, *The Response to Prostitution in the Progressive Era*, (Chapel Hill, 1980), p. 7.

28 Connelly, *op. cit.*, p. 7. [One argument holds that by concentrating their emphasis upon prostitution, the most sensational and overt form of prohibited sexual relation as well as the most stigmatized sort of female life beyond patriarchal authority and protection, reformers had in fact discovered a means to relieve their anxieties and avoid confronting more compromising social and economic issues. See: Walkowitz, Judith K., *Prostitution and Victorian Society: Women, Class, and the State*, (1980)]

29 *Nashville Tennessean and American*, November 22, 1915; Rosen, *op. cit.*, pp. 14-15, 40, 51-68; Connelly, *op. cit.*, pp. 114-35.

30 *Nashville Banner*, November 13, 1915, and; Nashville *Tennessean and Nashville American*, November 22, 1915.

31 Rosen, *op. cit.*, p. 23: (Rosen continues: "The term *feeble-minded*, [sic] then, became a way of classifying aggressive female sexuality, as well as expressing the growing class and cultural conflicts between penal reformers, eugenicists, and antivice crusaders and the target of their efforts, prostitutes and sexually 'deviant women.'") See also: Connelly, *op. cit.*, *Response*, pp. 41-44.

32 *Nashville Banner*, November 17, 1915.

33   *Ibid.*

34   Connelly, *op. cit.*, pp. 4-5, 15-16; Rosen, *op. cit.*, pp. 14-37, 72.

35   Memphis *Public Ledger*, February 23, 1874.

36   *Daily Memphis Avalanche*, October 1, 1885.

37   Miller, William D., *Memphis During the Progressive Era, 1900-1917*, (Memphis, 1957), p. 87.

38   Handy, W.C., *Beale Street Blues*, (New York: 1917).

39   Miller, *op. cit.*, p. 89.

40   *Ibid.*, p. 144.

41   *Ibid.*, p. 186.

42   Memphis *Commercial Appeal*, July 15, 1917.

43   Connelly, *op. cit.*, pp. 5-7, 143-146. See also: Snow, William F., MD, "Social Hygiene and the War," *Social Hygiene*, 3 (July 1917): 417-50, and: Martin, Franklin, "Social Hygiene and the War," *Social Hygiene*, 3 (October 1917): 605-27.

44   Boyer, *op. cit.*, *Moral Order*, 195; Memphis *Commercial Appeal*, July 12, 1917.

45   Connelly, *op. cit.*, pp. 5-7, 143-146. See also: Snow, *op. cit.*, 417-50, and: Martin, *op. cit.*, 605-27.

45   Memphis *Commercial Appeal*, July 16, 18, 19, 22, 25, 28, 31, August 7, 15, 19, 1917; Miller, *op. cit.*, 188.

46   Miller, *op. cit.*, 188.

47   Supreme Court, East Tennessee Division, *M. G. Weidner, et al., vs. Irene Friedman, et al.,* Tennessee State Library and Archives, Box 1184, Manuscripts Division: Deposition of W. B. Walker, and: Deposition of Benjamin Kerr. Manuscripts Section of the Tennessee State Library and Archives.

48   Supreme Court, East Tennessee Division *op. cit.* Deposition of J. M. James.

49   *Ibid.*, Deposition of J. L. Whiteside, March 24, 1911.

50   *Chattanooga Daily Times*, June 26, 1885. See also *Ibid.*, June 27, 1885.

51   *Ibid.*, July 11, 1885.

52   *Ibid.*, July 12, 1885.

53   *Ibid.*, July 13, 15, 19, 20, 22, 24, August 7, 8, 1885.

54   *Ibid.*, July 16, 1885

55   *Ibid.*, July 19, 1885.

56   *Ibid.*, July 13, 1885.

57   *Ibid.*, July 19, 1885.

58   *Ibid.*, September 1, 1887.

59   *Ibid.*, January 25, 31, February 3, March 2, 21, April 3, 24, May 16, 1888, and October 22, 1889; *Nashville American*, December 24, 1900.

60   Supreme Court, East Tennessee Division, *op. cit.*, Deposition of W. B. Walker, and: Deposition of Benjamin Kerr. Manuscripts Section of the Tennessee State Library and Archives.

61   Supreme Court, East Tennessee Division, *op. cit.*, Deposition of J. M. James. Testimony of W. B. Walker, April 8, 1911.

62   Rosen, *op. cit.*, p. 5.

63   *Chattanooga Daly Times*, April 13, 1911.

64   Supreme Court, East Tennessee Division, *op. cit.*, Affidavit of J. M James., June 11, 1910. The assertions concerning attire in the district include the testimony that

prostitutes wore "… loose fitting mother hubbard dresses in that section.…" Another witness stated "… sometimes they have regular dresses on and sometimes in the evening … they have loose ones on." Another witness, a seventy-two-year old insurance agent, complained that half-clad women stood in doorways as he drove his family to church on Sunday mornings. The prostitutes' dresses, he said knowingly, were designed so that at the "pull a string … all their clothes drop off…" See: *op. cit.*, Testimony of J. J. Sullivan, March 24, 1911. J.C. Jumper, March 24, 1911, and Deposition of F .E. Tyler, April 8, 1911.

65 *Ibid.*

66 *Ibid.*, Testimony of W. B. Walker, April 8, 1911.

67 *Ibid.*, Testimony of N. B. Hynes, April 8, 1911.

68 *Ibid.*, Testimony of Captain Will Burk, J. L. Whiteside, and Deposition of A. J. Geisman, April 8, 1911.

69 *Ibid.*, Deposition of Irene Friedman, December 12, 1911.

70 *Ibid.*, Deposition of Nellie Hood, December 12, 1911. See also: Rosen, *op. cit.*, p. 101, and: Barker-Benfield, G. J., *The Horrors of the Half-Known Life: Male Attitudes Toward Women and Sexuality in Nineteenth-Century America,* (New York: Harper and Row, 1976).

71 Supreme Court, East Tennessee Division, *op. cit.*, Opinion of the Court, June 24, 1912.

72 *Chattanooga Business Directories*, 1907-1910, 1912, 1913, 1915, 1917, 1920, Tennessee State Library & Archives. (The abbreviation "Mad" is never defined in the directories, yet its meaning seems clear and is verified by lists of prostitute's names in court records.)

73 *Chattanooga Daily Times*, May 26, 1917. See also: Livingood, James W., *A History of Hamilton County, Tennessee,* (Memphis, 1981), pp, 353-60.

74 *Chattanooga Daily Times*, May 17, 24-25, 1917 and, Rosen, *op. cit.*, 35, 36, 62. See also: *Chattanooga News*, May 17, 25, 26, 1917.

75 *Ibid.*, May 26, 1917.

76 *Ibid.*

77 *Ibid.*, May 27, 1917.

78 *Ibid.*, October 22, 1889.

79 *Ibid.*, September 9, 1917.

80 Minutes of the Common Council of the City of Knoxville, Book B-1/2, Meeting of May 16, 1838, p. 24.

81 Minutes of the Common Council of the City of Knoxville, *op. cit.*, Book D, Meeting of May 10, 1867, p. 399, and: *op. cit.*, Meeting of February 17, 1868, p. 466. See also: *Knoxville Daily Chronicle*, August 14, 1885.

82 Minutes of the Common Council of the City of Knoxville, *op. cit.*, Book D. Meeting of June 4, 1869, p. 533.

83 *Knoxville Daily Chronicle*, August 8, 1885.

84 *Ibid.*, August 10, 11, 14, 1885.

85 *Ibid.*, August 11, 1885.

86 *Ibid.*, August 10, 1885.

87 *Ibid.*, August 13, 1885.

88 *Ibid.*, August 8, 13, 14, 1885.

89 *Ibid.*, August 18, 1885.

90 Minutes of the Common Council of the City of Knoxville, *op. cit.*, Book J, *op. cit.*, Meeting of September 26, 1890, p. 252. See also *Knoxville Journal*, September 27, 1890.

91 Rothrock, Mary U., ed., *The French Broad-Holston Country*, (Knoxville, 1948), p. 424: McDonald, Michael J. and Wheeler William Bruce, *Knoxville Tennessee: Continuity and Change in an Appalachian City*, (Knoxville, 1983), p. 36.

92 *Knoxville Journal and Tribune*, May 5, 1914. (A search by the Tennessee State Library and Archives Manuscript Division staff failed to locate the records for this case, most likely because they apparently were never indexed. A similar search by the Knoxville Archives staff failed to reveal anything but docket numbers.)

93 Minutes of the Common Council of the City of Knoxville, *op. cit.*, Book 2, Meeting of March 20, 1914, 692-93.

94 *Knoxville City Directories, 1910*, McClung Collection, Knoxville Public Library, p. 748; 1911, p. 817; 1912, pp. 743-744; 1913, p. 721.

95 Minutes of the Common Council of the City of Knoxville, *op. cit.*, *Book 2*, Meeting of March 20, pp. 693.

96 *Ibid.*, Meeting of June 13, 1913, p. 240, and; *Knoxville Journal Tribune*, June 13, 1913 and; *Public Acts of the State of Tennessee* Fifty-Eighth General Assembly, 1913 (Nashville, 1913), pp. 665-66. [Ministers in Bristol, Virginia, pursued a different course in June 1913. There was a coalition of Protestant ministers who "quietly secured evidence against several houses ... swore out warrants ... [and] ... secured convictions in every case. Women were given the alternative of leaving the city or serving their sentences." See: *Knoxville Journal and Tribune*, June 16, 1913.

97 *Knoxville Journal and Tribune*, June 14, 1913.

98 *Ibid.*, June 16, 1913.

99 *Ibid.*, March 28, 1914. See also: *Ibid.*, March 21, 1914.

100 *Ibid.*, April 27, 1914.

101 *Ibid.*, May 5, 14, 1914.

102 Minutes of the Common Council of the City of Knoxville, *op. cit.*, Book 3, Meeting of May 8, 1914, p. 9.

103 *Knoxville Journal and Tribune*, May 5, 1914.

104 *Ibid.*

105 Minutes of the Common Council of the City of Knoxville, *op. cit.*, *Book 3*, Meeting of May 4, 1914, p. 754.

106 Boyer, *op. cit.*, pp. 191, 195-197, and; Rosen, *op. cit.* pp. 44-49, and; Connelly; *op. cit.*, p. 7.

107 *Chattanooga Daily Times*, June 26, 30, 1885, November 1, 1888, and; Supreme Court, East Tennessee Division, *op. cit.*, and; Miller, *op. cit.*, 89, and; *Knoxville Daily Chronicle*, August 8, 10, 1885.

108 Memphis *Commercial Appeal*, July 25, 1917, and; *Chattanooga Daily Times*, July 19, 1885. See also: Rosen, *op. cit.*, pp. 102, 104, 105, and 163.

109 Rosen, *op. cit.*, pp. 86-111, quotation from 105. *Nashville Tennessean and Nashville American*, March 3, 1917; and, *Senate Journal of Sixtieth General Assembly for the State of Tennessee*, (Nashville, State of Tennessee, 1917).

110　*Nashville Tennessean and Nashville American,* March 3, 1917; and, *Senate Journal of Sixtieth General Assembly for the State of Tennessee,* (Nashville, State of Tennessee, 1917). There is no record of any debate by the Senate on this measure.

111　Boyer, *Moral Order,* p. 195. (The cities of Montgomery, Alabama, and Columbia, South Carolina, for example, also closed their red-light districts the same summer. See Memphis *Commercial Appeal, July 25, August 7, 1917.*)

112　Burnham, John C., "The Progressive Era Revolution in American Attitudes toward Sex," *Journal of American History,* (March 1973), pp. 888, 901.

113　Rosen, *op. cit.,* 28.

114　Mayer, Joseph, *The Regulation of Commercialized Vice: An Analysis of the Transition from Segregation to Repression in the United States,* (New York: n. p., 1922), 91; Benjamin, Henry, and Masters, R. E. L., *Prostitution and Morality,* (London, 1964), p.76; Connelly, *op. cit.,* 26.

Chapter 3

1　Nashville *Daily American,* January 18, 1877; Jones, Jr., James B., "Shoot-Outs and Pseudo Duels in 19th Century Tennessee Journalism," a paper delivered at the 20th Symposium on 19th Century Press, the Civil War, and Free Expression, Chattanooga, TN, November 8-10, 2012.

2　*Ibid.,* and Jones, *op. cit.*

3　Coulter, E. Merton, *William G. Brownlow: Fighting Parson,* 1937, pp. 35-38.

4　Coulter, *op. cit., p,* 39.

5　*Ibid., p,* 39. See also: Nashville *Republican Banner,* May 27, 1840.

6　*Ibid.,* 40.

7　*Ibid.,* 41-46.

8　*Ibid.,* 46-52. See also: McIver, Stuart B. Dreamers, Schemers and Scalawags:," *Florida Chronicles Volume 1.* Pineapple Press. (1998). pp.3–8 and www.historynet. com/many-wives-ned-buntline.htm. See also Gidmark, Jill B., *Encyclopedia of American Literature of the Sea and Great Lakes.* Greenwood Publishing Group. 2001, 222–223._

9　*Nashville American,* May 1, 1897.

10　Nashville *Tennessean,* March 30, 1909.

11　*Memphis Daily Appeal,* August 26, 1852; Nashville *Daily American,* March 22, 1885. Quotation as cited in *Daily Scioto Gazette* (Chillicothe, OH), September 22, 1852 and, *Boston Daily Atlas,* September 27, 1852.

12　Nashville *Daily American,* March 22, 1885.

13　*Cleveland Herald,* August 23, 1852; *Weekly Herald* (NY), August 21, 1852; *Every Day* pp. 161-162.

14　*Nashville Patriot,* 6 October 1857; *Nashville Union and American,* 8 October 1857; Nashville *Republican Banner,* October 6, 1857.

15　*Nashville Banner Steam Press,* November 19, 1859; *New York Times,* December 6, 10, 1859; *Daily News* (Savannah, Ga., November 23, 1859; *Daily National Intelligencer,* November 19,.1859; *New York Herald,* November 19, 1859; www. SouthernHistory.net

16　Nashville Criminal Court Book G, December Term, 1859, 11.

17   Hall subsequently became the United States minister to Bolivia (1863-1867) where he died. *The New York Times* commented the affair "presents in a very strong light the ridiculous absurdity of the Southern code of honor," *The New York Times*, December 7, 1859. See also: Nashville *Republican Banner*, November 19, 30, December 1, 1859; *New York Herald,* November 19, 22, 1859; *Louisville Daily Journal*, November 19, 22, 1859; *New Orleans Daily Picayune (New Orleans)*, November 19, 20, 1859; *Memphis Daily Appeal*, November 19, 22, 1859; *Charleston Mercury*, November 23, 1859; *Nashville American*, March 18, 1902, March 21, 1909.

18   *The New York Times*, December 7, 1859.

19   Nashville *Tennessean*, March 30, 1909.

20   *The New York Times,* November 22, 1903.

21   September 30, 1819–November 27, 1895, he was a Confederate spy-master, and later a general in the Confederate army. See: en.wikipedia.org/wiki/Thomas_Jordan_(general).

22   Nashville *Republican Banner*, July 4, 1866; *The New York Times*, July 15, 1866; *Daily National Intelligencer*, July 6, 1866; *Freedom's Champion*, July 12, 1866; *The Daily Miners' Register* (Central City, CO), July 26, 1866.

23   Nashville *Republican Banner*, May 18, 19–20, 1883; Nashville *Daily American*, May 23, 1883.

24   *St. Louis Globe-Democrat*, May 24, 1883.

25   No copy of the *National Review* is known to exist.

26   *Nashville Weekly American*, December 28, 1887.

27   *The Milwaukee Sentinel*, December 29, 1887; *News and Observer* (Raleigh, NC) December 25, 1887; *St. Louis Globe-Democrat*, December 25-27, 1887; *Daily Inter-Ocean*, (Chicago), December 25, 29, 1887; *Daily Picayune (New Orleans)*, December 25, 1887.

28   Nashville *Daily American,* June 17, 1888, June 19, 1888; Nashville *Tennessean*, April 6, June 2, 7, 12, 1888, February 28, 1888, November 11, 1890; April 9, 1892.

29   Nashville *Republican Banner*, October 6, 1857.

30   *Knoxville Daily Tribune*, March 12, 1882.

31   *Knoxville Chronicle,* March 12, 1882.

32   *Knoxville Daily Tribune*, March 12, 1882.

33   *Knoxville Chronicle*, March 14, 1882. See also: *The St. Louis Globe*, March 12, 1882; *The North American* (Philadelphia), March 13, 1882.

34   *Knoxville Chronicle*, January 31, 1888.

35   *Ibid.*, January 31, 1888; Nashville *Daily American*, January 30, 1888; *The Daily Picayune (New Orleans)*, January 30, 1888; *Milwaukee Sentinel*, January 30, 1888; *Boston Daily Advertiser*; *The Daily Inter Ocean* (Chicago), January 20, 1888; *The News and Observer* (Raleigh), February 1, 1888.

36   Phelan, James, *History of Tennessee: The Making of the State* (Riverside Press: Cambridge, 1888); *Knoxville Sentinel*, April 10, 1890. Phelan, James, a Representative from Tennessee; born in Aberdeen, Monroe County, Miss., December 7, 1856; moved with his father to Memphis, Tenn., in 1867; attended private schools and the Kentucky Military Institute near Frankfort in 1871; entered the University

of Leipzig, Saxony, in 1874 and was graduated in February 1878; returned to Memphis; studied law; was admitted to the bar and commenced practice in 1881; elected as a Democrat to the Fiftieth and Fifty-first Congresses and served from March 4, 1887, until his death in Nassau, Bahama Islands, on January 30, 1891; interment in Elmwood Cemetery, Memphis, Tenn. bioguide.congress.gov/scripts/biodisplay.pl?index=P000289.

37 Nashville *Daily American*, April 9, 1890; Knoxville *Sentinel*, April 10, 1890

38 *Knoxville Sentinel*, April 10, 1990.

39 *Los Angeles Times*, April 8, 1890

40 Nashville *Daily American*, April 9, 1890; *Los Angeles Times*, April 8, 1890; *The New York Times*, April 9, 1890.

41 Nashville *Daily American*, April 11, 1890. Phelan may well have known of this caveat, his older brother having been triumphant in a duel according to the code in 1870. Nashville *Banner*, June 29, July 1, 1870.

42 *Knoxville Sentinel*, April 8, 10, 11, 12, 1890, *The News and Observer* (Raleigh, NC) April 11, 1890; *Milwaukee Sentinel*, April 9, 1890; *The New York Times*, April 9, 1890.

43 *Ibid.*, April 10, 1890. *Milwaukee Sentinel*, April 9, 1890; *The New York Times*, April 9, 1890.

44 *Knoxville Sentinel*, April 8, 10, 12, 1890; *The New York Times*, April 9, 10, 12, 1890; *Rocky Mountain News* (Denver CO), April 12, 1890; *Los Angeles Times*, April 9, 1890; *Morning Oregonian* (Portland, Oregon) April 8, 1890; *Wisconsin State Register* (Portage WI), April 12, 1890; *Milwaukee Sentinel*, April 9, 1890; *Atchison Dally Globe* (Atchison KS), April 9, 12, 1890; *The Atchison Champion*, April 9, 1890; *The Daily Interocean*, April 9, 10, 14, 1890; *The News and Observer* (Raleigh, NC) April 11, 1890.

45 *Memorial Address on the Life and Character of James Phelan, February 28, 1891* (Washington: Government Printing Office, 1891), p. 7; *The New York Times*, February 9, 1890.

46 Nashville *Daily American*, November 3, 1890.

47 *Ibid.*, February 18, 1893; *Galveston Daily News*, February 18, 1893; *The Daily Inter Ocean*, February 18, 1893.

48 *Nashville American*, December 15, 1908.

49 *The Memphis Commercial Appeal*, May 7, 1893; *Nashville American*, December 15, 1908.

50 Ezzell Timothy P., "Edward Ward Carmack 1858-1908," tennesseeencyclopedia.net/.

Chapter 4

1 Nashville *Daily American*, January 18, 1877; *Nashville American*, July 8, 1880, July 3, 1904; *Nashville Tennessean and Nashville American*, September 17, 1911; John Lye Wilson, *The Code of Honor, or Rules for the Government of Principals and Seconds in Dueling* (1828), at www.gutenberg.org/files/6085/6085-h/6085-httm. Accessed May 28, 2016. Andrew Jackson's admonition to his nephew is found in:

Jones, James B., *History in Tennessee: Lost Episodes from the Volunteer State's Past*. (Charleston: Arcadia Publishing, 2018), 428.

2   Mark Twain, *Journalism in Tennessee* (ca. 1871), at americanliterature.com/author/ mark-twain/short-story/journalism-in-tennessee. Accessed June 23, 2018.

3   As cited in Owlcation.com, "3 Famous Duels Involving Andrew Jackson," accessed December 10, 2018.

4   Smith, Sam B., and Owsley, Harriet Chappell, eds., Rimini, Robert V., Consulting ed., MacPherson, Sharon C., Associate ed., Keeton, Linda D., staff assistant, *Papers of Andrew Jackson,* vol. 1, 1780—1803, (Knoxville: University of Tennessee Press, 1980), *Andrew Jackson to John Sevier*, October 2, 1803, 367-368.

5   Smith, *et al., op. cit.*, John Sevier to Andrew Jackson, October 2, 1803, 368.

6   Article IX, Section 3 of the first Tennessee Constitution (1796) stipulated: "Any person who shall, after the adoption of this Constitution, fight a duel, or knowingly be the bearer of a challenge to fight a duel, or send or accept a challenge for that purpose, or be an aider or abettor in fighting a duel, shall be deprived of the right to hold any office of honor or profit in this state, and shall be punished otherwise, in such manner as the Legislature may prescribe." Therefore it was necessary to travel outside the state to conduct a duel. See also: *Tennessee Acts*, 1801, Ch. XXIII, for the statute prohibiting dueling. .

7   Smith, *et al., op. cit.*, Andrew Jackson to the Public, October 10, 1803, 378-379.

8   Parton, James *Life of Jackson*, Vol. I, (Boston: Ticknor and Fields, 1866), 234-235. Another source claims the two men immediately began firing at one another with their flintlock-one-shot pistols, but missed, and thereafter became the best of friends. See: Nashville *Daily American*, September 1, 1891.

9   Parton, *op. cit.*, 286-291. See also: Allison, Burden, *Murder and Mayhem in Nashville*, (Charleston: History Press, 2016), 14. John Coffee would later serve as a senior officer with Jackson during the Creek Indian War (1813-1814) and at the battle of New Orleans, January 8, 1815 fought after the War of 1812 had been concluded by the Treaty of Ghent, December 24, 1814. News traveled slowly across the Atlantic Ocean.

10 *Ibid.*, 293-294

11 *Ibid.*, 296.

12 *Ibid.*, 296-297.

13 *Ibid.*, 298-300. It has been suggested that the pistols used in the Jackson-Dickinson duel were the same weapons used in the Coffee-McNairy affair.

14 Parton, *op. cit.*, 388.

15 *Ibid.*, 388-389.

16 *Nashville American*, January 21, 1900. (That is, Jesse had been shot in his ass.)

17 Marquis James, *Life of Andrew Jackson,* (Bobs-Merrill Company, Indianapolis, 1938) 152-154;' James Parton Life of Andrew Jackson, 3 voles, Vol. 1, (Boston Tucknor and Fields, 1866), 386-398: See also: Nashville *Republican Banner*, June 29, 1871.

18 Nashville *Daily American*, June 20, 1882.

19 *Ibid.*, April 4, 1878; June 13, 1878; December 27, 1879; January 15, 1890; Nashville *Tennessean*, September 19, 1909; www.politico.com/story/2009/09/ rep-sam-houston-fights-a-duel-sept-22-826-027389, accessed June 3, 2017; www.

politico.com/story/2018/09/22/this-day-in-politics-sept-22-1826-826300, accessed July 12, 2017. For the Smith-Brank duel see: Nashville *Daily American*, July 2, 1870; and, June 19, 1890; and, Nashville *Tennessean*, November 14, 1939. Information on the Bernards-DuPont story is found in: Nashville *Daily American*, December 22, 1878. For Judge Catron's lengthy and powerful analysis on dueling in *Smith v. Tennessee*, see Nashville *Republican Banner*, July 2, 1870.

20   *Memphis Enquirer*, May 20, 1837; *Memphis Press Scimitar*, November 9, 1951; Memphis *Commercial Appeal*, February 1, 1929, and May 3, 1931.

21   Memphis *Commercial Appeal*, September 15, 1854.

22   *The New York Times,* November 4, 1856.

23   Memphis *Commercial Appeal*, November 28, 1858.

24   *Memphis Argus*, December 29, 1864; *New Orleans Daily Picayune*, January 4, 1865.

25   *Memphis Argus*, July 13, 1866, and Nashville *Republican Banner*, July 15, 1866. *New York Times*, October 8, 1866.

26   *Nashville American*, July 27, 1896. Miss Caldwell unsuccessfully attempted to discover the identity of the romantic "black knight" for thirty years.

27   *Memphis Bulletin*, February 19, 1868; Nashville *Republican Banner*, February 21, 1868. On the Fentress County rifle duel see: *The New York Times*, May 4, 1868 and; *Nashville Press and Times* April 17, 1868.

28   The brother of James Phelan who had a dispute with John M. Fleming, editor of the Knoxville *Sentinel* in 1890. It was merely a war of words, however.

29   Memphis *Public Ledger*, June 29, 1870; *Memphis Daily Appeal*, June 29, 1870; Nashville *Republican Banner*, June 29, July 1, 1870; *The New York Times*, September 25, 1913.

30   *Memphis Appeal,* August 27, 1870; Nashville *Republican Banner*, August 27, 30, 1870.

31   *Knoxville Chronicle*, December 19, 1872 and; Nashville *Republican Banner*, 21 February, 1873.

32   *Knoxville Chronicle*, December 19, 1872. And; *Nashville American*, December 24, 1905.

33   Nashville *Republican Banner*, February 21, 22, 1873; and *Nashville American*, December 24, 1905.

34   *Dalton Citizen*, February 9, 1873; *Atlanta Constitution*, February 22, 1873.

35   *Cincinnati Gazette,* February 25, 1873.

36   The *Nashville American*, December 24, 1905, erroneously claimed that the legislature passed a law providing death as a punishment for dueling, this was not so, A bill spelling out such a consequence was defeated in the General Assembly. See: *Senate Journal of the First Session of the Thirty-Eighth General Assembly of the State of Tennessee at Nashville on the First Monday of January 1873*, 436. Article V of the 1870 Tennessee State Constitution provided a milder sentence of two to ten years for everyone convicted of dueling, and lesser punishments for all other ancillary activities associated with dueling, including "imputations of cowardice."

37   Nashville *Republican Banner*, November 4, 1850.

38   *Memphis Appeal*, August 27, 1870; Nashville *Republican Banner*, August 27, 30, 1870. See also: *The New York Times*, September 16, 1870

39   *Jackson Whig and Tribune,* May 30, 1874; Nashville *Daily American,* May 31, 1874, and; *The New York Times,* June 7, 1874. (Tennessee Historical Commission Historical Marker 4-D 3 9 memorializes the founding of Cotton Grove in 1819.)

40   *The New York Times,* January 2, 1885.

41   *The Morning Oregonian,* September 5, 1895; *Los Angeles Herald,* September 5, 1895; *The Cultivator & Country Gentleman,* Sept. 11, 1895, p. 675. Curiously research did not reveal notice of this event in any Tennessee papers or magazines consulted.

42   *Nashville American,* December 7, 1903. In the end three men were arrested for the murder of Patrolman Dowell. Because a mob threatened to lynch them, they were transferred to the relative safety of Chattanooga for later trial. *Ibid.,* December 8, 9, 10, 1903.

43   *Tennessee Encyclopedia,* "Edward Ward Cormack," by Timothy Ezell, at tennesseeencyclopedia.net/entries/edward-ward-carmack/ accessed December 15, 2017; and, *op. cit.,* "Cooper *v.* State," by Tara Mitchell Myelin, at tennesseeencyclopedia.net/entries/cooper-v-state/, accessed December 27, 2017. See also: *Nashville American,* November 10, 11, 1908, February 23, 1909, March 18, 1909, April 14, 16, 1909 May 16, 1909; Nashville *Tennessean,* February 23, 1909, March 22, 1909, April 16, 1909, February 3, 1910, April 14, 1910, April 19, 1981, October 3, 1983.

44   *Nashville American* December 16, 1908; for the Polk County affair, see: Nashville *Tennessean,* February 1. 1921.

45   *Nashville Tennessean and Nashville American,* February 3, 1914.

46   See Chapter 3.

Chapter 5

1   *Knoxville Daily Tribune,* December 28, 1881, *Knoxville Daily Chronicle,* December 27, 1881; Nashville *Daily American,* December 31, 1881 and September 9, 1885, and November 6, 1888.

2   *Knoxville Daily Chronicles,* December 28, 1881.

3   Jones, James B. "The Wild, Wild East: A Blood Feud in Nineteenth-Century Knoxville: The Mabry, Lusby, and O'Conner Killings, 1881-1882," *The Courier,* June 1993.

4   *Ibid.*

5   *Knoxville Daily Tribune,* August 27, 1882; *Knoxville Daily Chronicle,* August 27, 1882; Nashville *Daily American,* August 27, 1882; and Jones, *ibid.*

6   Jones, *op. cit.*

7   *Ibid.*

8   *Knoxville Daily Tribune,* October 20, 1882; Nashville *Daily American,* October 20, 1882; Jones *ibid.*

9   *Knoxville Daily Tribune,* October 20, 1882; Jones, *ibid.*

10   Jones, *op. cit.*

11   *Ibid.*

12   *Crossville Chronicle,* January 4, 2007; and Swofford, Thomas V., *The Swafford-Tollett Feud* (Pikeville, TN: Printing Partisans, 2003), 23-45; video production, August 11,

2014, "Bloody Bledsoe, 'Vengeance by Blood' the Swofford and Tollett Feud," at www.youtube.com/watch?v=JgqFfCtU6BU.

13   *Nashville American*, July 6, 1905.

14   *Ibid.*, July 6, 21, 1905.

15   *Ibid.*, August 12, 1895

16   *Ibid.*

17   *Chattanooga Daily Times*, June 8, 1915.

18   Nashville *Daily American*, November 24 1883.

19   *Chattanooga Times*, November 14, 1883; Nashville *Daily American*, November 17, 1883.

20   Nashville *Daily American*, November 24 1883.

21   *Ibid.*

22   Nashville *Daily American*, September 15, 1882, November 23, 1883; *The New York Times*, September 15, 1882.

23   Nashville *Daily American,* September 15, 1882.

24   The county seat of Leclede County, Missouri, was named after Lebanon, Tennessee, from which its original settlers originated in 1849. See: en.wikipedia.org/wiki/Laclede_County,_Missouri.

25   Nashville *Daily American*, April 19, 1883, and November 24, 1883.

26   Jones, James B., "John, Bob and Andy, Tennessee's Other Taylor Brothers: A Nineteenth Century Saga of Law and Order," *The Courier*, Winter 2018

27   *Ibid.*

28   Nashville *Daily American*, October 14, 1883; *The New York Times*, November 24, 1883.

29   *Knoxville Sunday Chronicle*, June 8, 1884; *Clarksville Weekly Chronicle*, June 7, 1884.

30   Nashville *Daily American*, June 5, 12, 13, 1884; 28, 1884; *Clarksville Weekly Chronicle*, June 7, 1884; Dr. Bellamy's wife was William Morrow's sister; see Nashville *Daily American*, November 26, 1884.

31   Nashville *Daily American*, June 8, 1894; Douglas, Joseph C., "A Note on the History and Material Culture of Bellamy Cave, Tennessee," *Journal of Spelean History*, Vol. 43, No. 2, Issue 136, (July-December 2009), 4-10 at caves.org/section/asha/issues/136.pdf; Today the cave is sealed to protect the gray bat, threatened with extinction due to "white nose" disease. See: www.youtube.com?v_881-ok?7112tw.

32   *Knoxville Sunday Chronicle*, June 8, 1884.

33   Nashville *Daily American*, June 3, 1884; *Clarksville Weekly Chronicle*, June 7, 1884.

34   *Clarksville Weekly Chronicle*, June 7, 14, 1884; *Knoxville Sunday Chronicle*, June 8, 1884; Nashville *Daily American*, June 13, 1884.

35   Nashville *Daily American*, June 3, 1884; *Knoxville Sunday Chronicle*, June 8, 1884; *Clarksville Chronicle*, June 21, 1884.

36   Nashville *Daily American*, June 11, 1894. The excitement over Bellamy's Cave, "the Cavern of Horrors," led to speculation that it would become "the scene of a great industry." According to promoters, the cave was a perfect spot to manufacture and store apple cider. The cave could be leased for a century while several thousand acres of land on the surrounding surface would serve as a vast grove, "the largest

apple orchard in the world." Harvested apples would be dumped into the mill in the cave where it would be converted to cider. Or, a fortune could be made out of the vast amounts of bat guano in the cave. See: Nashville *Daily American*, June 19, 1884. There were no venture capitalists interested in the scheme.

37 Nashville *Daily American*, July 29, 1884; *Clarksville Weekly Chronicle*, June 28, 1884.

38 *Ibid.*, June 8, 1884 November 26, 28, December 21, 1884, May 23, 1885. *Memphis Daily Appeal*, March 8, 1885.

39 *Ibid.*, January 5, April 2, 21, May 23, 1885.

40 *Ibid.*, June 20, 1885.

41 *Ibid.*, August 5, 1886.

43 *Chattanooga Daily Times*, February 26, 1915

43 *Ibid.*, February 27, 1915.

44 *Ibid.*, March 22, 1915.

45 *Ibid.*, April 5, 1915.

48 *Ibid.*, September 5, 1915

49 *Ibid.*, June 8, 1915

50 *Ibid.*, September 5, 1915.

51 *Chattanooga Daily News*, October 31, 1919.

Chapter 6

1 Friends of the Clay County, Tennessee, Library, *Corn from a Jar*, compiled and edited by Friends of the Clay County, Tennessee, Library (Friends of the Clay County, Tennessee, Library: 2014). Dr. Michael E. Birdwell, "Moonshine Made for Strange Bedfellow in the Upper Cumberland," pp. 122-124. Ellis, William E. , "Moonshine" at: tennesseeencyclopedia.net/entries/moonshine/. Accessed December 14, 2018. For the Supreme Court ruling in *Tennessee v. Davis*, see: supreme.justia.com/cases/federal/us/100/257/. For information regarding the legal distillation of spirits in Tennessee, see: www.sugarlands.com/?gclid=Cj0KCQjw4fHkBRDcARIsACV58_EFNvsflybZSCz-kSGBOHrp4CWd36DCU7SsURIT64Q-4UWf5QmIWucaAl_4EALw_wcB. See also: Internal Revenue Service, *Historical Study: IRS Historical Fact Book: A Chronology 1646-1992*, (Washington: GPO, 1997). P. 5. See: Nashville *Daily American*, October 18, 1879 for information on the blanket amnesty offered to moonshiners.

2 Memphis *Public Ledger*, September 4, 1871, and *Morristown Gazette*, September 15, 1871; *The Tennessean*, September 2, 2012, and May 21, 2017; Nashville *Republican Banner*, October 19, 1871; Nashville *Daily American*, February 15, 1878; for information on the eight collection districts in Tennessee, see: www.archives.gov/research/guide-fed-records/groups/058.html#58.5.42. Nashville *Daily American*, February 10, 1881, for use of U. S. soldiers as deputies.

3 Nashville *Daily American*, June 29, 1880.

4 Nashville *Republican Banner*, October 19, 1871.

5 Nashville *Republican Banner*, December 25, 1873. Nashville *Daily American*, March 2, 1873. *Knoxville Tribune*, March 1, 1871. Singlings are the first run, or crude spirits, which would later be further distilled into purer whisky.

6   Ellis, *op. cit.*; *The New York Times*, July 16, 1878.

7   *The New York Times*, August 29, 1878.

8   Nashville *Daily American*, August 25, 29, 30, 1878; April 27, 1879, October 18, 1879; October 22, 1883; August 15, 1888; April 10, 1906; *The New York Times*, August 29, October 8, 15, 1878. See also: Atkinson, George Wesley, *After the Moonshiners, By One of the Raiders; A book of Thrilling, Yet Truthful Narratives*, (Frew & Campbell: Wheeling W. VA. 1881), pp. 43-48, accessed March 5, 2017 at: books.google.com/books?id=7-tJAQAAMAAJ&pg=PA45&dq=peek's+fight&hl=en&sa=X&ved=0ah UKEwis-tzFidPhAhXnRd8KHTwWAZwQ6AEIMDAB#v=onepage&q=peek's%20 fight&f=false.

9   Nashville *Daily American*, July 18, 1878, March 12, 1879, April 5, 23, 29, 1879; *The New York Times*, November 5, 1886;

10 *Ibid.*, March 6, 14, 1879, April; 5, 23, 1879; April 23, August 7, 1879. See also, *Ibid.*, March 30, 1876; June 26, 1877; March 20, 1878; August 7, 1879, January 17, 1880; February 10. 1881; *The New York Times*, February 2, 1880, July 19, 1885. For Uncle Havre's soliloquy see: Malone, Joseph S., *Sons of Vengeance: A Tale of the Cumberland Highlands*, (New York: 1901), pp. 222-224.

11 *Ibid.*, April 20, 21, 1886.

12 *Ibid.*, August 7, 1879.

13 *Knoxville Tribune*, August 8, 11, 1878; Nashville *Daily American*, August 13, 1878.

14 Nashville *Daily American*, August 31, 1878.

15 *Ibid.*, February, 5, 1879. See also: Atkinson, *op. cit.* p. 48.

16 *Knoxville Tribune*, February 1, 1879; Nashville *Daily American*, January 19, February 2, 1879, November 10, 1880; Atkinson, *op. cit.*, 47-48.

17 Nashville *Daily American* November 10, 17, 1880; *Chattanooga Times*, November 16, 1880; *The New York Times*, November 18, 1880.

18 *The New York Times*, September 15, 1885.

19 Nashville *Daily American*, June 8, 1880.

20 *Ibid.*

21 For Mollie Miller see: *Bolivar Bulletin*, October 29, 1894; and, *Los Angeles Herald*, June 17, 1894; for Mahala Mullins, see: *Columbia Herald*, September 29, 1898; and *The Comet* (Johnson City) September 1, 1888, 22, 1898: and, www.historical-melungeons.com/mmullins.html; and www.geni.com/people/Mahala-Collins-Mullins/6000000014999554659.

22 *Nashville American*, November 1, 1895.

23 *Ibid.*, May 21, 25, 29, 1878; June 11, 15, 28, 1878; August 25, 29, 30, 1878; December 12, 1880; March 14, 16, 1882. See also: www.odmp.org/officer/21923-deputy-collector-james-m-davis.

24 *The New York Times*, July 14, 1880; July 22, 1884.

25 *Nashville American*, December 22, 1895; October 10, 1896; June 19, 1901.

26 *Ibid.*, January 31, 1896; July 31, 1898; June 21, 1899.

25 *Ibid.*, February 17 1881.

26 *Ibid.*, December 22, 1895; June 21, 1899.

27 *Ibid.*, August 14, 1900.

28 *Ibid.*, June 10, 1901.

29   *Ibid.*
30   *Ibid.*, January 31, 1901, July 21, 1901; November 11, 1904; September 4, 1910;
     October 25, 1916; December 21, 1921; *The New York Times*, January 15, 1912,
     January 17, 1931.
31   *The Tennessean*, September 2, 2012, and May 21, 2017.

Chapter 7

1   Equal Justice Initiative (E .J. I.), Montgomery, Alabama *Lynching in America:
    Confronting the Legacy of Racial Terror,* Third ed., Chapter 1, "Session and
    Emancipation, 1861-1865" accessed April 30, 20019, lynchinginamerica.eji.org/
    report/.
2   E. J. I., op. cit., *Lynching in America.*
3   Civil Rights Movement Veterans Organization, http://www.crmvet.org/;"Direct
    Disenfranchisement," *Race, Voting Rights, and Segregation,* University of Michigan,
    www.umich.edu/~lawrace/disenfranchise1.htm, "Disfranchising Laws," *The Tennessee
    Encyclopedia*, Knoxville: University of Tennessee Press, 2012 tennesseeencyclopedia.
    net/entry.php?rec=380; *The Fifteenth Amendment Site,* 15thamendment.harpweek.
    com/HubPages/CommentaryPage.asp?Commentary=03Ratification; *History Matters,*
    George Mason University, historymatters.gmu.edu/d/5352; *The History of Jim
    Crow,* www.jimcrowhistory.org/history/creating2.htm; Jim Crow Laws Denied
    Blacks Dignity, Vote," Jackson *Sun,* orig.jacksonsun.com/civilrightssec1_crow.
    shtml; Kousser, J. Morgan. *The Shaping of Southern Politics: Suffrage Restriction
    and the Establishment of the One-Party South, 1880-1910,* (New Haven: Yale
    University Press, 1974);Lacayo, Richard. "Blood at the Root," *Time,* April 2, 2000;
    Rabinowitz, Howard N. *Race Relations in the Urban South, 1865-1890.* Athens,
    GA: University of Georgia Press, 1996.
4   www.blackpast.org/african-american-history/jim-crow-laws-tennessee-1866-1955/.
    Perhaps the best source for understanding the impact of segregation in the Volunteer
    State is found in Cartwright, Joseph H., *The Triumph of Jim Crow: Tennessee,
    Race Relations in the 1880s,* (University of Tennessee Press, 1976).
5   Laska, Louis L, *Legal Executions in Tennessee: A Comprehensive Registry,
    1782-2009,* (McFarland; 2011), 186.
6   *Milwaukee Morning Sentinel,* May 16, 1861, as cited in Laska, *op. cit.,* p. 58..
    The phrase "Confederate authorities" most likely meant the local Committee of
    Safety or Vigilance Committee. See: Jones, Jr., James B., "'The Reign of Terror of
    the Safety Committee Has Passed Away Forever,'" A History of Committees of
    Safety and Vigilance in West and Middle Tennessee, 1860-1862." *West Tennessee
    Historical Society Papers,* Vol XLII, 2009.
7   Laska, *op. cit.,* p. 59 and; Nashville *Daily American,* September 9, 1885.
8   Ellis, Daniel, *Thrilling Adventures of Daniel Ellis, the Great Union Guide of East
    Tennessee, for a Period of Nearly Four Years during the great Southern Rebellion
    Written by Himself, Containing a Short Biography of the Author,* (New York, Harper,
    1867) pp. 107-110. See also: Jones, James B., *History in Tennessee: Lost Episodes
    from the Volunteer State's Past,* (Charleston: Acadia Press, 2018), pp. 26-27.

9   Jones, James B., comp. "LIST OF 213 LYNCHINGS IN TENNESSEE, 1821-1946" research findings in the author's possession (see below in text). For the Baker lynching, see: *The Boston Herald*, September 8, 1865 and; Jones, *op. cit.*, "LIST OF 213 LYNCHINGS."

10 www.commercialappeal.com/story/news/government/state/2016/02/19/ state-historical-marker-to-commemorate-1866-memphis-race-riotmassacre /90445802/. See also: www.npr.org/sections/codeswitch/2016/05/02/476450908/ in-memphis-a-divide-over-how-to-remember-a-massacre-150-years-later; www. seattletimes.com/nation-world/150-after-memphis-massacre-marker-shows-continued-conflict/; www.memphisdailynews.com/news/2016/may/7/massacre-1866-and-the-battles-over-how-memphis-history-is-told/; and Ash, Stephen V., *A Massacre in Memphis: The Race Riot That Shook the Nation One Year After the Civil War*, (New York: Hill and Wang, 2013.)

11 Memphis *Commercial Appeal*, August 26, 1874. Memphis *Public Ledger*, August 27, 1874 and; Nashville *Republican Banner*, August 27, 28, 1874.

12 *The New York Times*, June 21, 1878.

13 Nashville *Daily American*, September 16, 1880.

14 *The New York Times*, February 20, 1881.

15 Nashville *Daily American*, February 17, 19, 1881.

16 *Ibid.*, May 27, 1882.

17 *Acts of the State of Tennessee, Passed by the Second Session of Thirty Sixth General Assembly. For the Years 1869-1870, Section XXXIX*, (Nashville: 1870), pp. 69-70. The stereotypical racist concept that black men were primitive sexual predators was invented by white slave owners who promoted the notion that male slaves were animalistic in nature. They stressed, for example, that African American males were largely controlled by passions and emotions, and were almost entirely obedient to their sexual drive. This idea of the oversexed black male in turn played into idle gossip that African-American men had "oversized macrophallic penises." See: Van Deburg, William L. *Slavery and Race in American Popular Culture*, (Madison: University of Wisconsin Press; 1984), p. 149 and Davis Gary L, and Cross, Herbert J., "Sexual Stereotyping of Black Males in Interracial Sex" *Archives of Sexual Behavior*, vol. 8, 1979, pp. 269-279. Ida B. Wells also pointed out that while black on white rape was a justification for lynching African-American men, white on black rape went unpunished, if not exclusively unreported. She demonstrated that the black community had no "license to lynch and thus intensified her argument that lynching and mob violence were unjust on several counts."

18 Nashville *Daily American* July 18, 1889; and Royster, Jacquelyn Jones, ed. and intro., *Southern Horrors and Other Writings: The Anti-Lynching Campaign of Ida Be Wells, 1892-1900*, (Boston: Bedford/St. Martin's, 1997), p. 31.

19 Nashville *Republican Banner*, September 17, 1872.

20 *Nashville American*, January 12, 1878; February 17, 1884; March 17, 1887; April 12, 1890; May 31, 1895; March 4, 1896; March 22, 1894; March 31, 1895; June 5, 1895; July 23, 1895; March 28, 1896; March 29, 1896; July 13, 1896; August 23, 1896; June 4, 1897; March 11, 1898; June 3, 1898; June 11, 1898; July 11, 1898; June 3, 1899; February 22, 1903; February 22, 1905; April 21, 1907: Nashville *Daily American*, February 27, 1877; August 8 1879; August 20,

1879; August 23, 1879; March 16, 1886; February 11, 1894; February 26, 1885; January 16, 1893; June 17, 1893; April 2, 1894; October 16, 1898; October 23, 1898: Nashville *Republican Banner*, October 25, 1865; July 1, 1866; November 24, 1866; November 4, 1871; July 24, 1872; November 13, 1873; June 3, 1874; July 1, 1874; August 10, 1874; October 16, 1874; December 3, 1874; November 11, 1874; June 13, 1877; November 7 1894: *Nashville Tennessean and Nashville American*, December 7, 1912: Nashville *Tennessean*, July 19, 1967,

21 In Winchester on August 25, 1891, a suspected black murderer was "burned to a crisp" in Winchester. See Nashville *Daily American*, August 26, 1891. According to the *Nashville American*, October 17, 1895, Ellis' "private parts" were likewise cut from his body. The Mississippians in the mob took his head as a trophy. See: Memphis *Commercial Appeal*, October 16, 1895; *New York Times*, October 17, 1895; Jones, *op. cit.*, pp. 355-356.

   A similar macabre blood-lust lynching, also justified on the belief the black victim had raped a white girl, occurred in Memphis on May 22, 1917. Upon his capture, local papers announced he would be burned the next morning. By eight o'clock on the morning of the lynching, reporters estimated that 3,000 people had gathered to watch. Some people had been camped out at the bridge for over 24 hours. See: www.memphisflyer.com/memphis/memphis-burning/Content?oid=4438125. See also: *Nashville Tennessean Nashville American*, May 23, 1917.

22 *Nashville Tennessean and Nashville American*, November 8, 1913.

23 *Clarksville Tobacco Leaf Chronicle*, Dec. 21, 1892. (Emphasis added.)

24 Nashville *Republican Banner*, February 4, 1869.

25 Nashville *Daily American*, September 5, 1885.

26 *Ibid.*, June 28, 1892. No copies of this photograph are known to exist.

27 *Ibid.*, May 28, 1891.

28 Memphis *Commercial Appeal*, September 2, 1894; Nashville *Daily American*, September 1, 3, 4, 5, 6 10, 11, 18, 20, 21, 22, 25, 27, 28; October 6, 12; November 12, 16, 18, 25, 27, 29; December 1, 2, 12, 15, 1894. See also *Inter Ocean*, (Chicago), December 15, 1894; and, and www.thiscruelwar.com/cold-blood-and-copnspiracy-this-week-in-historical-lynchings; and Royster, *op. cit.*, pp. 2-4.

29 Nashville *Daily American*, February 10, March 20, 21, 22, 25, 1906; June 7,12, 15, 1907; *The New York Times*, May 29, October 16, 1906; January 17, June 23, 1907; May 25, June 1, September 26, November 2, November 16, 1909; January 5, 30, 1910; February 27, 2000; *Chattanooga Times Free Press*, March 18, 2017.

30 Nashville *Republican Banner*, August 23, 25, 26; September 2, 3, 4 5, 6, 9, 13; November 4, 1874. *The New York Times*, September 7, 1874.

31 Nashville *Daily American*, February 5, 1892.

32 *Ibid.*, August 19, 20, November 23, 1886; and Jones, Jr., James B. Jr, *Every Day in Tennessee History*, (John F. Blair: Winston-Salem, NC, 1996), pp. 160-161.

33 Nashville *Daily American*, March 10, 1892; *Memphis Appeal Avalanche* March 5, March 28, 1892; Memphis *Commercial Appeal*, March 7, 1991; *The New York Times*, March 11, 1892. See also: tennesseeencyclopedia.net/entries/lynching/; daily.jstor.org/peoples-grocery-lynching/; lynchingsitesmem.org/archives/appeal-avalanche-drawings-calvin-mcdowell-and-thomas-moss-3281892; lynchinginamerica.eji.org/explore/tennessee.

34 Nashville *Tennessean*, December 16, 17, 1924.

35 Nashville *Tennessean*, December 29, 1933; *The New York Times*, December 16, 1933.

36 *Ibid.*, July 19, August 25, 1940. www.tn.gov/content/dam/tn/environment/ historic-commission/courier/thc_courier_jun15.pdf; www.cnn.com/2018/08/09/ us/elbert-williams-homicide-case-reopened/index.html; www.usatoday.com/ story/news/nation-now/2018/08/09/elbert-williams-civil-rights-murder-case-reopened/945320002/; www.foxnews.com/us/reopening-of-1940-elbert-williams-case-part-of-national-effort-to-bring-justice-to-civil-rights-heroes; www. elbertwilliamsfirsttodie.com/.

37 *Ibid.*, February 28, March 1, 3, 1946; *The New York Times*, November 3, 1946; *Nashville Retrospect*, February 2016; teva.contentdm.oclc.org/digital/collection/ p15138coll23/id/423/; "Columbia Race Riot, 1946," by Carroll Van West @ tennesseeencyclopedia.net/entries/columbia-race-riot-1946/.

38 List compiled by James B. Jones, © 2018. The Equal Justice Initiative (E. J. I.) presents the figure of 237 lynchings in Tennessee. Further research may reveal information resolving the deficit of twenty-three lynchings in the Volunteer State. This is a list generated from research conducted in Nashville, Tennessee, and may or may not represent the true number of lynchings. Unlike the E. J. I., however, this is a list, not an interactive map. (See: lynchinginamerica.eji.org/explore/tennessee). The E. J. I. map presents the number of lynchings per county, but unlike this list, does not provide dates, names (when known), places (when known) and crimes alleged (when known) nor the number of lynching victims. With the cooperation of the E. J. I. the differences in the two calculations may be resolved.

Bibliography

Primary and Secondary Sources

Acts of the State of Tennessee, Passed by the Second Session of Thirty Sixth General Assembly. For the Years 1869–1870 (Nashville: 1870)

Atkinson, G. W., *After the Moonshiners, By One of the Raiders; A book of Thrilling, Yet Truthful Narratives* (Wheeling, 1881)

Ball, J. C., Chambers, C. D., comps., *The Epidemiology of Opiate Addiction in the United States,* (Springfield)

Barker-Benfield, G. J., *The Horrors of the Half-Known Life: Male Attitudes Toward Women and Sexuality in Nineteenth-Century America* (New York, 1976)

Benjamin, H., and Masters, R. E. L., *Prostitution and Morality* (London, 1964)

Boyer, P., *Urban Masses and Moral Order in America, 1820–1920* (Cambridge, 1978)

Cartwright, J. H., *The Triumph of Jim Crow: Tennessee, Race Relations in the 1880s* (University of Tennessee Press, 1976)

Chambers, W. M., *Sanitary Report of the Condition of the Prostitutes of Nashville,* January 31, 1865, (William P. Palmer Collection, Western Reserve Historical Society, Cleveland)

Chattanooga Business Directories, 1907–1910, 1912, 1913, 1915, 1917, 1920 (Tennessee State Library & Archives)

Chestnut, M. B., *A Diary from Dixie,* ed. Ben Ames Williams (Boston, 1949)

Corlew, R. E., *Tennessee: A Short History,* 2d ed. (Knoxville, 1981)

Congress, U.S., *House Report No. 140: Report of the Committee on Military Affairs, to Which Were Referred the Correspondence and Documents from the War Department, in Relation to the Proceedings of a Court Martial, Ordered for the Trial of Certain Tennessee Militiamen, February 11, 1822*

Connelly, T. L., *Civil War Tennessee: Battles and Leaders* (Knoxville, 1990)

Coulter, E. M., *William G. Brownlow: Fighting Parson* (New York, 1937)

Doyle, D., *Nashville in the New South: 1880–1930* (Knoxville, 1985)

Gidmark, J. B., *Encyclopedia of American Literature of the Sea and Great Lakes* (Greenwood Publishing Group, 2001)

Gunn, J. C., *Gunn's Domestic Medicine: A Facsimile of the First Edition, Tennesseana Editions* (Knoxville, 1986)

Handy, W. C., *Beal Street Blues* (New York, 1917)

Hofstadter, R., *The Age of Reform: From Bryan to FDR* (New York, 1960)

Internal Revenue Service, *Historical Study: IRS Historical Fact Book: A Chronology 1646–1992* (Washington: GPO, 1997)

Jones, J. B., *Every Day in Tennessee History* (Winston-Salem, 1996)

Knoxville City Council Minute Books

Kousser, J. M., *The Shaping of Southern Politics: Suffrage Restriction and the Establishment of the One-Party South, 1880–1910* (New Haven, 1974)

McDonald, M. J., and Wheeler, W. B., *Knoxville Tennessee: Continuity and Change in an Appalachian City* (Knoxville, 1983)

Memorial Address on the Life and Character of James Phelan, February 28, 1891 (Washington: Government Printing Office, 1891)

Memphis City Council Meeting Minutes

Miller, W. D., *Memphis During the Progressive Era, 1900–1917* (Memphis, 1957)

Morgan, H. W., *Drugs in America: A Social History, 1800–1980* (Syracuse, 1981)

Minutes of the Nashville Board of Aldermen

Musto, D. F., MD, *The American Disease: Origins of Narcotic Control* (London, 1973)

Minutes of the Common Council of the City of Knoxville

Napheys, G. H., *The Transmission of Life; Counsels on the Nature and Hygiene of the Masculine Function*, fourteenth edition (Atlanta, 1873)

Official Records of the War of Rebellion, Series 1, vol. 30, pt. 3 (Washington, 1895)

Phelan, J., *History of Tennessee: The Making of the State* (Cambridge, 1888)

Public Acts of the State of Tennessee by the Fifty-Eighth General Assembly, 1913 (Nashville, 1913)

Rose, A., *Storyville, New Orleans: Being an Illustrated Account of the Notorious Red Light District* (Tuscaloosa, 1978)

Rosen, R., *The Lost Sisterhood: Prostitution in America, 1900–1918* (Baltimore, 1982)

Rothrock, M. U., ed., *The French Broad-Holston Country* (Knoxville, 1948)

Royster, J. J., ed. and intro., *Southern Horrors and Other Writings: The Anti-Lynching Campaign of Ida Be Wells, 1892–1900* (Boston, 1997)

Sears Roebuck Catalog 1897

Supreme Court, East Tennessee Division, M. G. *Weidner, et al., vs. Irene Friedman, et al.*, Tennessee State Library and Archives

Thomas, M., *The Response to Prostitution in the Progressive Era* (Chapel Hill, 1980)

Thomas, Miss J., *Old Days in Nashville: 1800 to 1899* (Nashville, 1899)

Van Deburg, W. L., *Slavery and Race in American Popular Culture* (Madison, 1984)

Walkowitz, J. K., *Prostitution and Victorian Society: Women, Class, and the State* (1980)

War Department, U.S., Office of the Surgeon General, *Military and Surgical History of the War of the Rebellion* Parts 1-3 Washington, GPO, 1890

Wolfe, M. R., *Lucius Polk Brown and Progressive Food and Drug Control: Tennessee and New York City, 1908–1920* (Lawrence, 1978)

Newspapers

Atchison Daily Globe
Bolivar Bulletin
Boston Daily Atlas
Cleveland Herald, August 21, 1852
Charleston Mercury
Chattanooga Daily News
Chattanooga Daily Times
Clarksville Tobacco Leaf Chronicle
Clarksville Weekly Chronicle
Columbia Herald
The Comet
Crossville Chronicle
The Daily Miners' Register
Daily National Intelligencer
Jackson Sun
Knoxville Chronicle
Knoxville Daily Tribune
Knoxville Chronicle
Knoxville Sentinel
Knoxville Sunday Chronicle
Los Angeles Herald
Los Angeles Times
Louisville Daily Journal
Memphis Daily Avalanche
Memphis Daily Bulletin
Memphis *Public Ledger*
Memphis Daily Appeal
Milwaukee Sentinel
Milwaukee Morning Sentinel
Morning Oregonian
Morristown Gazette
Nashville *Daily American*
Nashville Patriot
Nashville *Tennessean*
Nashville Tennessean and Nashville American
Nashville Union
Nashville Union and Dispatch
Nashville Daily Press
Nashville Daily Press and Times
Nashville Weekly American
Nashville Retrospect
New Orleans Daily Picayune
New York Herald
New York Times

New York Weekly Herald
St. Louis Globe-Democrat
Wisconsin State Register

Internet Sources

Davis James M. @: www.odmp.org/officer/21923-deputy-collector-james-m-davis.

"Direct Disenfranchisement," *Race, Voting Rights, and Segregation,* University of Michigan, @ www.umich.edu/~lawrace/disenfranchise1.htm

"Disfranchising Laws," *The Tennessee Encyclopedia,* @ tennesseeencyclopedia.net/entry. php?rec=380

Douglas, Joseph C., "A Note on the History and Material Culture of Bellamy Cave, Tennessee," *Journal of Spelean History,* 2009. @ caves.org/section/asha/issues/136.pdf.

Ellis, William E., "Moonshine," @ tennesseeencyclopedia.net/entries/moonshine/.

Equal Justice Initiative, Confronting the Legacy of Racial Terror, Third ed., Chapter 1, "Session and Emancipation, 1861–1865 @ lynchinginamerica.eji.org/report/

Ezzell, T. P., "Edward Ward Carmack 1858–1908," @ tennesseeencyclopedia.net/.

Fifteenth Amendment Site, @ 15thamendment.harpweek.com/HubPages/CommentaryPage. asp?Commentary=03Ratification

The History of Jim Crow, @: www.jimcrowhistory.org/history/creating2.htm

History Matters, George Mason University, @ historymatters.gmu.edu/d/5352

daily.jstor.org/peoples-grocery-lynching/; lynchingsitesmem.org/archives/appeal-avalanche-drawings-calvin-mcdowell-and-thomas-moss-3281892; lynchinginamerica.eji.org/explore/tennessee

Lynching: @ tennesseeencyclopedia.net/entries/lynching/

Tennessee v. Davis, @ supreme.justia.com/cases/federal/us/100/257

Terry, C. E., and Pellens, M., The Opium Problem, @ w*ww.hoboes.com/Politics/Prohibition/Notes/Opium_Problem* 1928

Articles

Birdwell, M. E., "Moonshine Made for Strange Bedfellow in the Upper Cumberland," in Friends of the Clay County, Tennessee, Library, *Corn from a Jar,* 2014.

Boyer, J. C., "The Progressive Era Revolution in America Attitudes toward Sex," *Journal of American History,* March 1973.

Brown, L. P., "Enforcement of the Tennessee Anti-Narcotics Law," *American Journal of Public Health,* 1915.

Burnham, J. C., "The Progressive Era Revolution in American Attitudes toward Sex," *Journal of American History,* 1973.

Courtwright, D. T., "Opiate Addiction as a Consequence of the Civil War," *Civil War History* 1978.

Davis, G. L., and Cross, H. J., "Sexual Stereotyping of Black Males in Interracial Sex" *Archives of Sexual Behavior,* 1979.

Degler, C. N., "What Ought To Be and What Was: Women's Sexuality in the Nineteenth

Century," *American Historical Review*, December 1974.

Jones, J. B., "Municipal Vice: The Management of Prostitution in Tennessee's Urban Experience. Part II: The Examples of Chattanooga and Knoxville, 1838–1917," *Tennessee Historical Quarterly* 1991; "The Wild, Wild East: A Blood Feud in Nineteenth-Century Knoxville: The Mabry, Lusby, and O'Conner Killings, 1881–1882," *The Courier*, June 1993; "Drug Abuse and Prostitution in Tennessee History," self-published, 2014; "Shoot-Outs and Pseudo Duels in 19th Century Tennessee Journalism," 20th Symposium on 19th Century Press, the Civil War, and Free Expression, Chattanooga, 2012; "John, Bob and Andy, Tennessee's Other Taylor Brothers: A Nineteenth Century Saga of Law and Order," *The Courier*, 2018; "Chronological List of 213 Lynchings in Tennessee, 1821-1946." (Author's Research Findings, in possession of the author.)

Kaser, D., "Nashville's Women of Pleasure in 1860," *Tennessee Historical Quarterly*, 1964.

Lacayo, R., "Blood at the Root," *Time*, April 2, 2000; "Blood at the Root," *Time*, April 2, 2000 Lacayo, Richard. "Blood at the Root," *Time*, April 2, 2000

LeHever, H. G., "Prostitution, Politics and Religion; The Crusade Against Vice in Atlanta in 1912," *Atlanta Historical Journal*, September 1980.

Lubove, R., "The Progressives and the Prostitute," *Historian*, 1962.

McIver, S. B., "Dreamers, Schemers and Scalawags," *Florida Chronicles* Volume 1 (Pineapple Press, 1998)

Martin, F., "Social Hygiene and the War," *Social Hygiene*, 1917.

Pearre, M. L. P., "A Diary Kept through 1863 and into 1864," Nashville, Tennessee State Library and Archives.

Petrik, P., "Capitalists with Rooms: Prostitution in Helena Montana, 1865–1900," *Montana*, 1981

Snow, W. F., "Social Hygiene and the War," *Social Hygiene*, 1917.

Terry, C. E., and Pellens, M., "The Extent of Chronic Opium Use in the United States Prior to 1921," in Ball, J. C., and Chambers, Carl, D., eds., *The Epidemiology of Opiate Addiction in the United States* (Springfield, Ill. 1921).

Thomason, P., "The Men's Quarter in Downtown Nashville," *Tennessee Historical Quarterly*, 1982.

Whitt, W., "Climax is Gone: Memories Linger," *The Tennessean Magazine*, July 8, 1973

Williamson, J. C., ed., "The Civil War Diary of John Coffee Williamson," *Tennessee Historical Quarterly*, 1956.

Wynn, L. T., "The Little Known Saga of Elbert Williams and the Fight for the Franchise in Haywood County," *The Courier*, 2015.